THE
# Ambassadors

*America's Diplomats on the Front Lines*

## PAUL RICHTER

Simon & Schuster

NEW YORK · LONDON · TORONTO
SYDNEY · NEW DELHI

Simon & Schuster
1230 Avenue of the Americas
New York, NY 10020

First Simon & Schuster hardcover edition November 2019

SIMON & SCHUSTER and colophon are registered trademarks
of Simon & Schuster, Inc.

For information about special discounts for bulk purchases, please contact
Simon & Schuster Special Sales at 1-866-506-1949
or business@simonandschuster.com

The Simon & Schuster Speakers Bureau can bring authors to your
live event. For more information or to book an event contact the
Simon & Schuster Speakers Bureau at 1-866-248-3049
or visit our website at www.simonspeakers.com.

Manufactured in the United States of America

Photographs courtesy of U.S. Army, U.S. Air Force,
U.S. embassy in Iraq, and Brian Linvill

1  3  5  7  9  10  8  6  4  2

Library of Congress Cataloging-in-Publication Data is available.

ISBN 978-1-5011-7241-0
ISBN 978-1-5011-7242-7 (ebook)

*For Karen*

# CONTENTS

Chris Stevens walking with an elderly Libyan he's just befriended on a visit to Ras al-Hilal in eastern coastal Libya.

Anne Patterson delivering American military precooked meals for humanitarian relief to a Pakistani general.

Ryan Crocker meets with U.S. three-star General Ray Odierno
and an Iraqi general in the first days of his posting
as U.S. ambassador to Iraq in 2007.

Robert Ford shares a meal with Marsh Arabs in southern Iraq.

# CAST OF CHARACTERS

**Ryan C. Crocker,** ambassador to Afghanistan, 2011–12; ambassador to Iraq, 2007–9; ambassador to Pakistan, 2004–7; deputy assistant secretary of state, 2001–3; chargé d'affaires, U.S. embassy in Afghanistan, 2002; ambassador to Syria, 1999–2001; ambassador to Kuwait, 1994–97; ambassador to Lebanon, 1990–93.

**Robert S. Ford,** ambassador to Syria, 2010–14; deputy chief of mission, U.S. embassy in Iraq, 2008–9; ambassador to Algeria, 2006–8; political counselor, U.S. embassy in Iraq, 2004–6; deputy chief of mission, U.S. embassy in Bahrain, 2001–4.

**Anne W. Patterson,** assistant secretary for Near Eastern affairs, 2013–17; ambassador to Egypt, 2011–13; ambassador to Pakistan, 2007–10; assistant secretary of state for international narcotics and law enforcement affairs, 2005–7; acting U.S. ambassador to the United Nations, 2005; ambassador to Colombia, 2000–2003; ambassador to El Salvador, 1997–2000.

**J. Christopher Stevens,** ambassador to Libya, 2012; U.S. special representative to the Libyan rebel coalition, 2011; deputy chief of mission, U.S. embassy in Libya, 2007–9; deputy principal officer and chief of political section, U.S. consulate, Jerusalem, 2002–6; killed in terrorist attack on U.S. diplomatic mission in Benghazi, September 11, 2012.

## At the State Department

**Richard L. Armitage,** deputy secretary of state, 2001–5.

**Richard A. Boucher,** assistant secretary for South and Central Asian affairs, 2006–9; assistant secretary of state for public affairs, 2000–2005.

**William J. Burns,** deputy secretary of state 2011–14; undersecretary of state for political affairs, 2008–11; assistant secretary for Near Eastern affairs, 2001–5.

**Hillary R. Clinton,** secretary of state, 2009–13.

**Jeffrey D. Feltman,** assistant secretary for Near Eastern affairs, 2009–12.

**Marc I. Grossman,** special representative for Afghanistan and Pakistan, 2011–12; undersecretary of state for political affairs, 2001–5; director general of the U.S. Foreign Service, 2000–2001.

**Richard C. A. Holbrooke,** special representative for Afghanistan and Pakistan, 2009–10.

**A. Elizabeth Jones,** acting assistant secretary for Near Eastern affairs, 2012–13.

**John F. Kerry,** secretary of state, 2013–17.

**Colin L. Powell,** secretary of state, 2001–5.

**Condoleezza Rice,** secretary of state, 2005–9.

**Wendy R. Sherman,** undersecretary of state for political affairs, 2011–15.

## At the White House

**Joseph R. Biden,** vice president, 2009–17.

**George W. Bush,** president, 2001–9.

**Richard B. Cheney,** vice president, 2001–9.

**James F. Dobbins,** Bush administration senior representative on Afghanistan, 2001–2.

**Zalmay Khalilzad,** ambassador to Iraq, 2005–7; ambassador to Afghanistan, 2003–5; special presidential envoy for Afghanistan, 2001–3; ambassador-at-large for the Free Iraqis, 2002–3.

**Prem G. Kumar,** senior director for Middle East and North Africa on the National Security Council staff, 2013–15; director for Israeli, Palestinian, and Egyptian Affairs, 2009–13; political officer, U.S. consulate, Jerusalem, 2002–4.

**Denis R. McDonough,** chief of staff to President Obama, 2013–17; deputy national security adviser, 2010–13.

**Barack H. Obama,** president, 2009–17.

**Benjamin J. Rhodes,** deputy national security adviser, 2009–17; top communications aide to President Obama.

## At the Defense Department

**General Martin E. Dempsey,** chairman of the Joint Chiefs of Staff, 2011–15.

**Douglas J. Feith,** undersecretary of defense for policy, 2001–5.

**Robert M. Gates,** secretary of defense, 2006–11.

**Leon E. Panetta,** secretary of defense, 2011–13.

**Donald H. Rumsfeld,** secretary of defense, 2001–6.

**Paul D. Wolfowitz,** deputy secretary of defense, 2001–5.

## *In Afghanistan*

**Abdul Rashid Dostum,** ethnic Uzbek warlord from the country's north who served as deputy defense minister in 2003; vice president since 2014.

**Karl W. Eikenberry,** a career U.S. Army officer; ambassador to Afghanistan, 2009–11; commander of U.S. and coalition forces in Afghanistan, 2005–7.

**Muhammad Qasim Fahim,** ethnic Tajik warlord who led the U.S.-allied Northern Alliance forces that drove the Taliban out of Kabul in 2001. Vice chairman, Afghan interim government, 2001–2; vice president, 2009 until his death in 2014.

**Gulbuddin Hekmatyar,** brutal leader of the Hezb-i-Islami Islamist militia; two-time Afghan prime minister during the 1990s. During the civil war of 1992–96, forces under his command destroyed much of Kabul.

**Hamid Karzai,** chairman of the interim government, 2001–2; interim president, 2002–4; president, 2004–14.

**Ismail Khan,** ethnic Tajik warlord from western Afghanistan; minister of water and energy, 2004–13; governor, Herat Province, 2001–4.

**Atta Muhammad Noor,** ethnic Tajik warlord from northern Afghanistan; commander in the U.S.-allied Northern Alliance militia coalition during the 2001 campaign to oust the Taliban; governor, Balkh Province, 2004–18.

**Abdul Rahman,** onetime Northern Alliance official, appointed minister of aviation in December 2001 but beaten and stabbed to death, allegedly by political rivals, in February 2002.

**Abdul Rahim Wardak,** defense minister, 2004–12; senior representative in negotiations with U.S. officials, 2011–12.

**Amanullah Khan Zadran,** a minister of tribal and border affairs, 2001–2; militia leader and younger brother of warlord Pacha Khan Zadran.

**Pacha Khan Zadran,** ethnic Pashtun warlord; nominal U.S. ally in the 2001 campaign against the Taliban who also battled the U.S.-supported government in Kabul.

## U.S. Team in Afghanistan

**General John R. Allen,** commander of U.S. and coalition forces, 2011–13.

**James B. Cunningham,** deputy chief of mission, 2011–12; ambassador to Afghanistan, 2012–14.

**Eileen O'Connor,** director of communications, U.S. embassy, Kabul, 2011–12.

**Ronald E. Neumann,** ambassador to Afghanistan, 2005–7; ambassador to Bahrain, 2001–4; political adviser to coalition forces in Iraq, 2004–5.

## In Iraq

**Adel Abdul-Mahdi,** economist and Shia politician who held a series of high posts in postwar Iraq, including vice president, 2005–11. He became Iraq's prime minister in October 2018.

**Masoud Barzani,** president of the Iraqi Kurdistan region, 2005–17; longtime leader of Kurdish Democratic Party, one of two main political groupings in Iraqi Kurdistan.

**Karim al-Burjas,** governor of Anbar Province, 2003–4; quit his post to free three sons who had been kidnapped by Al Qaeda in Iraq.

**Ahmad Chalabi,** controversial Iraqi expatriate financier who lobbied in Washington for the Iraq invasion and sought unsuccessfully afterward to become the country's leader. He held a series of high posts, including deputy prime minister, in the post-invasion government.

**Major General Mehdi al-Gharawi,** Shia police commander accused by U.S. officials of torturing and killing Sunni prisoners in a secret prison.

**Ali Radhi al-Haidary,** successful businessman; governor of Baghdad Province, 2004–5; assassinated in 2005 in the eighth attack on his life by insurgents.

**Tariq al-Hashimi,** top Sunni politician; a leader of the Iraqi Islamic Party; vice president of Iraq, 2006–12.

**Ibrahim al-Jaafari,** physician and leader of the Dawa Party, a small but influential Shia faction; Iraqi prime minister, 2005–6.

**Abdel Nasser al-Janabi,** top Sunni lawmaker; adherent of a harsh Islamist ideology.

**Nouri al-Maliki,** Iraqi prime minister, 2006–14; exiled dissident during Saddam Hussein's reign; a leader of the Dawa Party.

**Mahmoud al-Mashhadani,** hard-line Sunni politician; speaker of the Iraqi parliament, 2006–8.

**Saleh al-Mutlaq,** Sunni politician; onetime member of Saddam Hussein's Baath Party; deputy prime minister, 2010–15.

**Saddam Hussein,** strongman ruler of Iraq, 1979–2003.

**Abdul Sattar Abu Risha,** sheikh from Anbar Province and cofounder of the Awakening movement, whose members joined U.S. forces to battle insurgents; assassinated September 2007.

**Moktada al-Sadr,** firebrand leader of Jaish al-Madhi, a Shia militia that challenged U.S. forces and U.S.-backed government in Baghdad.

**Grand Ayatollah Ali al-Sistani,** the most revered Shia religious figure in Iraq.

**Abu Musab al-Zarqawi,** Jordanian extremist who led Al Qaeda in Iraq from 2004 until his death in 2006.

## U.S. Team in Iraq

**Jeffrey Beals,** Arabist and former CIA analyst; U.S. embassy political officer, 2004–6; political officer under Chris Stevens at U.S. consulate in Jerusalem, 2002–4.

**L. Paul "Jerry" Bremer III,** leader of the Coalition Provisional Authority, Iraq's occupation government from April 2003 to June 2004.

**Patricia A. Butenis,** deputy chief of mission, 2007–9.

**J. Adam Ereli,** minister-counselor for public affairs, 2008–9.

**Jay Garner,** director of Office of Reconstruction and Humanitarian Assistance, U.S. agency organized with plans to oversee a quick transition to Iraqi rule in 2003. The agency was shut down after four months.

**Christopher R. Hill,** ambassador to Iraq, 2009–10.

**Ali Khedery,** special assistant to five U.S. ambassadors in Iraq, including Ryan Crocker, 2003–9.

**Thomas C. Krajeski,** senior adviser to Ambassador Ryan Crocker on northern Iraq, 2008–9; ambassador to Yemen, 2004–7; political adviser to Coalition Provisional Authority, 2003; deputy director, then director, office of Northern Gulf Affairs, Bureau of Near Eastern Affairs, 2001–4.

**John D. Negroponte,** deputy secretary of state, 2007–9; director of national intelligence, 2005–7; ambassador to Iraq, 2004–5.

**General Raymond T. Odierno,** commander of coalition forces in Iraq, 2008–10.

**General David H. Petraeus,** CIA director, 2011–12; commander of U.S. and coalition forces, Afghanistan, 2010–11; commander, U.S. Central Command, 2008–10; commander, U.S. and coalition forces, Iraq, 2007–8.

**Charles P. Ries,** minister for economic affairs, 2007–8.

**Marcie B. Ries,** minister-counselor for political-military affairs, 2007–8.

**Lieutenant General Ricardo Sanchez,** commander of U.S. and coalition forces in Iraq, 2003–4.

**Emma Sky,** British Mideast specialist; adviser to U.S. general Raymond T. Odierno, 2007–10; occupation government's representative to the city of Kirkuk, 2003–4.

## In Pakistan

**Benazir Bhutto,** two-time prime minister; leader of left-leaning Pakistan Peoples Party until her assassination in 2007.

**Iftikhar Muhammad Chaudhry,** three-time chief justice of the Pakistani supreme court between 2005 and 2013; political rival of Presidents Pervez Musharraf and Asif Ali Zardari.

**Yousaf Raza Gilani,** prime minister, 2008–12.

**General Ashfaq Parvez Kayani,** chief of army staff, 2007–13; Pakistan's most powerful figure.

**Pervez Musharraf,** president of Pakistan, 2001–8; chief of army staff, 1998–2007.

**Maulana Fazlur Rehman,** leader of the pro-Taliban religious political party Jamiat Ulema-i-Islam.

**Nawaz Sharif,** three-time Pakistani prime minister; leader of a center-right party, the Pakistan Muslim League-Nawaz.

**Asif Ali Zardari,** son of a wealthy landowner; president of Pakistan,

2008–13; swept into power after his wife, former prime minister Benazir Bhutto, was assassinated in 2007.

## U.S. Team in Pakistan

**Gerald M. Feierstein,** principal deputy assistant secretary for Near Eastern affairs, 2013–16; ambassador to Yemen, 2010–13; deputy chief of mission, Pakistan, 2008–10.

**Kevin Hulbert,** CIA station chief, Islamabad, 2004–5.

**Vice Admiral Michael A. LeFever,** top Defense Department representative in Pakistan, 2008–11.

## In Libya

**Wissam bin Ahmed,** leader of Libya Shield 1 militia in Benghazi.

**Ali Aujali,** veteran Libyan diplomat; served as Qaddafi government's ambassador to the United States from 2009 to February 2011; began serving as the rebel alliance's ambassador to Washington in August 2011; Libyan foreign minister, 2012–13.

**Muhammad al-Gharabi,** leader of the Rafa' al-Sahti Brigade and Libya Shield 2 militia in Benghazi.

**Mustafa Abdul Jalil,** chairman of the rebels' umbrella organization, the National Transitional Council, in 2011.

**Mahmoud Jibril,** U.S.-trained political scientist who served in early 2011 as the first emissary of the Libyan rebels and later the same year as the rebels' interim prime minister and minister of foreign affairs.

**Ahmed Abu Khattalah,** Benghazi militia leader who was sentenced to twenty-two years in a U.S. prison for leading the 2012 attack on the U.S. diplomatic mission in Benghazi.

**Muammar el-Qaddafi,** authoritarian leader of Libya from the moment he seized power in a coup in 1969 to 2011.

**Mohammed el-Qaddafi,** Muammar el-Qaddafi's oldest son.

**Seif al-Islam el-Qaddafi,** Muammar el-Qaddafi's second son and, until Muammar el-Qaddafi's death, his presumed heir.

**Abdul Fatah Younis,** top military leader of the rebels until he was assassinated on July 28, 2011, apparently by disaffected rebels.

## U.S. Team in Libya

**Lieutenant Colonel Gregory Arndt,** U.S. Army military adviser to the Libyans.

**Gene A. Cretz,** U.S. ambassador to Libya, 2009–12.

**Bubaker Habib,** teacher and translator from Benghazi who became adviser and fixer for Ambassador J. Christopher Stevens.

**Deborah K. Jones,** ambassador to Libya, 2013–15.

**Lieutenant Colonel Brian E. Linvill,** defense attaché, 2012.

**David McFarland,** political counselor; acting deputy chief of mission, U.S. embassy, 2012.

**Laurence E. Pope II,** chargé d'affaires, U.S. embassy, 2012.

**Scott Wickland,** diplomatic security officer on the team accompanying Ambassador J. Christopher Stevens during Benghazi attack.

## In Syria

**Hassan Abdul Azim,** head of the Democratic Arab Socialist Union, an Arab socialist party.

**Bashar al-Assad,** president of Syria since 2000; son of Hafez al-Assad, Syrian ruler from 1971 to 2000.

**Moaz al-Khatib,** imam from a prominent Damascus family; leader of the Syrian opposition's umbrella organization, 2012–13.

**Ghiyath Matar,** twenty-six-year-old Damascus tailor who led nonviolent demonstrations in 2011 and was tortured and killed by secret police.

**Faisal Mekdad,** Syrian deputy foreign minister since 2006.

**Colonel Abdul Jabbar al-Oqaidi,** commander and spokesman for the Free Syrian Army rebel group, 2011–13.

**Dhu al-Himma Shalish,** chief of presidential security in Damascus and a first cousin of President Bashar al-Assad.

**Razan Zaitouneh,** human rights lawyer widely considered the mother of the country's nonviolent protest movement. She is believed to have been kidnapped by a jihadist group in 2013 and her fate is unknown.

## U.S. Team in Damascus and Washington, DC

**Mounir Ibrahim,** political officer at U.S. embassy in 2011.

**Wa'el N. Alzayat,** worked with Robert Ford in Washington coordinating relations with Syrian opposition, 2012–14.

## In Egypt

**Essam el-Haddad,** foreign policy adviser to Mohamed Morsi, 2012–13.

**Hosni Mubarak,** president of Egypt from 1981 until his forced resignation in 2011.

**Mohamed Morsi,** engineering professor and Muslim Brotherhood official who was elected president of Egypt in 2012 and deposed in a military coup in 2013. He died on June 17, 2019, while still imprisoned.

**Ahmed Shafik,** former Egyptian air force general who ran unsuccessfully for president in 2012.

**Khairat el-Shater,** Egyptian tycoon; chief strategist and financier

xxii 	CAST OF CHARACTERS

of the country's Muslim Brotherhood organization during the revolution; imprisoned since the military coup of 2013.

**Abdel Fattah el-Sisi,** Egyptian general who made himself president in a military coup in July 2013.

**Field Marshal Mohamed Hussein Tantawi,** chairman of the Supreme Council of the Armed Forces, 2011–12.

## U.S. Team in Egypt

**Margaret Scobey,** ambassador to Egypt, 2008–11.

## In the Persian Gulf States

**Mohammed bin Zayed,** crown prince of Abu Dhabi and de facto ruler of United Arab Emirates.

**Yousef al-Otaiba,** United Arab Emirates ambassador to the United States since 2008.

## In Iran

**Hassan Kazemi Qomi,** first Iranian ambassador to postwar Iraq; believed by U.S. officials to also be a member of the elite Quds Force of Iran's Islamic Revolutionary Guard Corps.

**General Qassim Suleimani,** Iranian military mastermind; leader of the Quds Force of Iran's Islamic Revolutionary Guard Corps, a unit that spearheads Iranian military and intelligence strategy abroad.

**Mohammad Ebrahim Taherian,** Iranian diplomat who negotiated with U.S. officials over Afghan issues in 2001 and served as Iranian ambassador to Kabul in 2002.

**Mohammad Javad Zarif,** Iranian career diplomat and scholar; took part in secret negotiations with U.S. officials before Iraq war; Iranian foreign minister since 2013.

# TIMELINE OF EVENTS

**September 11, 2001**—Al Qaeda's attacks on the United States kill 2,977 and begin a new era of U.S. military involvement in the Middle East and South Asia.

**December 9, 2001**—U.S. and allied Afghan forces complete a nine-week campaign that topples the Taliban government, which supported the Al Qaeda fighters who carried out the 9/11 attacks.

**January 2, 2002**—RYAN CROCKER arrives in Kabul, Afghanistan, to serve three months as acting U.S. ambassador and to help set up a new Afghan government.

**March 19, 2003**—U.S. forces invade Iraq, taking control in one month.

**April 2003**—Crocker arrives in Baghdad, Iraq, to begin work helping the Iraqis organize a new government. In May he signs on for a three-month assignment with the newly formed U.S. occupation government. He leaves in August.

**August 2003**—ROBERT FORD arrives in Iraq for a four-month stint as the one-man U.S. occupation government for the central province of Najaf. He leaves in December.

**July 2004**—Ford agrees to return to Iraq as political counselor, in the second of five postings in the country.

**November 25, 2004**—Crocker takes over as U.S. ambassador to Pakistan, as the George W. Bush administration intensifies its campaign against militants in that country's wild tribal areas. He leaves in 2007.

**March 31, 2007**—Crocker arrives in Baghdad as U.S. ambassador to Iraq, with the Bush administration expanding the U.S. troop presence there in a final attempt to end ethnic fighting.

**June 2007**—CHRIS STEVENS begins a two-year assignment as the number two U.S. diplomat in Libya during a warming of U.S. ties with Libyan leader Muammar el-Qaddafi.

**July 2007**—ANNE PATTERSON succeeds Crocker as U.S. ambassador to Pakistan. She stays until October 2010.

**February 13, 2009**—With Iraq more peaceful and the Obama administration under way, Crocker leaves Iraq with plans to retire from the U.S. Foreign Service.

**April 2010**—Ford ends his final posting in Iraq.

**October 2010**—Patterson gives up her post as ambassador to Pakistan and is chosen to be ambassador to Egypt.

**January 2011**—Ford begins his posting as U.S. ambassador to Syria, weeks before the antigovernment demonstrations that in a few months will become a civil war.

**April 5, 2011**—Stevens secretly enters Libya as a U.S. envoy to rebel forces one month after the beginning of a NATO air campaign against the Qaddafi government.

**July 25, 2011**—Crocker takes over as ambassador to Afghanistan, with instructions to help draw down the U.S. military presence and reshape the U.S.-Afghan relationship.

**August 18, 2011**—Six months after a revolution, with Egypt still in upheaval, Patterson takes over as U.S. ambassador in Cairo.

**November 17, 2011**—Following the close of the Libya war, Stevens ends his role as envoy and leaves Libya.

**February 2012**—Ford leaves Damascus because of the growing threats from the Syrian civil war but continues in Washington, D.C., as the State Department's lead official on Syria.

**June 7, 2012**—Stevens returns to Libya after his confirmation as the new ambassador.

**July 23, 2012**—Crocker quits his post as ambassador to Afghanistan.

**September 11, 2012**—Stevens is killed in a terrorist attack on the U.S. diplomatic mission in Benghazi, Libya.

**August 31, 2013**—Patterson gives up her post as ambassador to Egypt. On December 23 she is confirmed as top State Department official for the Middle East.

**February 2014**—Ford gives up his role as point man to Syria, saying he can no longer defend the U.S. approach to the war, and quits the Foreign Service.

**January 6, 2017**—Patterson retires from the Foreign Service as the Obama administration winds down.

**February 2017**—James Mattis, the Trump administration's first defense secretary, asks Patterson to serve as the Pentagon's number three. In March, however, some officials in the Trump White House and conservative senators block the nomination, arguing Patterson was too close to Islamists during her service in Egypt.

THE
# Ambassadors

CHAPTER 1

# The Best People for the Worst Places

On a mild day in February 2009, President Barack Obama appeared before 2,000 camouflage-clad Marines in Camp Lejeune, North Carolina, to announce plans to wind down the Iraq war. American and foreign audiences had been waiting for months to hear how the new president would deal with the six-year-old conflict, and his remarks drew worldwide attention. Almost unnoticed in the text was a line thanking a career diplomat who as ambassador to Iraq helped shape a successful effort to check the country's bloody insurgency. Americans owed a debt of gratitude to Ryan C. Crocker, an "unsung hero" who had always sought the toughest assignments and was "an example of the very best our country has to offer," Obama said.

Crocker and a small number of seasoned diplomats like him were central players throughout the long campaign that America waged in the greater Middle East in the decade and a half after the September 11, 2001, terrorist attacks. In the aftermath of 9/11, the country began dispatching waves of troops and civilian specialists to the Middle East and South Asia to try to overcome security threats and steady fractured societies. These ambassadors, practicing a new diplomacy of the front lines, became Washington, D.C.'s preeminent troubleshooters and primary links to foreign leaders. Presidents and secretaries of state sometimes heeded their advice and sometimes didn't. But even when they chose a different path, they continued to seek out these ambassadors to ask their guidance and recruit them for new assignments. Although their names were unknown to most at home, they became a crucial line of national defense.

The American leaders these diplomats served never solved the puzzle of the greater Middle East. Two presidents of different parties blundered getting into conflicts and stumbled trying to exit or avoid them. They were overwhelmed by the dysfunction of the world's most volatile region and buffeted by the pressures of U.S. domestic politics. Now Americans yearn for an end to the "forever wars" in the Muslim world. Yet the nation can't retreat from the effort to stabilize weak countries. This mission, the foremost task of these diplomats, is more important than ever. Unstable lands continue to threaten—not only those in the Muslim world's long arc of instability, but also in Central and South America, sub-Saharan Africa, and other regions. Washington needs to find ways to steady these countries using diplomacy and political and economic leverage, if not American armies. Left alone, they will menace their neighbors and the distant American homeland, too, with extremist violence, mass migration, economic turmoil, and transnational crime. The threat they pose remains among the most urgent of security challenges.

The story of these diplomats' experiences offers a window onto the history and lessons of America's long struggle. Dispatched repeatedly to the most important and difficult posts, these foreign service hands saw the conflicts from all angles. They met with warlords and terrorist chiefs and witnessed bloody civil strife from street corners. They heard the whispered secrets of Arab rulers and took part in White House strategy sessions. They did not have all the answers, they are the first to admit. But through their many tours they learned at closest range what happened in embattled capitals and on the far sides of the blast walls and razor wire. They saw which of Washington's decisions brought progress and which led to disaster. After decades in the region, they returned home with an unmatched understanding of the capabilities and limits of American power.

The diplomats were present as the new era of U.S. involvement began after the shock of the September 11 attacks. As years passed

and Washington's interests in the region shifted, they moved from capital to capital and remained at the center of the action.

The first American intervention came within a month of 9/11 when U.S., British, and Afghan forces routed the Taliban government, which had provided a haven for the Al Qaeda terrorists who attacked the United States. Within days after the Taliban fled the capital of Kabul, a small landing party of U.S. diplomats arrived there to help set up the replacement government that had been organized by world powers.

Eighteen months later, 177,000 U.S. and allied troops invaded Iraq to oust Saddam Hussein, whom they incorrectly believed to be developing nuclear arms that threatened the world. Saddam's fall left the country in chaos and opened years of bloody struggle among Iraq's ethnic and religious groups. The Pentagon was first put in charge of running postwar Iraq, but U.S. diplomats took an ever-larger role over the next eight years in efforts to build a functioning state.

By the end of the decade Washington's attention turned back to South Asia, where the Taliban and allied militant groups again threatened the weak Afghan government from the countryside and havens in neighboring Pakistan. The Bush and then Obama administrations added U.S. troops and turned to a new style of counterinsurgency warfare that relied on armed drone aircraft and special forces troops. U.S. diplomats helped guide the new war in the shadows.

In 2011, Washington's attention shifted to a wave of popular uprisings in the Middle East that came to be called the Arab Spring. In February 2011, crowds of thousands in Cairo's streets forced the resignation of Hosni Mubarak, Egypt's ruler for the past thirty years. For the next two years U.S. diplomats tried to steer the most populous Arab country toward a more democratic government. But in the summer of 2013 the military seized power from a democratically elected Islamist government and imposed the harshest rule the country has had in modern times.

In 2011 the Obama administration was also drawn into a revolution in Libya, which had been ruled since 1969 by the erratic Muammar el-Qaddafi. U.S. forces joined a Western bombing cam-

paign that protected the rebels from Qaddafi and enabled them by August to topple his government. But after the war ended and world powers turned their attention elsewhere, the country descended into bloody factional fighting and lawlessness that continues.

The Obama administration sought to avoid a large military role in the civil war that broke out in Syria in the summer of 2011. As the war became the most devastating of the new century, a divided administration carried on a prolonged internal debate about military involvement. It chose to focus instead on unsuccessful attempts to negotiate a peace between President Bashar al-Assad and the rebel opposition. By the close of Obama's second term, the Assad government and its Iranian and Russian allies had gained the upper hand in the war.

The Obama administration found getting out of wars was harder than getting into them. After withdrawing the last U.S. troops from Iraq in 2011, the administration was compelled to return some forces to the region in 2014 to halt the advance of a new insurgent group that was seizing land in Iraq and Syria. The so-called Islamic State, heir to the Sunni insurgents who ignited civil war after the Iraq invasion, controlled at its peak territory as large as Britain. U.S., Iraqi, and allied forces gradually reclaimed the land. President Donald Trump, who campaigned in 2016 on bringing an end to the Middle Eastern wars, was still wavering in the third year of his presidency on how quickly to withdraw the last U.S. forces from Syria and Afghanistan.

The diplomats sent on the Middle Eastern missions were a small part of the more than 3 million Americans on the expeditions. The vast majority were military, but they also included intelligence officers, aid specialists, drug agents, and others. The biggest frontline embassies—in Iraq, Pakistan, and Afghanistan—were sprawling frontier forts with thousands in staff from more than thirty U.S. agencies. In 2008, when the U.S. embassy in Baghdad was the largest in U.S. history, the country was host to 170,000 U.S. troops and 154,000 U.S. contractors, but had only 140 officers handling the core diplomatic work.

Yet the top foreign service officers were mainsprings of these missions. In battle zones where most in the U.S. military knew nothing of the locals, the ambassadors understood language and custom and could lead Washington around the blind curves of local politics. They were confidants of local leaders, able to steer them through crises. They sat with U.S. generals and spy chiefs to decide how to wage war, as well as how to end it. When Washington had no plan for dealing with a country on the edge, they could improvise.

This style of statecraft did not resemble diplomacy as outsiders imagined it—a decorous pursuit carried on in the gilt halls of foreign ministries and at glittering dinner parties. The foreign service officers who thrived in sandstorms and the smoke of battle became known among insiders as "expeditionary diplomats." They were the best people for the worst places.

Ryan Crocker was one of them. The son of an Air Force bomber pilot from Spokane, Crocker became a rising star in the U.S. Foreign Service with his first assignment, in provincial Iran in 1972. Before the September 11 attacks, Crocker was already a three-time ambassador, with experience tangling with Saddam Hussein's regime and Hafez al-Assad's Syrian police state. He was nearly killed in the 1983 terrorist bombing of the U.S. embassy in Beirut. After the Taliban was ousted in 2001, Crocker was sent to run the U.S. embassy in Kabul and help organize a fragile new Afghan government. He was among the first U.S. diplomats detailed to Baghdad after the 2003 invasion to help run the chaotic occupation. In 2004 he was appointed ambassador to Pakistan, which had become a key player in the fight against Islamist militants. President Bush sent him back to Iraq in 2007 as ambassador and partner to General David Petraeus as Bush began a high-stakes strategy to suppress the insurgency with a surge of U.S. troops. In 2011 he was brought out of retirement by President Obama to again lead the U.S. embassy in Afghanistan and to help lay the groundwork for an exit from America's longest war.

Another drawn to the toughest jobs was Anne W. Patterson, an

Arkansan who learned to wrap Washington's demands in the soft accents of her native state. Patterson made her reputation leading the embassy in Colombia from 2000 to 2003 when the government in Bogotá was buckling under a drug-financed Marxist insurgency. The multibillion-dollar aid program overseen by Patterson seemed to bring it back from the brink. The assignment made her reputation and earned her appointments to a series of the State Department's toughest and most important posts. In 2007 she was made ambassador to Pakistan, replacing Crocker, when Washington was expanding its campaign against the country's militants. Patterson was dispatched as ambassador to post-revolutionary Egypt in 2011, at a desperate moment when the Obama administration was divided on how to promote democracy while preserving an essential alliance. In 2013, when her tour was done, she served for three years as the top State Department official for the Middle East.

Robert S. Ford, the son of a Colorado geologist, was first noticed by the State Department brass for the insightful reports he wrote while a one-man provincial government in Iraq in 2003, in the dark early days of the U.S. occupation. Like Crocker, Ford ended his first Iraq tour in despair over the chaotic mission and vowed never to return. But his bosses wanted him back and he accepted four more assignments in the country. As the embassy's top political official and then its deputy chief, he decoded Iraqi politics for Washington and found ways to open a dialogue with the insurgency's supporters. In 2011, Ford earned a worldwide reputation as the American ambassador who stood up to Syrian president Bashar al-Assad when Assad began slaughtering protesters at the start of the Syrian civil war. Ford fled Damascus in early 2012 amid threats from the regime, but he continued for two years in Washington as the administration's chief point man on Syria.

J. Christopher Stevens became the country's most well-known frontline diplomat when he was killed in the terrorist attack on the U.S. mission in Benghazi, Libya, on September 11, 2012. A charismatic Californian, Chris Stevens served three tours in Libya, which for Americans had long been unknown and hostile terrain. In his first tour, which began in 2007, Stevens sought to improve ties with a country that had been for four decades one of America's chief foes in the region. His second tour came during the 2011 Western air campaign against the Qaddafi government, when Secretary of State Hillary Clinton enlisted him to sneak into the country to serve as Washington's link to the Libyan rebels. The following year, after Qaddafi's fall, Stevens returned as U.S. ambassador to try to steady the country. After he and three other Americans were killed in the terrorist attack, Stevens's name became a partisan war cry for Republicans who blamed Clinton. In Benghazi's aftermath, the State Department tightened security rules and made diplomats stick closer to their fortified embassies. But inside the diplomatic service he remained a symbol of the opposite philosophy: to do the job right, diplomats needed to get past the barricades and make face-to-face contact.

These four diplomats crossed paths repeatedly. Ford worked as Crocker's number two in Iraq after serving with him at the start of his career as a junior officer in Egypt. Patterson succeeded Crocker as ambassador to Pakistan when Crocker was sent to Iraq in 2007. Crocker had a long friendship with Stevens, starting when they both worked in Washington in the 1980s.

All four had long experience in the kind of assignments that led Ronan Farrow, a State Department official turned journalist, to write that the diplomat's life could have the feel of "Thanksgiving dinner with your most difficult relatives, only lasting a lifetime and taking place in the most dangerous locations on earth."[1]

U.S. diplomats in the Middle East had faced risk since the day in 1786 when consul general Thomas Barclay arrived in Morocco to begin negotiating with the Barbary pirates. But this generation of foreign service officers lived with danger like none before. In this era American diplomats were always on the extremists' kill lists. Like the troops working alongside them, they lived with the daily reality of truck bombs, rocket barrages, and sniper fire. Since 2001 there have been more than four hundred "significant" attacks on U.S. diplomatic facilities and personnel, data from the Bureau of

Diplomatic Security suggest.[2] Terrorists have killed more than 166 diplomatic personnel, contractors, and local hires since the 1970s.[3] In 2012, Al Qaeda's branch in Yemen offered 6.6 pounds of gold to anyone who could assassinate the U.S. ambassador, Gerald M. Feierstein. U.S. diplomats are injured or killed far more often than American generals.

Even before 9/11, top State Department officials understood that the diplomatic corps was going to have to find new ways to deal with the growing threats from disorderly states that were breeding grounds for extremism. Marc Grossman, the top manager of the Foreign Service in 2000 and 2001, proposed creating a corps of rough-riding diplomats who would be the civilian equivalent of the military's elite Navy SEALs, Army Rangers, and Delta Force. They would be an advance guard tasked to do more than the traditional observing and reporting. "We were going to have to find ourselves a group of people who were going to go to the hardest places and do the hardest things," Grossman said. Grossman's boss, Secretary of State Colin Powell, and the three secretaries who followed all gave priority to this new diplomacy of crisis.

Three of these diplomats, Crocker, Ford, and Stevens, rose through the ranks as part of the State Department's tight-knit community of Mideast specialists, sometimes called Arabists. Patterson began as a Latin American specialist. But she lived in Saudi Arabia for three years, early in her career, because her husband, David, was a foreign service officer and Mideast hand.

The Mideast specialists had a celebrated history and group culture. They were drawn by the romance of a region that seemed full of nobility and savagery and infinitely far from home. In recent decades the Middle East was the world's most turbulent region and the Mideast bureau was always at the center of the action. Top State Department officials spent their days worrying about the multiple wars that raged at any moment, Arab-Israeli frictions, counterterrorism campaigns, civil upheavals, and ethnic strife. About half the paper flowing to the department's mahogany-paneled executive floor was about the Middle East. Young foreign service officers were told that the Near Eastern Affairs bureau, known to insiders as the "mother bureau," was a club that admitted only the best. Mediocre talents would not stand up to the demands and pace of these jobs. "It was drilled into us: you're part of an elite group," said former ambassador R. Nicholas Burns, who began his career as a Mideast specialist and rose to number three in the department. "And that's what drew me."

The State Department's Mideast specialists were a small tribe, a fraction of a foreign service that itself is compact. Of the 75,000 State Department employees, only about 8,000 are the so-called foreign service generalists who do the core diplomatic work. Until recently that was fewer than the number of musicians in U.S. military bands. Only a handful speak the difficult language of Arabic well enough to conduct top-level diplomacy. The Mideast hands have long been known as proud, loyal to each other, and a bit insular. They see themselves as diehards who work long hours in blast-furnace heat, risking dysentery and terrorist attack while their colleagues in more stable regions knock off at dusk for cocktails. (Other bureaus have a different view, of course.)

The chaos was the attraction. Former ambassador A. Elizabeth Jones, a Mideast veteran, recalled a colleague telling her: "I want to be able to go down the hall and say, 'I'll be goddamned—guess what's happened now?' If you can't say that, what's the point?" Even after years in the region, the Mideast hands remain fascinated by its romance. When they arrive in a new country, they gravitate toward the tribal leader in a flowing gold-trimmed robe rather than the government functionary who might have more influence. "You go into the Foreign Service to meet a sheikh, not some bureaucrat in an ill-fitting polyester suit," said former ambassador Gordon Gray III.

Their role as regional experts didn't always make them popular. They often had to deliver bad news that Washington's plans would take longer and cost more than expected, and sometimes wouldn't work at all. Often their superiors didn't want to hear it.

Under the code of the Foreign Service, the diplomats were entitled to disagree with top officials during initial debates over policy. Once the policy was set, they were supposed to salute smartly and help figure out how to make the approach succeed. They were part of a nonpartisan professional service, and that's the way it was supposed to work.

That was sometimes easier said than done. All of the ambassadors wrestled with their consciences over what they considered disastrous policy blunders. They always had a choice. They could quit, as some diplomats and military officers did. Or they could stay on the job, hoping they would make more of a contribution by using their skill to make the policies work. Crocker and Stevens came close to quitting over the Iraq invasion. Stevens refused repeated requests to serve in Iraq, at some risk to his career. Patterson considered joining a new management at the Pentagon in 2017 in hopes of setting right mistakes of the Obama administration. Ford, after years of misgivings, finally decided he could no longer support administration policy and had to quit.

The rule requiring foreign service officers to support all policies "is simple in concept—a lot harder in practice," Crocker said after he retired.[4]

Other Americans who risked all on the front lines won acclaim for their contributions. The exploits of generals, spies, and sharpshooters were chronicled in bestselling books, movies, and TV series. But the complicated business of steering relations between nations didn't stir the public's passions. It never had. "There are no ticker tape parades for diplomats," said Richard N. Haass, who headed the State Department's policy planning office under Secretary of State Powell.[5]

When the Trump administration arrived in 2017, the Foreign Service's problem wasn't indifference but hostility. Skeptical of traditional foreign policy and its practitioners, the Trump team sought to cut the State Department's budget by 30 percent in its first year, 25 percent in its second, and 23 percent in its third. It shuttered offices that had been occupied by diplomats and gave top foreign policy posts to military officers and cable news personalities. Two years into the administration, almost one half of the State Department's top jobs remained unfilled.[6] It was "perhaps the foreign service's greatest crisis," Crocker and former ambassador Nicholas Burns warned in an op-ed column.[7]

Among those who had been closest to the action, there was no doubt about the value of the diplomats at the battle's edge. The presidents and secretaries of state who preceded Trump had relied on them as caretakers of the most sensitive overseas relationships and consulted them before making the weightiest foreign policy decisions. During emergencies they talked to them many times a day. They enlisted them, because of their nonpartisan credibility, to sell controversial policies to a skeptical Congress. When these diplomats left the service, the top administration officials continued to seek their advice and sometimes tried to rehire them or recruit them for secret missions.

As the presidents knew, you had to hear their take on the mess in the Middle East. You couldn't understand it without them.

CHAPTER 2

# Go Figure Something Out

Ryan Crocker had just returned to Washington from the Middle East on the day after Christmas 2001 when he was summoned to the executive floor of the State Department. Deputy Secretary of State Richard Armitage, a bull-necked and famously gruff former Navy officer, had marching orders. "Crocker, we need you in Afghanistan now!" Armitage barked.

The U.S.-led military campaign that had ousted the Taliban government after the 9/11 attacks was winding down and U.S. troops were leaving. The administration needed someone to lead the newly reopened Kabul embassy and help organize the Afghan government that had been conceived only that month at a conference of world powers in Bonn, Germany. The mission would be difficult, the country dangerous and chaotic, and the living conditions primitive. It was just what Crocker wanted.

Seven days later, Crocker got off a military plane at Bagram Air Base, thirty miles north of Kabul, and was driven to the capital across a muddy ribbon of road through a postapocalyptic wasteland. He passed the blackened carcasses of abandoned tanks, collapsed homes, and uncleared minefields. Kabul in 2002 was the worst place he ever saw during his career—worse than Beirut or Baghdad in their worst days. The city didn't seem like the scene of a developing-world struggle as much as Berlin in 1945, with block after block of crushed buildings that looked like so many broken teeth. Broad boulevards that had once been shaded by stately chinar trees were pitted with craters and carpeted in rubble. No cars were on the roads, most shops were closed, and the few pedestrians who dared venture out seemed dazed and fearful. Most of the damage was caused not by the Taliban or American invaders but by Afghans fighting each other in block-by-block tank battles during the devastating civil war of 1992 to 1996. Crocker surveyed the damage and thought: *My God, we've got quite a job in front of us.*

The U.S. embassy had been closed in 1989 because of fears that a civil war would erupt as the Soviets pulled out after their bloody nine-year occupation. It had been reopened three weeks before Crocker arrived, after the U.S. forces and their Afghan allies entered the city. There were signs of the embassy staff's hurried departure: documents remained stacked on desks under coatings of dust, and old ashtrays were half-full. On the walls were faded pictures of former secretary of state George Shultz. In the cafeteria the menu listed hot dogs at a 1980s price of 25 cents.

The embassy had had more than its share of trouble. The last ambassador posted there was Adolph Dubs, who had been kidnapped in 1979 by Afghan militants disguised as police, then killed during a botched rescue attempt. Washington didn't send an ambassador for a decade after that incident, leaving it instead to be run by lower-ranking diplomats.

The embassy had no electricity, heat, or water. There was no regular phone or telegraph service, Internet, or any of the classified links governments depend on. Communications with the outside world were, in the early days, entirely by satellite phone. Some staff meetings were held in the first-floor lobby in almost total darkness, except for the light of a single candle.

For sleeping quarters, much of the staff was jammed into a six-room underground concrete bunker across a field from the main building, the chancery. Crocker made do with a sleeping bag in his office. Many of the windows in the embassy building were broken, and the winds knifing through them made it hard to ever feel really warm.

The Taliban had melted away, but the Americans never knew for sure the intentions of the armed militiamen who roamed the capi-

tal's streets. The company of ninety young Marines and sailors who
protected the embassy were mostly teenagers on their first deploy-
ment, learning on the job. They came with all the gear needed to
sustain the embassy: medical kit, equipment for gathering intelligence and engineering tasks, missiles to fight off a tank attack.
They gave Afghan streets American names for their use because
they couldn't read Afghan script. Here and there across the city,
tiny metal tail fins poked from the soil, looking like some form
of science fiction plant life. They were unexploded ordnance, and
they claimed hundreds of lives in Afghanistan every year.

The danger and disorder were a tonic for Crocker. The vibra-
tion he gave off was " 'This is a great adventure. Aren't we lucky?
Man, we're in the action,'" recalled Jonah Blank, then an aide to
former senator Joseph Biden (D-Del.), who visited the embassy
only weeks after it reopened. If Crocker had been uncomfortable,
Blank said, the staff would have sensed it, with damaging effects
on morale. But they could see Crocker was where he wanted to be,
and found him reassuring.

Crocker set a brisk pace. He had developed a running habit in the
1970s and during postings in Washington had jogged every morning the eight miles from his home in Alexandria, Virginia, to State
Department headquarters. The streets of Kabul were still too dangerous for an early-morning run, so fifty-two-year-old Crocker got
in the habit of running a tight circle around the embassy, followed by
pull-ups on a set of outdoor bars. The commander of the Marine unit
had been excusing his troops from their usual dawn exercise because
of the city's dangers. Then he spotted the gray-haired ambassador,
his thin face flushed and dripping as he labored in Kabul's morning
cold. The officer issued a new order: Do like the old guy.

Crocker was a natural choice for the assignment because of his
long history in danger zones. Serving in Lebanon in 1982 during
the country's bloody civil war, he risked his life investigating the
slaughter of at least eight hundred Palestinians by right-wing Christian militias in Beirut's Sabra and Shatila refugee camps. Crocker
drove himself to the camps in the middle of the night to investi-

gate rumors of a massacre while gunmen were still present. The same year a band of teenage militiamen abducted him on a street in Beirut and threatened his life. The following year he was working in the U.S. embassy in Beirut when the militant group Hezbollah set off a 2,000-pound truck bomb at the embassy's entrance, killing sixty-three. Crocker was shadowed by Saddam Hussein's secret police during a posting in Baghdad in the late 1970s and had his home attacked and looted while he was ambassador to Syria in 1998.

The brushes with danger convinced him he belonged in the field. He took only two managerial jobs at State Department headquarters in Washington during his career and tried to keep those short. He and his wife, Christine, also a State Department staffer, decided they would have no children because of the difficulty of juggling family and frequent postings abroad.

"Ryan would look around for wherever the worst crisis was, the hardest place to go, and he'd wave his hand and say, 'I'll go there,'" said former ambassador Thomas C. Krajeski, who served in the Mideast and Washington with Crocker.[1]

Insiders differentiated between two types of Mideast hands. One group were the "indoor Arabists," who spent their time in Washington working on long-running diplomatic problems, such as the Israeli-Arab conflict. The other were the "outdoor Arabists," who jumped in their cars to drive through gunfire and sandstorms to interview sources in the local dialect. Crocker was in the second group.

The reopened U.S. embassy in Kabul got a ceremonial blessing on January 17, 2002, when Secretary of State Colin Powell thundered in on a Chinook helicopter, with machine gunners in front and rear, for a six-hour visit. Crocker greeted Powell at the embassy and described the diplomats' mission in military terms. "The men and women of this mission are very happy to be your forward element," Crocker told the retired general.

Powell met with Hamid Karzai, an opposition leader of the Pashtun ethnic group who a month earlier had been made interim head of the new government by world powers at the conference in Bonn, Germany. Among the chandeliers and rose-marble columns of the faded royal palace, Powell clasped hands with Karzai, who had a courtly bearing, a shiny bald head, and a beak-like nose. Karzai was wearing the lambskin hat and shimmering emerald and blue cape that became his signature formal dress. Powell assured him the Bush administration was "doing everything we can to assist you in this time of transition to a new Afghanistan."

In truth, the administration wasn't doing all it could, and intended to do even less. While Powell and State Department officials wanted more money and troops to ensure the success of the new government, officials at the White House and Pentagon were determined to step back from the chronic troubles of one of the world's poorest countries. They wanted the Afghans to rely on the United Nations mission that had been set up to help. They wanted U.S. forces focused on completing the counterterror fight and not involved in the kind of postwar rebuilding the Clinton administration had undertaken in the Balkans and elsewhere in the 1990s. The Afghans resented foreigners, they argued, and a large troop presence would only anger them and inflame resistance. The administration ruled out any U.S. contribution of troops to the 4,000-soldier British-led international peacekeeping force taking shape in Kabul. Officials agreed to spend about $1 billion for reconstruction and humanitarian relief in 2002, a figure that Pentagon comptroller Dov Zakheim considered about $500 million short of what was needed.[2] "We're not there to fix their problems," President Bush told Zalmay Khalilzad, his special envoy for Afghanistan.[3]

But even though White House and Pentagon officials were determined to limit U.S. spending on Afghanistan, the State Department was happy to have its low-cost foreign service team do what it could. Crocker was dispatched with orders to help make a government in name only, a real one. He was given full freedom to do it as he wished—more freedom, really, than he wanted. "I did not arrive with a detailed set of instructions on what the administration wished to have accomplished in those initial months," Crocker

said. "In fact, I arrived without any instructions—just, 'Go figure something out.'" The assignment was a rush job, and the State Department didn't have time to get the Senate to confirm Crocker as ambassador. He led the mission as the chargé d'affaires, the fill-in mission chief.

His key partner was Karzai, the interim leader. The day after Crocker arrived, he visited Karzai and discovered that the leader's offices in the former royal palace were ice-cold. The two wrapped themselves in blankets and launched into the first of many meetings. "We just sat down and started to map through all the steps we would need to take to ensure that there was an Afghan government that could function like a government," he said.

Crocker and Karzai got in the habit of meeting at dawn, when the rest of the city was still asleep, and huddling next to a space heater, sipping traditional *chai shireen*. The palace, known as the Arg, was a once-grand nineteenth-century stone citadel with eighty-three acres of gardens, courtyards, and decorative pools, enclosed in high walls with ramparts, battlements, and turrets. Now the gardens were overgrown, the roof leaked, and the plumbing was busted. The office of the new head of state smelled faintly of sewage.

"Every conversation we had would begin with the phrase, 'What the hell do we do now?'" Crocker said.

Crocker understood when he arrived that this diplomacy would be far different from the craft as outsiders imagined it. Though a civilian, he could not avoid becoming deeply involved in the continuing military struggle.

In early March U.S. commanders decided to send a column of tanks owned by allies of the Tajik ethnic group from the country's north to a valley south of Kabul. U.S. forces had no tanks, and they desperately needed big guns to blast Al Qaeda and Taliban forces from a stronghold in the remote Shah-i-Kot Valley. But when the tanks reached the city of Gardez, 80 miles south of Kabul, they were blocked by a rival Pashtun warlord. The warlord, Pacha Khan Zadran, also a U.S. ally, was incensed that the Tajiks wanted to cross his territory. He threatened to attack with his 3,000-man force, unless the Tajiks turned around. It appeared that in their search for more firepower U.S. commanders had touched off an ethnic confrontation that might split their coalition.

It fell to Crocker to find a way out. In U.S. battlefield strategy sessions, CIA officers and special forces commanders towered over him. But he had dealt with militia chiefs in earlier postings. He was willing to try it again.

Crocker tracked down Zadran's brother and senior aide, a bearded, scowling commander called Amanullah. Then he spent a night with him in a bullet-scarred, unheated building in Kabul, arguing by the light of a single kerosene lamp.

Crocker made the case that the Tajik force would help the Zadrans beat their common enemies, the Taliban. The Tajiks had no designs, he insisted, on the Pashtun territory. But as the hours dragged on, Zadran came up with a series of reasons why the armored column could not advance. Zadran, it was clear, had made up his mind and was simply offering excuses. Crocker finally broke off the negotiation. He conferred for a last few minutes with his U.S. team and Afghan allies. Then he returned and played his last card.

The United States would give its guarantee that the Tajik forces would withdraw after the fight, he told Zadran. But if the warlord continued to resist, the Tajiks would advance anyway. "If we have to fight our way through, we will," he said. "And if we find your brother in those circumstances, we will kill or capture him. You will be fighting us." The U.S.-Afghan force had overwhelming power, he pointed out: not just tanks, but F-16 fighter aircraft.

The giant Pashtun "had his awakening moment," Crocker recalled later. "I finally had something he could comprehend." Pacha Khan Zadran ordered his force to stand down and the tanks passed. Crocker had won the day, on the edge of the battlefield, by threatening the life of an ally.

Another of Crocker's chief tasks was helping Karzai figure out how to set up a working political structure and run a country. World leaders had made Karzai Afghanistan's interim leader in part because he was well-spoken, peace loving, inclusive, and presentable. In a country of rough-hewn and often violent leaders, Karzai could describe in eloquent English, Pashtun, and Dari how his country yearned to emerge from thirty years of civil war to become a modern society. Karzai relished his ceremonial role and was delighted at his unlikely ascent to power. But he had no clue how to run a government. The product of a family of tribal leaders from the southern city of Kandahar, he had spent his adult life as an English teacher and then a public relations aide for an opposition politician. When Karzai was sworn in in December, he inherited a state that had no police force, military, or government bureaucracy, and was nearly broke. When he chose ministers, they sat alone in battle-scarred buildings in Kabul. The country was chronically wracked by sectarian warfare and had never had an effective central government.

In those first days of his thirteen years as the country's leader, Karzai needed some prodding to do his part. Karzai wanted to bring back the functioning Afghanistan of his youth, "but he was oddly passive about doing so," wrote Zalmay Khalilzad, the Afghan-born scholar and diplomat who was made U.S. presidential envoy to the country in December 2001 and U.S. ambassador two years later. "He knew what needed to be done. The problem was he wanted America and the rest of the world to do it."[4] The CIA officials who had led the U.S. effort in Afghanistan since the fall told Crocker when he arrived he would need to push Karzai to start organizing the government, build support from provincial leaders, and figure out how to spend his meager budget.

Crocker, eager to build a personal tie with the Afghan leader, listened patiently to Karzai. He called him "sir" and showed him the deference Karzai craved. But Crocker was also persistent in reminding him what needed to be done. Crocker understood that "if you didn't tell Karzai what to do, he wouldn't do anything," said a former senior intelligence officer who was in Afghanistan at the time. "You had to say, 'Do this, appoint this guy, get rid of

this guy'. . . Ryan was the first one to really kick Karzai in the ass."
Unlike some U.S. diplomats, Crocker wasn't queasy about telling
officials of the host government what to do, the intelligence official said.

One of Karzai's top priorities was building support for the new
government from warlords and other regional leaders who were the
real power in the country. Karzai needed to distribute some posts
in the new government to the regional bosses to strengthen their
support for Kabul and to allow him to keep tabs on what they were
doing. But the field of candidates was not inspiring, and sometimes
Crocker and other U.S. officials would discover Karzai had chosen
Afghans who were too corrupt or too closely tied to the drug trade
or the Taliban. They would tell Karzai he needed to cancel their
appointments. He was usually amenable.

Through Karzai's office and sitting room flowed a constant
stream of Afghans, prominent and obscure, lobbying for money,
security forces, appointments, or the arrest of a rival. Karzai was
always ready to hear their supplications and sometimes too willing
to grant them. He had the bad habit of "listening to the last corrupt
Afghan official he saw in his office," said the former intelligence
official. Sometimes, after these sessions, Crocker would have to
meet with Karzai to explain that he would have to take back what
he had just promised.

All issues, big and small, ended up in Karzai's in-box. One morning, over an Afghan breakfast at the palace, Karzai told Crocker he
wanted to discuss the design of a new Afghan flag. He sketched his
idea on a napkin. He wanted to restore the traditional red, green,
and black color scheme used by the old Afghan monarchy, sending
a signal of continuity that he thought would be popular. He wanted
also to add, in Arabic script, the *Shahada*, the Muslim profession
of faith: "There is no God but Allah and Muhammad is Allah's
messenger." Karzai summoned an aide to take his doodle to the
bazaar, to see what it would look like when turned into a flag. The
aide eventually returned with the flag, and Karzai was pleased.

Crocker helped Karzai try to defuse frictions between the warlords. When the Taliban was ousted, militia leaders filled the vacuum of power, leaving them controlling vast stretches of the country. Some of the most aggressive among them began maneuvering to expand their fiefdoms. Around the northern provincial capital of Mazar-e-Sharif, warlords General Atta Muhammad Noor, an ethnic Tajik commander, and General Abdul Rashid Dostum, an Uzbek, quickly began a confrontation over control of the city.

Soon after he arrived, Crocker traveled to the north to visit Atta and urge him to settle his differences with Dostum. Atta told Crocker there would be no trouble—not because he was willing to compromise, but because he intended to overwhelm Dostum. "The response was basically: 'I'm going to annihilate that guy and everybody who's shaken hands with him,'" Crocker said. The rivalry between them raged for years.

The rivalries sometimes exploded into violence in the capital. In February 2002, the minister of civil aviation, Abdul Rahman, was beaten to death by a mob at the Kabul airport. Crocker learned about it one night during a meeting with Karzai when the defense minister Muhammad Qasim Fahim, who was also commander of the Northern Alliance forces, burst into the room giggling with the news. Karzai and Crocker were stunned. The first reports had it that Rahman had been attacked by Muslim pilgrims angry that their flight to Mecca had been canceled. Karzai soon concluded the killing was the work of officials in his intelligence, defense, and justice ministries who had long been Rahman's rivals. Karzai held a press conference to denounce the crime and announce the launch of an investigation. But the accused were never brought to trial, and several retained high-level posts in the government. The incident was the ultimate example, Crocker thought, of the poisonous rivalries that swirled in Kabul.

Crocker carried on a continuing round of meetings with local and tribal leaders. Some were near the capital, but to reach others he had to fly by helicopter across the mountains to remote landing strips and struggle across rocky terrain to reach the leaders' homes. Intelligence officials recommended that he avoid risky travel, "but

Crocker was clamoring to go to iffy areas," said a former senior U.S. intelligence official. He wanted to wear jacket and tie to show respect for the Afghan leaders, even though formal dress could make him a target for enemy snipers. CIA officers wore beards and Afghan clothes to reduce that risk.

On arrival, Crocker's team would be waved into the leader's walled compound and greeted in the courtyard with handshakes and embraces. Then they would step inside to talk for hours, sipping tea and eating raisins and nuts. They would sit on pillows and simple rugs or Chinese-made polyester carpets, often in concrete walled rooms with diesel-burning heaters. The leaders were rarely well off but generous with their hospitality, following Afghan tradition. In those months the Americans were still popular for ousting the Taliban.

American diplomats often make one of two mistakes in such introductory meetings. Sometimes they are too deferential, an approach that invites their new contact to press them with demands. In other cases, they lecture the local leader on what America expects of them. Crocker tried to convey that he understood the pressures on the leaders and, without promising more than he could deliver, wanted to work out solutions that could benefit both sides, colleagues said.

The local leaders usually had a wish list: weapons, water wells, medical help, garbage trucks. Sometimes they would tell the American team that they were under attack by the Taliban, when their skirmishes were actually not with militants but with their longtime local rivals. Crocker had to know enough about local politics not to be snowed.

"Crocker would say 'Thanks for telling me that. Maybe they're Taliban. But don't they also happen to be that group you're historically at war with?'" recalled a former U.S. official who worked with him. "'How about you make it a priority to reconcile with that guy, so that you both can use the highway and the mountain pass? Then you'll both get help from us.'"

Sometimes the local leader got the message right away. In other cases, it took them longer. Sometimes an emissary would show up later in Kabul asking Crocker: What about the aid you promised? In one case, Crocker answered: Why are we still hearing reports that your militia is still fighting with your neighbor on the highway? Although Crocker was new to the region, he had heard similar pitches for thirty years in the Mideast. Word got around among the local leaders that Crocker knew what he was doing and had pull in Washington.

When Crocker arrived, the new government was almost without cash. The Taliban had raided the central bank's vault before leaving town, and the country's primitive financial system was barely functioning. Crocker spent one of his first nights in the embassy on a satellite phone, shivering in the draft, trying to get Federal Reserve officials to send cash to Karzai to jump-start the government.

Many of Karzai's cabinet ministers started their jobs with nothing more than what they were given by the United Nations: a single Land Rover and a satellite phone. The bombed-out official buildings they worked from had recently been occupied by the Taliban.

The new government faced tough choices in deciding how to spend its meager resources. Afghanistan's needs were overwhelming: 70 percent of the population was malnourished, and one quarter of children died before age five. But in addition to providing humanitarian relief, they needed to build credibility for the new government, both with Afghans and with the world powers that were helping to sustain it. "We had to create at least a plausible image of Afghanistan as a country that could succeed," Crocker said. They needed to show progress.

Education was an area where they could do that. Much of the world knew of the plight of Afghan girls and women who had been excluded from education by the Taliban. First Lady Laura Bush, among others, had championed their cause. And within weeks of its arrival, the new Afghan government, with U.S. help, was reopening schools for girls as well as boys, with gratifying results.

During Senator Joe Biden's early visit, Crocker led the delegation to a newly opened first-grade class in Kabul. The girls ranged in age from six to twelve, because the older ones had had no chance up to that point to go to school. Crocker asked one twelve-year-old if it bothered her to be in a class with girls half her age. She beamed. "I'm just so happy to be in school," she told him.

When Crocker arrived in January 2002, there were 900,000 pupils in Afghan schools, all boys. By September of that year, there were 3 million, far exceeding expectations, with about 30 percent of them girls. Over the next decade and a half, as the economy sputtered and violence raged, education remained a bright spot.

Crocker helped direct other aspects of the development program. The U.S. Agency for International Development, the lead U.S. foreign aid agency, had decided to give agriculture an early focus. But many of the agricultural projects would not produce results for several growing seasons. Crocker pushed to have the money go instead to rebuilding the nation's roads, arguing that without them produce wouldn't get to market. Andrew Natsios, USAID's director, agreed.

Crocker, Karzai, and his team held a long brainstorming session trying to figure out how they could find skilled, culturally attuned, and reasonably priced help to build a new country. Their answer: enlist accomplished Afghan expatriates from Europe and America. They began reaching out.

One of Crocker's most important contributions was in enlisting the help of Iran. The Iranians were seen by the Bush administration as a chief regional foe and the world's foremost sponsor of terrorism, and the White House had barred high-level negotiations with them. But after the 9/11 attacks, Iran had stepped forward to offer Washington help in ousting the Taliban, whom they viewed as an enemy. Starting in late September 2001, Crocker had served repeatedly as a point man in secret talks about the military campaign and formation of the new government in Kabul.

Crocker's meetings with the Iranians after 9/11 had hopscotched from Geneva to Paris and New York. While Tehran was publicly denouncing the United States, its diplomats were lobbying Washington to send its troops into Afghanistan to install a new government.

One round of meetings was held in the United Nations offices in Geneva on weekends, when no one else was around. Crocker would slip out of State Department headquarters on Friday afternoons to catch flights so that the talks were known only to the smallest circle. The American and Iranian officials sometimes began their talks in the UN offices, then adjourned to hotel rooms, where they ordered room service for dinner, then continued talking until dawn. Crocker found the Iranians civil, professional, and fully informed on American culture, including the recent performance of the UCLA Bruins football team. Two of the three Iranian diplomats had been to school in the States. Crocker learned that the diplomats were being directed from Iran by General Qassim Suleimanei, leader of the elite Quds Force unit of the Iranian Revolutionary Guard Corps. Suleimani, a small man with sleepy dark eyes and a close-cropped silver beard, was feared and admired throughout the Middle East as Iran's military mastermind.

The Iranians, who had been helping the Taliban's Afghan opponents for years, offered a full range of military intelligence and advice. They produced a map detailing the location of Taliban troops and arms. "The Iranian thrust was, 'What do you need to know to knock their blocks off? You want their order of battle? Here's the map. You want to know where we think their weak points are? Here, here and here,'" Crocker said.

The Iranians grew impatient only when they thought the Americans were dragging their heels on the invasion. One of the Iranian officials blew up at Crocker during a long discussion on how to organize a new government in Afghanistan. There was no point in debating a new government, he declared, unless Washington was going to move against the current one. He stomped out of the room.

The Iranians listened to briefings from U.S. intelligence on Al Qaeda's presence in Iran and arrested some of the group's members there. In November 2001, when world powers met in Bonn, Germany, to help organize a new Afghan government, the Iranians played a key role. They were even agreeable to having an international peacekeeping force in the country after the war.

When Crocker arrived in Kabul, he discovered that Mohammad Ebrahim Taherian, the Iranian official who had led the fall weekend talks in Geneva was now ambassador to Kabul. So the U.S.-Iranian talks simply picked up where they had left off. They made plans to collaborate on a ring of highways that would link the country. The plan was for the Iranians to start building in Herat, in the country's west, and work eastward toward Kandahar in the south. The Americans would start in Kabul, in the east, and work westward. The two sides even discussed using a similar composition for asphalt so that their roads would join seamlessly.

The talks led to a discussion of more sensitive issues, such as how to reduce threats from the more aggressive warlords to other provincial leaders. The Americans worked on limiting Abdul Rashid Dostum's ambitions in the north by giving him a role in the new central government while the Iranians applied pressure to restrain Ismail Khan, a Tajik power broker who ran much of western Afghanistan. The plan worked reasonably well for a time.

Crocker passed on to the Iranians the location of an Al Qaeda official who was living in Mashhad, in eastern Iran. The Iranians arrested him and turned him over to Afghan officials, who in turn passed him to U.S. officials.

The Iranians were also taking care to avoid run-ins with the U.S. and allied forces in the country. Tehran's Islamic Revolutionary Guard Corps, a chief executor of the regime's foreign policy, was present all over the country. But unlike in Iraq, where they became a deadly threat to U.S. forces, "they never interfered with us," said a former senior intelligence officer. "They never attacked us and we never attacked them."

But the U.S.-Iranian cooperation unraveled quickly after January 29, 2002, when President Bush declared in his State of the Union speech that Iran was a member of the "axis of evil" and threatened to attack its nuclear program. Crocker's next meeting with his Iranian counterparts was ugly. An Iranian official demanded to know how, after their collaboration on Afghanistan, Washington had seemed to turn on them so abruptly. "What are you

guys doing?" the Iranian demanded. He told Crocker that his standing at home had been damaged by the speech. Suleimanei, too, felt
jeopardized by the speech, and was in a "tearing rage," the diplomat said.[5] Crocker had no good answer. He stammered something
like "I'm the guy in Kabul. We've got to focus on the issues we've
been dealing with."[6]

Crocker was most upset because it appeared the speech had
destroyed a chance for improved relations between the two states.
The Iranian diplomat told Crocker that Suleimanei had been weighing a complete re-evaluation of the relationship. "One word in one
speech changed history," Crocker said.[7]

The Iranians were now thinking about payback. The Americans
and Iranians had been discussing what to do with former Afghan
prime minister Gulbuddin Hekmatyar, who had ties to Osama bin
Laden and had been one of the country's most brutal warlords in
the 1980s and 1990s. Hekmatyar was then in luxurious house arrest
in Tehran. But U.S. officials feared he would try to seize power in
Afghanistan if freed and were urging that he be jailed and turned
over to Afghan authorities. They were also quietly lobbying to have
Iran jail any Al Qaeda fugitives they picked up.

After the speech, the Iranians made it clear they would not help
on either issue. The Iranian diplomat told Crocker they planned not
only to release Hekmatyar from house arrest but also to help him
surreptitiously reenter Afghanistan. U.S. troops tried but failed to
intercept him on his way in. In the years since, Hekmatyar's Hezb-
i-Islami insurgents have been among the most dangerous opponents of U.S. forces and the Afghan government.

In Crocker's view, the "axis of evil" speech marked a point of
no return where the Iranians decided they couldn't cooperate with
the Americans, even where interests overlapped. "It was the point,
I think, where the Iranians made the decision, 'Can't work with
those sons of bitches. Told you all along, can't do it,'" Crocker said.
The hard-liners in Iran gradually took control of the Afghan portfolio from more moderate officials in the foreign ministry. While the
U.S.-Iranian talks continued intermittently until May 2003, they

were passed to lower-ranking Iranian officials and yielded less and less. The speech "killed the diplomatic channel that Ryan Crocker had so skillfully developed with the Iranians," William J. Burns, then the State Department's assistant secretary for the Middle East, wrote in his memoir, *The Back Channel*.[8]

Karzai and many other Afghan leaders remained worried about security. Afghan delegations from around the country were always asking him for troops to protect them from warlords or criminal gangs. Karzai believed warlords were a threat to the country, to the new government, and to him personally. Pacha Khan Zadran, the Pashtun warlord who tried to prevent the tanks reaching the battle in the Shah-i-Kot Valley, repeatedly defied Karzai. In May his militias launched a rocket attack on the city of Gardez in an attempt to seize power. Another threat came from defense minister Muhammad Qasim Fahim, who swaggered around Kabul as if he and his 15,000 troops, rather than Karzai, were running the government. Fahim made himself at home in Karzai's palace, sometimes sitting in the leader's chair even when Karzai was in the room. He joked darkly that if Karzai arranged the government in a way he didn't like, he would send his guards to kill him.[9] Karzai confessed to American officials he feared he could be killed at any time. When American officials visited, Karzai would invariably press them for more American troops.

But the Pentagon was dead set against sending more U.S. troops and didn't want the allies to send more of their troops, either. Defense Secretary Donald Rumsfeld and other Pentagon officials opposed expanding the mission of the international force in Kabul, believing that would discourage the Afghans from figuring out how to protect themselves.

After a few weeks in the country, Crocker began to fear that a clash between rival warlords could cripple the new government before it got started. The U.S. forces in the country then consisted of a single Marine expeditionary unit, usually 2,200 troops, and a scattering of special forces teams. The administration's bywords in the anti-Taliban campaign had been "small footprint" and "economy of force." "This was economy of force to the nth degree," Crocker said. Was this smart strategy, Crocker wondered, or simply an effort to pull off regime change on the cheap? If the government fell, Afghanistan could once more become a lawless state and Washington could again face the same militant threat that brought American troops there in the first place, Crocker thought. U.S. forces might be compelled to return.

Crocker's worries were shared by the leader of the international force, British Army major general John McColl. He as well as Karzai and Lakhdar Brahimi, the United Nations special envoy for Afghanistan, favored a larger force that could take on threats outside of Kabul.

Crocker and McColl came up with a plan to strengthen the force. Their idea was to have an expanded company of troops in each of four cities in corners of the country. The companies would be backed up by an airmobile battalion—a helicopter force with massive firepower—that could reach the cities within an hour or two if a threat appeared. The force would deter warlords from attacking the Kabul government or fighting among themselves. The message would be "We're here to develop a unified Afghan state and if you have different views you'll be chopped up into hamburger," Crocker said.

Crocker and McColl cabled their proposals to Washington and London at the same time. And they both got replies that were emphatic and negative. Officials in Washington and London called back in the middle of the night telling them, essentially, "'We're shredding this: Don't ever send in anything like this again,'" Crocker recalled.

Other officials, including Secretary of State Powell and former U.S. envoy James F. Dobbins, also pushed to add more troops and were also rebuffed. In truth, most top officials in Washington were no longer thinking about Afghanistan but focused on preparing for the coming war against Iraq. As former envoy on Afghanistan, Dobbins had been recruited to oversee Afghan issues from Washington between January and April 2002, while Crocker was in charge in Kabul. During that period Dobbins didn't have a single inquiry about Afghanistan from top administration officials. There were only two interagency meetings on Afghanistan at the White House during the period.[10]

On April 3, Crocker wrapped up his mission in Kabul and boarded a plane at Bagram Air Base to return to Washington. But the three months had convinced him that the administration had misunderstood the outcome of the campaign and bungled the aftermath. U.S. officials didn't appreciate the complexity of the situation, the intensity of local rivalries, or the resistance to the new government, he feared.

The battle in the Shah-i-Kot Valley, which began after Crocker's negotiation over the tanks, had turned out to be the largest American battle since the Persian Gulf war. The American and allied forces had destroyed the militants' mountain stronghold. General Tommy Franks, the Army four-star who led the U.S. military effort in Afghanistan, described the battle as "an absolute and unqualified success." Bush administration officials were convinced that their minimal-force strategy had been brilliant. In Washington they were already preparing to use it in their next war, against Saddam Hussein's Iraq.

Crocker had a different view. He believed the battle showed that the enemy was stronger and more tenacious than expected and that America's Afghan allies were weaker and more divided. Eight Americans had been killed in the battle, and eighty wounded. The enemy was presumed to have had many casualties, but few bodies were ever found in the valley. By the time the attackers had gathered enough force to destroy the enemy, Crocker believed, most of the Al Qaeda and Taliban fighters had escaped to havens in Pakistan's wild border areas. There they would join others to rearm, recruit, and begin raids on U.S. and allied forces in Afghanistan.

Crocker's effort to get the tanks to Shah-i-Kot Valley had convinced him that the war had been dangerously under-resourced. He saw another troubling sign when he learned that U.S. forces had been picking up a steady flow of young Afghans who were trying to cross their lines to get into the battle. They were trying to join not the American side but the Taliban's. It looked like resistance to the new government might be far stronger than Washington had expected. "It was another uh-oh moment for me," Crocker said. The war in Afghanistan might be just getting started.

# CHAPTER 3

# The Perfect Storm

Ryan Crocker returned to Washington, D.C., from Afghanistan in April 2002, ready to resume his job at State Department headquarters helping manage the difficult U.S. relationships with Iraq, Iran, and the Persian Gulf emirates. But his job had been completely transformed. The Bush administration was edging toward a war with Iraq. And for the next year Crocker was caught up in an acrimonious internal debate over whether to go to war and how to run the country once U.S. forces had taken control. It was one of the most agonizing periods of his career.

Secretary of State Colin Powell, the department's Mideast hands, and many military and intelligence officials thought an invasion unwise and unnecessary. But others, including civilian officials in Defense Secretary Donald Rumsfeld's Pentagon, and in the office of Vice President Dick Cheney, believed the country needed to reassert its military might after 9/11. And they had the president's ear.

Deputy Secretary of State Richard Armitage would head off to top-level meetings about the war and return hours later growling about how the skeptics had been rolled by advocates for the invasion. State Department officials were seen by the other side as not just doubters on the war, but active opponents. To observers, the split between the two sides looked like the chasm that opened in the following year between rival Muslim groups in Iraq. "It was Sunni and Shia, but in Washington," said Charles Duelfer, who was working with both groups at the time as part of his mission as a United

Nations weapons inspector for Iraq. "They could never agree on a shared strategy or set of facts."[1]

Crocker was one of the government's most knowledgeable sources on Iraq, a repository of its institutional memory. He had been posted there from 1978 to 1980, when Saddam seized absolute power. He had been sent to Baghdad in 1998—the first U.S. official inside Iraq since the Persian Gulf war—as part of the United Nations effort to find Saddam's banned weapons programs. But Crocker wasn't included in most of the planning sessions for the war and remained in the dark on the most important decisions. It all worried him. He got in the habit of prowling by the executive-floor office of Marc Grossman, the State Department's number three, to try to find out what the administration leadership was contemplating. "What's going on?" he would ask Grossman. "Where is all of this going?"

Crocker had been picking up hints since the beginning of the administration that the inner circle was already committed to a war to oust Saddam. A few days after the 9/11 attacks, when officials were planning the campaign to oust the Taliban government in Afghanistan, one of Crocker's counterparts in the Pentagon told him ruefully that the campaign in Afghanistan was shaping up as a troublesome distraction. "All this Afghan stuff is really going to slow us down on Iraq," the official grumbled.

As the months passed, almost all the State Department's Mideast specialists became skeptics on the war. The Near Eastern Affairs bureau came to be seen by the war's champions as "a den of defeatists and Cassandras," Bill Burns, who then led the bureau as assistant secretary of state for the Middle East, wrote in his memoir.[2] Crocker was the most skeptical.[3] In the summer of 2002, he initiated a bureau effort to lay out all that could go wrong in an intervention. The result was a ten-page, single-spaced memo titled "The Perfect Storm" that warned that, once Saddam's iron grip was lifted, sectarian warfare could erupt between Iraq's sectarian factions. Violence and looting could occur if Saddam's military and police disappeared, it said, and Iraq's neighbors, including

Iran, could use the vacuum of power to meddle and expand their influence in and around the country. If Iraq slid into chaos, the United States would bear the burden and cost of restoring order, it predicted. The memo was signed by Crocker and Burns and sent in July to Secretary of State Powell and Deputy Secretary of State Armitage.

"I was scared," Crocker said. "We hadn't thought this through: we hadn't thought of the fortieth and fiftieth order consequences of bringing down a regime in the center of the Middle East." The memo's goal was not to forecast what would happen but to lay out some of the unhappy possibilities "and ask: Is it worth it?" he said. But if the memo's goal wasn't to predict, it did foresee the invasion's unhappy results, according to Armitage. "From my point of view, it was dead on the money," he said four years later, when Iraq's civil war was raging at peak intensity.[4]

Since April, Crocker had also been overseeing a yearlong State Department effort to enlist skilled Iraqi expatriates to help figure out how to deal with the challenges of a post-Saddam Iraq. The project was inspired by Crocker's recent three months in Afghanistan, where he sought to mobilize skilled Afghan expatriates to help build a state from scratch. The new effort, known as the Future of Iraq Project, enlisted more than two hundred participants, mostly Iraqi exiles, and generated a seventeen-volume report touching on key issues from agriculture and the economy to security and government formation. But the effort was seen as a threat by Ahmad Chalabi, a wily Iraqi expatriate financier whom the administration's pro-war faction wanted to put in charge of the post-invasion government. Chalabi and his allies in Washington worked to sideline the effort, while the Pentagon ignored it and began a separate planning process. "When Saddam was toppled, those seventeen volumes continued to gather dust," wrote Burns.[5] The war's advocates in the administration contended later that the study had little policy value. But a study completed in February 2009 by a U.S. watchdog agency, the Office of the Special Inspector General for Iraq Reconstruction, found that the project's "richly developed

id Crocker was following the rules. "As an FSO, you can debate
ad oppose, but when the decision is made, it's your job to try to
ake it right," said Grossman. "That's what he did."

Even before the invasion, Crocker had been helping to make
aplomatic preparations. He had the delicate task of trying to line
a the support of Mideast governments for a war with Saddam,
though officially the Bush administration had still made no final
ecision on an invasion. He spent time in the Kurdish territory in
orthern Iraq, trying to convince the Kurds' two rivalrous political
actions not to do anything that would complicate the approach-
ag war. They shouldn't start a fight with Saddam, he told them, or
another new war with each other. They agreed.

Crocker traveled to Ankara on the eve of the war to try to talk
ae reluctant Turks into cooperating with the American invasion
lan. The Bush administration had been seeking for months to
ersuade the Turks to allow 15,000 troops from the U.S. Army's
ourth Infantry Division to attack Iraq from Turkey. Such an
nfantry thrust from the north could have divided Saddam's army
nd ended the war more quickly and with fewer casualties, mili-
ary planners believed. The administration had offered the Turks a
ile of sweeteners, including $19 billion in cash and loans. But on
March 1, supporters of cooperation fell just short of gathering the
otes they needed in the Turkish parliament, dealing the U.S. plans
heavy blow.

With the Pentagon holding troops on ships in the eastern Med-
terranean in case the Turks changed their mind, Crocker made a
inal appeal to the Turks to help their NATO allies. In meetings
vith W. Robert Pearson, the U.S. ambassador to Turkey, Crocker
marshaled every argument of logic and sentiment. He recalled the
ong history of the United States and Turkey, the joint effort to
tand up to the Soviets in the Cold War, and how Ankara had sent
roops to fight side by side with Americans in the Korean War. The
Turks wouldn't budge.

Despite the vote, Washington still had enormous leverage over
Turkey. Crocker told his superiors in Washington that he was will-

reports were the single most rigorous assessment conducted by the
U.S. government before the war."[6]

Crocker thought the most regrettable outcome of the effort lay
in the Pentagon's decision not to use the dozens of knowledgeable
Iraqi-Americans who were ready to help in Iraq. Crocker asked
defense officials to allow the study's director, Tom Warrick, to
enter Iraq so that he could begin arranging for their return. But
Warrick was refused entry and the Iraqi-Americans never made it,
either. "Rumsfeld never wanted it to happen—at what cost is very
difficult to calculate," Crocker said.[7]

He also regretted that Secretary of State Colin Powell and Deputy Secretary Richard Armitage didn't use the report to help bolster
their case against the invasion. Powell never passed along to the
White House the "Perfect Storm" memo, although he told Burns
he cited it in a conversation with Bush.[8] It seemed to Crocker that,
in their anger at the war's advocates, Powell and Armitage had lost
interest in figuring out how Washington was going to deal with
post-war Iraq. "Persuaded it was a bad idea and that they couldn't
turn the decision around, they basically carped and criticized from
the sidelines," he said. "They redefined 'passive-aggressive.'"
Their attitude sharpened the frictions within the administration and
made it tougher for the State Department team who were trying to
help manage the occupation, he said.

Crocker's doubts about the war were noticed, with displeasure,
by the war's advocates. "I was spending a lot of time making a lot
of enemies," he said. "It could get nasty." In interagency meetings,
officials who favored the war would bring up Crocker's misgivings, implying that they had doubts about his loyalty to the country. Why, they asked, did he want to aid and abet the enemy? The
war's advocates read State Department officials' doubts about the
war as excessive sympathy for one of the region's most brutal
regimes. They were the "Department of Nice," said Douglas Feith,
the undersecretary of defense.[9]

At one meeting at the Pentagon, Crocker forecast that, once the
old Iraqi order collapsed, the country would fracture as ordinary

Iraqis began looking not to the state but to their tribes and families for security. Feith pushed backed, insisting that the State Department's supposed experts had it all wrong. Iraq was an educated, urbanized country, he said, and once Saddam's inner circle was removed, the country's elite would restore order and organize a new and better government. Crocker didn't press his case. "Crocker never ever argued," recalled a State Department official who was present. "He hated those meetings."

Pique at the dissenters went all the way to the top. Condoleezza Rice, then President Bush's national security adviser, viewed them as arrogant members of the permanent bureaucracy. "The inclination of some at State to display what they regard as their superior expertise was especially strong in the turbulent first years of the Bush administration. . . . There is a tendency of foreign service officers to regard the president and his political advisers as a passing phenomenon without the deep expertise that they, the professionals, bring to diplomacy," Rice wrote in her memoir, without naming names.[10]

Crocker and his team assumed that a U.S. embassy would be needed in Baghdad after the invasion and, in the fall of 2002, began preparing to open one once the war was over. They assumed Crocker would head the mission initially as chargé d'affaires, the interim ambassador. But President Bush ultimately gave overall control of the mission in post-invasion Iraq to the Pentagon, reasoning that only the Defense Department had the numbers and budget needed to do the job. And defense officials vetoed the idea of an embassy, which they believed would only provide a beachhead for their ideological rivals. "State will not send an embassy until defense says. Defense is going to run it," a State Department official told the Mideast team.[11]

Jay Garner, a retired Army general, was made head of the Office of Reconstruction and Humanitarian Assistance, a U.S. agency that was created to oversee Iraq after the invasion but lasted only three months. When Garner turned to State Department officials to lead two of his office's three key units—for humanitarian relief,

reconstruction, and government operations—Rumsf[...] demanding that Pentagon officials be put in charge. [...] ning gun battle with the Defense Department over [...] put in charge of each of these pillars," Garner recoun[...]

Feith picked Michael H. Mobbs, a corporate lawy[...] law partner, to head the unit that would deal with [...] ment in Iraq. Grossman, the undersecretary of state, [...] ing Garner that Mobbs was unqualified and the job sh[...] experienced State Department official. Garner worke[...] promise under which his organization took on forme[...] Barbara Bodine, a Mideast specialist, to make up for N[...] perience.[13]

The friction continued even as U.S. forces moved [...] to attack. A week before the invasion, Rumsfeld blo[...] from hiring seven ambassadorial-level State Departm[...] three of whom were Mideast experts. Powell called [...] protest. "Don, we're trying to help," he said.[14]

Five of the seven were eventually hired. But Garne[...] to fill many of his positions with professional diplomat[...] instead to State Department retirees, military reservists [...] ers. Some slots were never filled. George Ward, a forme[...] mat who joined the group, said there was a conspicuou[...] enthusiasm or cooperation with the mission from top S[...] ment officials. "It was, 'If you don't want us, we're [...] play the game,'" Ward said.[15]

Crocker was one who agreed to go. In a late-night [...] State in late 2002, Crocker told his team that a decisio[...] made to invade, although there had been no official a[...] ment of it. "This is going to be the biggest fucking n[...] any of us will ever be involved in," Tom Krajeski, a me[...] team, recalled Crocker saying. "We're each going to ha[...] a decision whether we can support this, whether we can [...] He added that he personally decided to help out. "I'm a [...] vice officer; I'm going to serve my president."[16]

Marc Grossman, then undersecretary of state for polit[...]

ing to build further pressure on the Turks by threatening to withdraw U.S. military and economic support. His bosses told him no: Turkey was an essential ally in the Middle East, and the relationship was too important. "I was ready to do some threatening," Crocker said. "But they didn't want that. I think they were right." Crocker left Ankara brooding over the failure.

In the first months of 2003, Crocker joined Zalmay Khalilzad, then President Bush's envoy to Iraq, in a series of secret meetings with the Iranians to discuss the approaching war. The meetings were a top priority, since the Iranians, as Iraq's neighbors, had the ability to greatly complicate American war plans. The sessions were held in Geneva with a delegation headed by Mohammad Javad Zarif, a suave, U.S.-educated career diplomat who twelve years later negotiated a nuclear arms deal with the Obama administration and other countries.

Khalilzad tried to convey to the Iranians, without saying so directly, that Washington had no intention of making war on Iran after toppling Saddam, as many Iranians feared. When he asked for a commitment that Tehran wouldn't fire on U.S. aircraft that strayed into Iranian airspace, Zarif agreed. But the two sides differed on postwar Iraq. The Iranians wanted to see the Americans out of Iraq as soon as the last shot was fired. Zarif asserted that Washington should form a government of Iraqi exiles before the war and turn over control of the country to them immediately after the invasion, with no American occupation.

Khalilzad wrote later that he wished he had taken more seriously Zarif's warning that Iraq would be dangerously unstable after the war.[17] Crocker took it seriously: he had been saying the same for months.

U.S. and allied troops began their invasion of Iraq on March 19 and had taken Baghdad by April 9. A week later Crocker was back in Iraq, trying to help arrange a quick transition to a new government. Colin Powell had asked him to help Khalilzad, who had the lead in arranging the new government. The first step in the process was an April 15 meeting with Iraqi leaders in the southern city of

Nasiriyah, near the birthplace of Abraham, with the goal of encouraging the Iraqis to begin organizing for an interim government and elections. The gathering took place in a vast air-conditioned tent, near the Ziggurat of Ur, a 4,000-year-old terraced temple, now scarred with bullet holes. Iraqi expatriates, tribal leaders, and local politicians took part, and the event had the atmosphere of a political rally.

Khalilzad, standing with Crocker on the dais, told the group: "We have no intention of ruling Iraq. We want you to create your own democratic system." By the end of the conference, the group had approved a thirteen-point joint statement advocating a government with a distinctly American cast: it would be a democratic, federal state, grounded in the rule of law and with respect for diversity and the rights of women.

But the difficulties facing the project were clear even that day. Dozens of political activists of varying affiliations milled outside the tent, complaining that the Americans had invited the wrong Iraqis inside. In nearby Nasiriyah, thousands of Shias gathered to hear Sheikh Mohammed Bakr Al-Nasri, the white-bearded leader of the long-banned Dawa Party, denounce the U.S. effort to organize an interim government. Ahmad Chalabi, an expatriate Iraqi financier who was expected to become leader of the new government, avoided the U.S.-organized gathering entirely.

In Washington, meanwhile, top officials of the Bush administration were rethinking their original plan for a quick handover of power to an interim Iraqi government. Iraq was simply too chaotic: ministries were being looted and burned, the army was melting away, sewage was overflowing onto the streets, and the electric grid was near collapse. Organizing an effective government in this environment seemed a remote hope. When Crocker and Khalilzad returned to the White House in early May to provide a status report on their effort to jump-start a government, National Security Adviser Condoleezza Rice told them the plan for a quick handover of power was being scrapped.

President Bush had decided to replace Garner and his agency

with a new organization, the Coalition Provisional Authority, which was going to assume broad authority over the country and hunker down for a longer stay. As the new group began to get organized, Colin Powell proposed Crocker lead a unit that would start trying to set up a democratic government. The idea did not thrill Crocker, but he agreed to stay to work for the occupation's new overseer, L. Paul "Jerry" Bremer III.

A dashing figure in crisp blue suits and tan desert boots, Jerry Bremer was a former foreign service officer who had been chief of staff to Secretary of State Henry Kissinger. He was a specialist in Europe, spoke no Arabic, and had never laid eyes on Iraq. But when he arrived in Iraq, on May 12, he quickly grasped the country's condition. As his Air Force C-130 descended into Baghdad, Bremer counted half a dozen columns of smoke rising at intervals from the city's dun expanse. They were blackening the skies above government buildings set afire by looters. A few minutes later, in an armored limousine heading toward the city center, Bremer caught sight of looters speeding by in a pickup truck piled high with stolen furniture. Another Iraqi fired forlornly after them.[18]

Bremer's first order of business was to take over the office space in Saddam's former Republican Palace, then occupied by the Office of Reconstruction and Humanitarian Assistance, the U.S. government organization he was replacing. The palace, located in an eighty-acre compound on a bend in the Tigris River, was a hive of U.S. troops and civilians that operated around the clock, with no air-conditioning and spotty electricity.

Crocker was one of several officials who had come to work with Garner's operation and whom Bremer wanted to keep on. When Crocker arrived at the palace, the two reached an agreement. Crocker would serve as head of the Coalition Provisional Authority's governance team only until the team could put together an advisory committee of Iraqis who would help lead the transition to a sovereign Iraqi government. Crocker set up the team's operations in the palace's former kitchen, a spacious, somewhat battered hall with green ceramic tiles, a five-minute walk from Bremer's office.

The adjoining corridors were jammed with beds, like a wartime hospital, because of the shortage of housing.

Crocker found the new job an exercise in frustration. Bremer centralized authority in his own hands and, in his desire for quick action, did not rely heavily on the regional specialists. "He wasn't turning to very many of us, nor very often," Crocker said. One source of tension between the two men was a controversial order, known as CPA Order No. 2, that disbanded Saddam's Iraqi army. Crocker disagreed with parts of it, and raised his misgivings with Bremer. But the occupation chief had made up his mind and signed it on May 23, his eleventh day in the country.[19] The order was debated for years afterward, with critics contending that by leaving thousands of Sunni soldiers jobless it became a major driver of the new insurgency.

Emma Sky, a British Mideast expert who advised U.S. generals and served later with Bremer's governance team, wrote in her 2015 memoir that the occupation chief "relied heavily on those who shared his convictions and marginalized the serious and skilled diplomats who had their doubts."[20]

Crocker found himself amid a swirl of newly appointed American officials who were enthusiastic about shaping a new Iraq but had little or no background in the region. One was Bernard Kerik, the former New York City police commissioner, who was a hero of 9/11 and a loyal Republican. Kerik had been asked to take charge of the crucial task of training new police. He was a media favorite who generated flattering news stories for the administration and enjoyed going on nighttime police raids. But when he left after three months, he had made almost no headway on police training.[21] "He knew nothing about the region," Crocker said. With the first round of appointees, "you had that up and down the line."

Meanwhile, the top Pentagon officials who oversaw the chaotic opening months of the occupation were working to limit the influence of the State Department's Middle East hands, fearing the diplomats would try to seize control of the mission. A week after Bremer asked Crocker to come out, Crocker realized his unit was going to be grossly understaffed for the huge job assigned to it. Crocker put in a request to have some of his staff in Washington reassigned to Baghdad. He was told: Not just yet. "That was the climate of the time," he said. The Pentagon "would allow you to be out here, but they wouldn't countenance bringing any State Department fifth column into the effort." Eventually, as the chaos in Baghdad and the occupation authority's desperation grew, Crocker was given the staff he wanted.

Crocker had a similar experience a month earlier, when he was working with Khalilzad. Crocker had asked Khalilzad to put in a request to the State Department for communications gear, armored cars, support staff, and other resources. The proposal prompted an angry call from Paul Wolfowitz, the deputy defense secretary, to Khalilzad. Wolfowitz suspected that Crocker's request meant the State Department was trying to undercut Pentagon authority by setting up an American embassy. "Paul, don't we work for the same government?" Khalilzad asked him.[22] When Khalilzad told Crocker about it, he apologized for getting the envoy in trouble.

Within weeks of his arrival, Crocker was wrestling with the problems caused by Bremer's first order, CPA Order No. 1, which aimed at purging from the Iraqi government the top four levels of Saddam Hussein's Baath Party. It was popular with the Shia and Kurds, who had been oppressed by Saddam, and bitterly resented by Saddam's fellow Sunni Iraqis, who saw it as evidence that Iraq's formerly dominant faction would be marginalized in the new order.

Crocker realized that the policy was excluding from government many ordinary Iraqis, in addition to hard-core Saddamists. It was being applied unevenly, he saw, and ignoring many Iraqis who wanted to appeal their exclusion. Crocker wrote a memo to Bremer on July 9, suggesting that implementation be handed to Iraqis, who, he argued, would be better attuned to the nuances of a complex issue.[23] Bremer agreed. Unfortunately, the body that was created after Crocker's departure to manage the policy was headed by Ahmad Chalabi, the expatriate financier, a Shia. Chalabi, try-

ing to consolidate his political influence, purged more than 50,000
Sunni Iraqis, including low-level functionaries and schoolteachers,
further hobbling the government. Bremer "gave it to the Iraqis, and
said, 'You guys sort out how you want to see it administered,'"
Crocker said. "The problem was that Chalabi glommed onto it and
used it as a lethal weapon against all his political opponents." Soon
there was wide agreement that the harsh implementation of the de-
Baathification order was also a major contributor to the insurgency.

Crocker's principal job of organizing an interim Iraqi leadership became more urgent every day. With the country descending
into lawlessness, Iraqis were angry that the Bush administration
appeared to have reversed its original plans for a quick return of
power to Iraqis. Protesters demonstrated almost every day outside
the CPA headquarters, demanding elections.

The American team spread out across the country, looking to
select an Iraqi council that would represent all the important Iraqi
groups and set in motion plans to write a constitution and move
toward an elected government. Choosing the right people was a tall
order, Crocker quickly learned, especially in the Sunni community.

When the Americans arrived, there was no clear leadership
among Sunnis, but squabbling and rivalries. Even among the chief
tribes like the Shammar and Dulaim, multiple figures vied for leadership. "And they all hated each other," Crocker said. "Trying to
sort out who had real weight and legitimacy became almost impossible as we set up the council." To further complicate the task, in
June, Grand Ayatollah Ali Sistani, Iraq's ranking Shia leader, issued
a fatwa, or religious edict, condemning the occupiers' plans to have
an unelected body write the country's new constitution.

Crocker decided that the composition of the new advisory body
was a topic he needed to discuss with the Iranians. Iran had a powerful influence on Shia Iraqis and needed to be consulted on any new
leadership, he believed, just as Iran had been consulted on the new
leadership of Afghanistan in 2001 after the Taliban were ousted.
Once again, Crocker found himself in an indirect dialogue with
Qassim Suleimani, the powerful leader of the Iranian Revolution-

ary Guard Corps' Quds Force unit. Crocker would pass the names of possible Shia selections to Iraqi officials, who during visits to Tehran would pass them on to Suleimani. If Suleimani objected to a choice, Crocker would drop the candidate. "The formation of the governing council was in essence a negotiation between Tehran and Washington," Crocker said later.[24]

After several rounds of negotiations, UN and U.S. officials announced on July 13 the formation of the twenty-five-member Iraqi Governing Council, which included representatives of six major political parties, thirteen Shias, five Kurds, and five Arab Sunnis. Nine of the seats were given to former expatriates. The U.S. team picked them in part because the Americans knew more about them than about the Sunnis who had remained in the country.

It soon became clear that the council would not be the ideal face for the new Iraq. When Bremer asked the group to choose a leader to address the press that day, the members argued for twenty minutes. The twenty-five Governing Council members were a "raucously divided group reflecting the political fissures of the country," Condoleezza Rice wrote.[25] Unable to agree on who should lead, the group decided to rotate the presidency of the council to a new member of the group every month. It became tough for Bremer to even bring them together for meetings, because many of them enjoyed traveling abroad in their role as representatives of the new Iraq.

As Crocker prepared to leave Iraq, the U.S. effort suffered another blow. On August 20, a bombing at the United Nations headquarters in Baghdad killed Sergio Vieira de Mello, the UN's top official in the city, and twenty-three others. Vieira de Mello had been working on organizing the Governing Council and, as representative of an international body, had given a measure of legitimacy to the American presence. The loss was "catastrophic," Crocker wrote later. "With the U.N. pulling out, there was no neutral force to shepherd the political process." Now it was easier for insurgents to describe this as a struggle of American occupiers versus Iraqis.

In other postings, Crocker had been able to establish good relations with the local U.S. military commanders. But in these months his relations with the brass were often strained. In the aftermath of the invasion, the military found itself the default government of a country in upheaval, a job it wasn't prepared for and didn't want. Rather than trying to sort out the conflicts between warring sects, criminals, and society's helpless, the officers tried to focus narrowly on their security duties. Their goal was "How do I get through this day?" Crocker said. Part of the problem was that the generals had never been told that they would need to get involved with Iraqi political leaders to ensure that the country was functioning. Crocker recalled trying to explain to one senior officer the problems that Iraqis—and his troops—would face if the occupiers didn't find a way to deal with the economic social and political issues. "This isn't our mission here," the officer told him. "The things you're telling me are interesting, but they have nothing to do with me."

Crocker got into a screaming argument with Lieutenant General Ricardo Sanchez, the commander of coalition ground forces. The issue was security for members of the new Iraqi Governing Council. The Iraqis' security guards spoke little or no English, and they were having heated arguments at American security checkpoints. Crocker asked Sanchez to assign bilingual officers to travel with the Iraqis to avoid angry arguments that might lead to gun battles. When Sanchez refused, Crocker warned him that "somebody's going to get killed out there, and this whole political effort is going to collapse. And you're going to be in a bigger war than you're in now." Sanchez was unmoved. He wouldn't be taking orders, he made clear, from the striped-pants set.

When Crocker prepared to leave Iraq in August of 2003, Bremer didn't try to keep him on.[26] Crocker told friends he was thinking about retiring from the Foreign Service. "You could just see Iraq going bad," he said. His goal now was "to get Iraq into my rearview mirror as soon as I could."

CHAPTER 4

# A Government of One

I n the spring of 2003, Robert Ford was the second-ranking diplomat at the U.S. embassy in Bahrain, a dot-sized monarchy on
an island off the western edge of the Persian Gulf. It was a sweet
gig. The Bahrainis were rich, pro-American, and easy to get along
with. He was living in a spacious four-bedroom villa just outside
the capital city of Manama, with his every need met by an atten-
tive staff. His cook, an Indian named Ivan, had trained at a five-star
hotel. He produced a memorable lemon mousse, a superlative stro-
ganoff, and a full repertoire of Indian dishes. The greatest threat to
Ford's health was from extra pounds.

But Ford's life changed after Secretary of State Colin Powell sent an urgent memo to all foreign service officers. The Bush
administration needed help organizing an Iraqi government to
replace the fallen regime of Saddam Hussein. The work was difficult and dangerous, Powell acknowledged. Mideast hands were
badly needed. Especially ones with good Arabic.

Ford was a forty-five-year-old Coloradan who had been in the
Foreign Service for eighteen years, almost entirely in hardship
posts in remote corners of the Middle East. He had grave doubts
about the American invasion of Iraq. But he knew he was among
the best Arabic speakers in the State Department, and he volunteered for a three-month tour. Two months later, in late August, just
as Ryan Crocker was departing Iraq, Ford left the placid waters
of the Persian Gulf for the parched Middle Euphrates. He arrived
in Baghdad on a military plane, carrying only a few wrinkled

clothes in a duffel bag. He reported to Saddam's former Republican Palace, now the pulsing center of the occupation government. The Americans who had entered the city triumphantly in March were adjusting to the idea that they were running a country without an economy, functioning infrastructure, or law and order. With an insurgency taking shape, they had barricaded the 4.4 square miles of the Green Zone, the occupation center, behind miles of barbed wire and concrete blast walls that were yards thick and, in some places, more than twenty feet high.

American officials had little time to talk. Ford was given a pile of American bills worth $20,000, and nothing else. The U.S. staff in Baghdad was already joking that the initials of the interim government, the Coalition Provisional Authority, really meant "can't provide anything." Ford caught a ride with a U.S. official who was headed south, and was soon in Najaf, ninety miles away. With a population of 1 million, Najaf was an important city. For the Shia, the branch of Islam that includes 60 percent of Iraqis, the city was the holiest in the country. It was the home of Grand Ayatollah Ali al-Sistani, a reclusive cleric who was the Iraqi Shias' most revered figure. But for the moment Ford was the occupation government's only civilian representative in the city. His marching orders were to help the Marine battalion that was the default government of the region repair war damage, restore public services, and police the streets. In a tough year for U.S. diplomats in Iraq, Ford had drawn the shortest of straws. Tom Krajeski, the foreign service officer who was then assigning staff to Iraq's regions, said later that the Najaf job was arguably the toughest in the service that summer. "It was a dangerous, hard place without a lot of support," he said.[1]

Ford's escort deposited him outside the gate of Najaf's university, where the Marines had set up base, and told the sentry that Ford had come to help. Ford wandered around in the 120-degree heat until he found the battalion commander.

"We've been expecting you," the lieutenant colonel said. "Where's the rest of your team?"

"It's just me," Ford told him.

"When are they coming?" the officer said.

"I have no idea," Ford replied. "It's just confusion in Baghdad."

Najaf was the site of one of the world's first universities. But in the aftermath of the U.S. invasion, faculty and students had fled and looters had carted off everything of value. They didn't just take books and furniture. They stripped wiring from the buildings, chipped ceramic tiles from the walls, and wrenched off doorframes and doors. Tarpaulins fluttered in their place.

Ford was assigned a bunk in a small dust-coated room already occupied by several others. He stood in line with the seven hundred Marines to share a few toilets and bathroom sinks. To shower, he made his way across an open field to a small wooden platform set over a deep hole. A water hose had been laid next to it. There was no hot water and no shower curtain. Ford soaped up and surveyed the desolate fields, whose vegetation had long since shriveled in the sun. *What*, he wondered, *have I gotten into?*

Meals were at a Marine mess a half mile down the road. Ford, wearing a blue blazer and open-collared shirt, got in line. A knot of young Marines, coated in grime and glistening with sweat, gawked at the diplomat in preppy duds.

"Who are you?" asked one Marine. "I haven't seen anybody dressed like that in months."

Ford got a ride over to the municipal government building, hoping to make his first contact with Iraqi officials. Most of them had disappeared when U.S. forces arrived and had remained out of sight. Army Major General David H. Petraeus had entered the city as commander of the 101st Airborne Division in the fourth day of the war and had no luck finding a mayor or other officials to restore a semblance of public order.

The municipal building was a four-story edifice with hundreds of offices that had been looted of furniture and office equipment. Only a handful of staff were present and working listlessly in the heat.

"Where is everybody?" he asked.

"They ran away," one told him. "We see them at the end of the month when they come to get their pay."

Ford had gotten into the Foreign Service because of his fascination with languages, history, and the Arab world. He was drawn by the image of Peter O'Toole leading Arab cavalry in *Lawrence of Arabia*. In 1980, after college, he took a Peace Corps job teaching English to teens in a fly-blown Moroccan village between Casablanca and Marrakesh. The kids rode to class barefoot on donkeys and knew almost nothing about the West, although Europe was only 400 miles away. One day a teen came to class with a battered VHS tape of *Saturday Night Fever*. The class was intrigued but baffled by Brooklyn teens in platform shoes and three-piece polyester suits. Ford was just as happy that they hadn't been reached by the tendrils of Western popular culture. Like generations of Arabists before him, he enjoyed the halting process of making friends, mastering a language, and discovering the unaccountable quirks of a society so different from his own.

Ford also enjoyed his cultural immersion in Najaf. He began rounds of meetings with Iraqi officials and tribal and religious leaders, sometimes holding a half dozen sessions a day. After his first week he emailed his wife, Alison Barkley, who was at the U.S. embassy in Abu Dhabi, to say that his fifteen-hour days were frantic but also fascinating. He was doing what foreign service officers come to do.

"I spent the whole day speaking in Arabic—very satisfying," Ford wrote. "I understand about 90% of what they are saying and they seem to understand all of what I'm saying. Their leaders are all younger than me, inexperienced, scared, and very serious."

He related how a group of clerics had served up a wonderful meal of kebabs, rice, bread, and tomatoes. But sitting cross-legged on pillows in the Arab style for a three-hour meeting would take some adjustment. The meeting "left me so stiff I could barely get up again." In all, it was a bit like his days Morocco, he wrote. "A very Peace Corps–like experience."

He told Alison that in his first days he had seen some encouraging signs from the Shia in Najaf, who had been glad to see Saddam's regime fall. He told her of children waving at the Americans and giving them the thumbs-up. At one school, children greeted him with chants of "Bush, Bush, Bush!" The Americans received friendly waves and honks from wedding processions, too.

Najaf authorities held a local election that seemed to go off reasonably well. Ford visited a polling station and found Iraqis enthusiastic about their venture in democracy. He saw one man voting twice—but only one. It was probably not much worse than what had once gone on in his adopted home of Baltimore, he thought. "They're doing as well as Baltimore did in 1850," Ford wrote afterward. "It's a start."

He wrote in the first days of his tour: "I don't have the sense at all from the people we met and saw that Najaf is on the boil against the coalition." Yet, "I also have the strong sense that there are some bad people here, too."

He soon learned more about them, and realized that security issues would be his biggest challenge. The region was in the crossfire between hard-line Sunni followers of Saddam Hussein and newly forming Shia militias. Within a few days of his arrival in Najaf, Sunni hard-liners set off two car bombs at the entrance of the landmark Imam Ali Mosque, killing ninety-five, including Ayatollah Muhammad Bakr al-Hakim, a moderate cleric who had struggled against Saddam.

Two Shia militias were expanding their local influence. One was the Badr Corps, the armed wing of the leading Shia party, then called the Supreme Council for the Islamic Revolution in Iraq (SCIRI). The other was the militia of Moktada al-Sadr, a thirty-year-old populist firebrand from a celebrated Shia family.

Sadr, who spent much of his time in Najaf, was a special problem. He had begun denouncing the American occupation and trying to set up a separate government, including courts. Iraqi government courts had evidence he had personally ordered the killing of an ayatollah. His troops were stockpiling arms, carrying out kidnappings and murders, and occasionally organizing marches to the home of Grand Ayatollah Ali al-Sistani, alarming Sistani's circle. Sadr "is muscling people and making us look irrelevant," Ford emailed his superiors in Baghdad in September.[2] A confrontation with Sadr's followers, he thought, was inevitable.

Three weeks after Ford arrived, the Marines pulled out, leaving south-central Iraq in the hands of Spanish, Honduran, and other coalition forces, along with a small detachment of 250 U.S. military police. Ford decided he needed to convince the militias to keep their men off the streets and turn over policing of Najaf checkpoints to the American military police.

One evening in early September, Ford set off with a Marine lieutenant to meet a local cleric who was a point of contact with the broader Shia religious leadership. He knew the trip might be risky. The meeting began well enough, with an exchange of pleasantries and the customary rounds of tea. Then, with no warning, about two dozen heavily armed militiamen appeared and broke open the front door. They dragged Ford's translator, a young dental student named Haidar, out of the room and began beating him savagely.

"Who are you?" they demanded of Ford.

"I'm the representative of Paul Bremer," Ford told him, referring to the occupation chief.

The militiamen, in their teens and early twenties, were members of the Badr Corps. It appeared they weren't going to shoot the Americans, but they seemed to be ready to hold them hostage.

As it happened, Ford also had an appointment to meet the head of the Badr Corps's local organization the same night at midnight. Ford realized the appointment gave him some leverage.

"I'm supposed to go meet Hassan Abtar in two hours," Ford told them. "But I can't make it if you're holding me. Why don't you go tell him?"

The comment seemed to confuse the captors. They didn't let the Americans go, but they stopped threatening them. Two hours later an older cleric appeared, with apologies. This was all a terrible mistake, he told them. They were free to go.

Ford wanted to go immediately to make his appointment with the militia leader. This was a great opportunity, he told the major, because Abtar would be embarrassed by the militia's behavior. That might make him more open to Ford's arguments that he should take the Badr Corps militiamen off the streets, he said.

The Marine had had enough excitement for one evening. "Are you fucking crazy?" he asked Ford. "This is my car, and we're going back to the base."

The run-in with the militia was a reminder that dangers were all around him. But Ford had a lot to do and did not want to be immobilized by security worries. On some trips he traveled in a protective convoy with a military escort. But at other times, when time was short and security unavailable, he went without. He had no bodyguards for much of his stay, and none of the armored sedans that soon became standard.

Ford stayed in regular touch via his personal Hotmail email account with his boss in Bahrain, Ambassador Ronald E. Neumann. Neumann, a Mideast veteran who had also been an Army officer in the Vietnam War, grew alarmed when Ford told him he was traveling without detailed advance planning and bodyguards.

"I gulped when I heard you were off to a meeting with no security," Neumann wrote him. He urged Ford to take a series of precautions, including checking his car for bombs before entering it after a meeting. "Of course, you can probably get away with anything once or twice," he wrote. He also encouraged Ford to buy or borrow a pistol and to get hold of enough ammunition so that he could practice using it. He signed the letter "your worried friend."

Ford promised to take precautions. He told Neumann he was keeping the dangerous trips to a minimum, because his supervisor at occupation headquarters in Baghdad "would kill me himself if he knew I was doing this."

The security threats were complicating everything else Ford was trying to accomplish. Officials in Baghdad wanted Ford to open a line of communications with Grand Ayatollah Ali al-Sistani, who lived an austere life in a tiny house in Najaf and made few public appearances. But when Ford asked for a meeting, an aide to Sistani launched into all the reasons why that would not be possible. The militias were threatening everyone in the community, including Sistani's people, he said. The Marines weren't protecting the public. The Iraqi police force was worthless. "All true," Ford acknowledged. As a result, the aide said, "it's just too dangerous for us to be seen with you." Ford was told to speak to an intermediary, an aide to Sistani's third-ranking deputy, who would pass his comments on to the ayatollah.

For a while it appeared that Ford had succeeded in convincing the Badr Corps to keep its militia off the streets. But on October 2 the Badr Corps held a march that drew 1,000 fighters to central Najaf and nearly exploded into a firefight with American troops.

The colonel leading the Spanish brigade, eager to avoid a confrontation with the Badr fighters, promised the Spanish troops would stay out of the way during the parade and gave them permission to carry arms. The Badr militia took this agreement as an invitation to take control of the city center. They flooded downtown, showing up at central intersections armed with assault rifles and rocket-propelled grenade launchers. Other armed fighters perched on rooftops overlooking the parade route.

Soon the American MPs showed up and, knowing nothing about the Spanish general's promise, confronted the militia. The Badr fighters tried to block the MPs' access to the city center, and the two sides seemed close to a firefight.

With no phone service available, Ford fired off an emergency email to the office of Bremer, the occupation chief. "We're giving away control of Najaf to this militia," he said. Bremer had Lieutenant General Ricardo Sanchez, the commander of coalition ground forces, tell the Spanish to rescind the order.

The immediate threat was defused, but the core of the problem remained. The U.S. and allied authorities didn't want to disarm the Shia militiamen, risking all-out war with groups that had a vast arsenal of arms and at least a measure of public support. But doing nothing carried risks, too. They could not afford to allow the militias to become a rival government.

Ford repeatedly appealed to American authorities to arrest Sadr. The cleric was twice detained at coalition security checkpoints but both times released. In one case, in October, Honduran troops stopped Sadr and released him without even raising the issue with Ford. No one had told them to pick Sadr up, the Hondurans said, or to notify American officials when they had done so. In another case, Sadr was stopped, and the question of Sadr's arrest went all the way to Defense Secretary Donald Rumsfeld, Ford said. Rumsfeld ordered his release.

As Ford feared, the Sadrist fighters only became stronger and more of a threat. In April of the following year, Sadr's militia, now called Jaish al-Mahdi, launched what turned into a bloody two-month battle against U.S. forces in Najaf, as well as in the cities of Karbala and Kufa and the Sadr City neighborhood of Baghdad. The Americans won the opening fight, but Sadr's militias, with Iranian support, grew to tens of thousands of fighters and remained for years one of the deadliest threats to U.S. forces.

Paul Bremer recalled later how Ford was among the handful of officials arguing in the summer of 2003 that Sadr needed to be arrested before his forces became more dangerous. The Marines, British troops, the CIA, and Lieutenant General Ricardo Sanchez, commander of coalition ground forces, all opposed an arrest. But the judgment of the U.S. diplomat in Najaf, Bremer said later, "was right. Whatever the military reasoning was—and I understand the operation was going to be difficult and lead to some American casualties—from a political point of view, we should have moved in August."[3]

Ford's efforts to restart government and rekindle the provincial economy were going only slightly better. Ford had access to piles of U.S. cash, flown in from Federal Reserve vaults in the United States, to finance small projects. He went around the region ordering work, some costing a few hundred dollars, others more than $100,000. It was reconstruction bit by tiny bit.

The provincial government was paralyzed, in part, because it was immobile. Ford went to examine the provincial government's motor pool and found dozens of cars inert under deepening layers of dust.

"How many of these work?" he asked the attendant.

"None," the man replied.

"See if you can get this one and that one fixed," Ford said. "Here's $400. I'll be back in a week."

He visited the provincial government finance office and asked to see the office's records of payments and disbursements. "We have no computers," he was told. "So how do you keep track?" An employee emerged from a storeroom with a huge, dusty ledger that looked like something from a Dickens novel. The entries were written in tiny Arabic script. The record-keeping system was the same across much of Iraq.

He visited forlorn-looking police stations and found walls crumbling and toilets busted. He peeled off a few American bills for painting, plumbing, and carpentry repairs. "I'll be back in a week to see what you've done," he said.

The region's economy needed much more than what Ford could do with his briefcase full of cash. Najaf's cement, soft drink, and textile factories were closed when he arrived for lack of electricity, and the workers jobless. He visited the power plant for a firsthand look at the problem and discovered a grim reality: it would cost tens of millions of dollars to restore enough electricity to get the factories working again. Meanwhile, the workers were jobless and angry. They aired their grievances in demonstrations, some right outside Ford's door.

Ford organized a public works program that aimed to employ 1,800 Iraqis in its first stage. He set up a task force consisting of a U.S. contractor and an Iraqi provincial official to guide the project. But he worried about the competence of the Iraqis and what he suspected were their schemes to profit personally from American largesse. He set up a system with careful record keeping to try to maintain some control over spending, but worried that it might not be enough. "I cannot begin to describe how utterly incompetent and corrupt the governorate bureaucrats are," he lamented in an email to Neumann.

It wasn't only Iraqis who were enriching themselves on the generosity of the U.S. taxpayer. Ford's money was coming from an American contract employee, Robert J. Stein Jr., who'd been designated the CPA comptroller for the south-central region of Iraq. Stein would drop off boxes of cash for officials like Ford. Stein was a striking figure, dressed all in black and wearing a sidearm slung low like a Western gunfighter. In that early period of the occupation, many civilian CPA officials toted guns and knives. "Everybody thought Stein was so interesting," said Stuart E. Jones, who was then a provincial official based in Ramadi and later became U.S. ambassador to Iraq. "He had this 'man in black' thing."

It turned out that Stein was an outlaw in more than wardrobe. Three years later a U.S. court sentenced Stein to serve up to nine years in prison and to forfeit $3.6 million for his role in a bribery and fraud scheme involving contracts in Iraq. The CPA had hired him, and entrusted him with control of $82 million, without knowing that he had been convicted of fraud in the 1990s, court filings disclosed.

Ford had almost no interaction with Washington. Rumsfeld had barred officials from communicating directly with the State Department, fearing meddling. And Ford's line to his superiors in Baghdad was also dead: they weren't telling him what to do and weren't listening to what he had to say about one of the country's most important areas.

In October, Bremer convened a meeting in Baghdad of U.S. military division commanders and top civilian leaders to review plans. Ford raised his concerns about the angry protests over the lack of jobs in his region and made a pitch for a greater effort to put young Iraqi men to work to head off unrest. "I didn't come here to set up a socialist economy in Iraq," Bremer told him. The subject was closed. The CPA leadership was running at a breakneck pace without little time for deliberation or input from its own people, Ford thought. "Everything was done on the fly," Ford told Neumann in an email.

There were frictions with U.S. military officers as well. While the foreign service staff chafed that they had been initially shut out of the Iraq effort, much of the military were outraged that the diplomats weren't there running the country, forcing the military to do it.

A few days after Ford's arrival, a Marine lieutenant colonel complained that foreign service officers were only then beginning to trickle into Iraq. Ford countered that the State Department had made plans in 2002 to open an embassy as soon as the war ended, but they were abandoned at the orders of Pentagon officials.

Ford worked hard to bring in additional foreign service officers to Najaf to help with his mission. It was not easy. Once he found candidates with Arabic skills or regional knowledge, he had to get on the phone with their families to persuade them it would be safe to come. Eventually he arranged the transfer of two talented young foreign service officers to the post. But talent was in short supply. As soon as his superiors in Baghdad learned about Ford's promising recruits, they had them quickly reassigned to the capital.

From time to time the violence touched close to home. In early December, seven Spanish intelligence agents, including two who had become Ford's close friends, were attacked and killed on the road from Baghdad. The men, driving in two cars, were fired on by a swarm of attackers in other vehicles. They finally lost control of their cars and lurched to a stop on the shoulder. They held off the attackers for about half an hour, until the attackers fired on them with rocket-propelled grenades that set their cars on fire. The Iraqi news channels carried video of young Iraqi men exulting over the Spaniards' deaths and kicking their charred corpses.

"I only hope their children will never see this," George Farag, a foreign service officer Ford had brought to Najaf, wrote colleagues. Farag was devastated by his Spanish friends' deaths. Alberto and Nacho had been scheduled to return to Spain in only two weeks.

By December, Ford was getting death threats from Sadr's militia, Jaish al-Mahdi. He began to feel that if he stayed, he would be risking his life to no purpose.

"I am not optimistic about the outlook in Iraq," Ford wrote Neumann. "I fear we have only a limited window to win the confidence of the Iraqis, and that time is slipping away."

Ford was implored by short-handed U.S. officials in Baghdad to extend his stay from three months to at least six. "Robert, you're doing a great job," Tom Krajeski wrote him after he'd been there a month. "What's your feeling on an extension? We need you to stay." But Ford resisted. He had watched Crocker, a respected colleague he had worked with in Cairo, grow frustrated in Iraq and leave. "I understand why Ryan was keen to go after four months," Ford wrote to Neumann. He held firm to his original agreement to leave in early December.

Ford was correct in his hunch that conditions were deteriorating in Najaf. The Shia militias were growing steadily more threatening to Americans. When his successor was sent down, U.S. intelligence soon began picking up chatter showing that the militias intended to kill him, too. Twice he narrowly escaped assassination.

Despite it all, Ford indulged in a bit of fun before he left. Following the example of the British Arabists T. E. Lawrence and St. John Philby, Ford dressed up in traditional Iraqi clothing—dishdasha, Arabian robe; keffiyeh on the head—and went for an evening stroll, without bodyguards, in the old city. A few of his Iraqi contacts, including the local leader of one of the Shia militias, did double takes. "It was a hoot," he emailed his wife.

On December 2, Ford pulled out. His bodyguards drove him the dusty 350 miles from Najaf to Kuwait. By then the insurgency was fully under way, and Ford understood they might be ambushed anywhere along the route. They set off in the morning before dawn, knowing that Iraqis tend to stay up late, so that there were likely to be few on the roads at that hour. After six hours they were approaching Kuwait, and it appeared they would make it. Then disaster struck. A huge black desert bird plowed into the grille of their car, severing the radiator line. Soon the engine overheated and died, leaving them vulnerable to whoever might come along. They were in luck, however: they had broken down within a mile of a Western military installation and were quickly rescued by Italian troops.

Their car was towed the rest of the distance to Kuwait, and Ford was dropped off at Kuwait International Airport. It was a dazzling sight to Ford: gleaming, spotless, modern—from a world he had not seen for months.

The next day he was dropped off by a taxi at his residence in Bahrain. His Sri Lankan housekeeper, Raj, opened the door. She saw his disheveled condition and let out a cry.

"Sir, what happened to your clothes?" she said.

"Raj, it's a horrible, horrible war, and I'm out of it," Ford told her.

CHAPTER 5

# With Us and Against Us

Ryan Crocker arrived in Islamabad in November 2004 to begin a new job as U.S. ambassador to Pakistan. He was already focused on his top priority. His first phone call, on the way into town from the airport, was to set up a meeting with the CIA's top two officials in the country to discuss the expanding U.S. campaign against Islamist militants. When he reached the embassy, the three sat down in the building's secure room for a lengthy session on "what we were doing, the challenges we faced, and where we thought it was all going," said Kevin Hulbert, then the station chief. Crocker and Hulbert, who had offices just down the hall from each other on the embassy's third floor, talked several times a day, every day, for the next two years.

Pakistan was a country that kept U.S. officials awake at night. It was a leading source of Islamist terrorism, the home of the world's fastest-growing nuclear program, and a central player in the continuing war next door in Afghanistan. Jihadists crossed the border to attack Afghan and U.S. troops, then retreated to the safety of havens in Pakistan's rugged northwest tribal lands.

U.S. officials had been demanding full Pakistani support for its war on militants since 9/11. Two days after the attacks, the U.S. ambassador to Pakistan, Wendy Chamberlin, presented Pakistani president Pervez Musharraf with an off-the-record document listing seven U.S. demands, including access by the U.S. military and intelligence to Pakistani territory, "as needed," to fight the war.[1] Musharraf, though bridling at some of the demands, promised President Bush full support. "We are with you," he said. But it was soon clear that the two countries had different views on who should be pursued, and different levels of enthusiasm for the battle. Crocker was there to try to keep the two countries in sync and to prod the Pakistanis to do as much as possible.

The assignment was only Crocker's second in the region, after his three-month mission leading the U.S. embassy in Kabul in 2002. He had studied up on Pakistan in advance, including a discussion with a group of South Asia experts at Meridian House, a private foundation in Washington, D.C. One of the Pakistan experts warned Crocker that he might find Pakistani officials less candid than others he had worked with, recalled Daniel Markey, a South Asia specialist then with the State Department's policy planning office. "Do you know where I've been?" Crocker told the expert, referring to his many postings in the Middle East. "It won't be a problem."

Crocker's approach on the counterterror campaign was to develop the closest possible relationship with Musharraf and top military and intelligence officials and to keep pressing them to move more aggressively against the militants. As he had been with Karzai in Afghanistan, he was respectful, soft-spoken, and willing to bang his head against the wall, making the same request over and over if necessary. Throughout his career, he was willing to sit with foreign leaders for hours, through countless arguments and cups of tea, to try to budge them. His approach was "all about persistence," said Richard A. Boucher, who was assistant secretary of state for South and Central Asia, and Crocker's boss.

In the first few years after 9/11, U.S. and Pakistani teams were especially successful in tracking down Al Qaeda in their sanctuaries in Pakistan's tribal areas. The military and intelligence agencies captured Khalid Sheikh Mohammed, the principal architect of the 9/11 attacks, in 2003, and Abu Faraj al-Libi, his replacement, in 2005. They killed or captured hundreds of Al Qaeda fighters and lost hundreds of their own troops in the process.

Five months before Crocker arrived, Bush administration officials had expanded their campaign in Pakistan with a deadly new weapon, the drone aircraft that rely on sophisticated cameras and missiles to locate and kill militants miles below. The White House had in June cleared the CIA's first Predator drone strike in the country.

The U.S. drone program began slowly, with only ten strikes between 2004 and 2007, the period Crocker was in Pakistan.[2] In the early stages the program wasn't the point of contention that it became in 2008, after Crocker left, when it was rapidly expanding. The U.S. team, including Crocker and top CIA officials, would meet with Musharraf and officials of the chief Pakistani intelligence agency, Inter-Services Intelligence, and describe their intelligence and plans for a strike. Usually the Pakistanis would approve the strike. In a few cases Musharraf objected—not because of a reluctance to go after the militants, but because the strike would violate treaties with the tribes or risked damaging relationships that were important to the Pakistani government. "If he said no, we wouldn't go," Crocker said. Crocker thought the Pakistanis understood the nuances of the situation in the frontier areas better than the Americans, and accepted Musharraf's arguments. At the same time, Crocker said, the Pakistanis understood that if U.S. officials came across a target of the highest value—such as Osama bin Laden—they wouldn't feel obligated to seek advance clearance from Islamabad. During Crocker's years in Pakistan, drone strikes killed Abu Hamza Rabia, a top Al Qaeda commander, and Haitham al-Yemeni, an Al Qaeda explosives expert.

Musharraf did sometimes resist when Crocker and other U.S. officials pushed him to send more troops into the tribal areas. "I'm sending my boys in there and they're getting killed," Musharraf protested to the Americans. But Crocker and the intelligence officials shared intel showing a continuing militant presence and kept arguing the Pakistani army needed to do more. "We were pretty unpleasant," a former senior intelligence official said. When Defense Secretary Donald Rumsfeld visited Islamabad on April 13, 2005, Crocker and CIA officials urged him to tell Musharraf that if the Pakistanis didn't deal with the threat and there was an attack on U.S. interests from the tribal areas, Washington would send in U.S. forces. "Rumsfeld went in there and blistered Musharraf, basically threatened him," the former intelligence official said. "Musharraf was not prepared for Donald Rumsfeld."

Although Crocker was new to it, officials in Washington recognized his long experience and deferred to his judgments more than they usually did with ambassadors. "He was very much at the core," said Daniel Markey, who was in charge of the South Asia portfolio in the State Department policy planning office from 2003 to 2007. "I thought that was a bit unusual and a reflection of the sense of people in Washington that he was that good."

Crocker started most days meeting with a dozen or so members of the U.S. country team in a surveillance-proof room in the embassy called the Bubble. The entrance to the room looked much like the heavy-gauge steel door to a bank vault. The interior was nothing special. If Hollywood had depicted this sanctum, said Kevin Hulbert, it would have been full of sleek computer consoles, dazzling lights, and high-tech maps. In real life it was a cramped space with a conference table surrounded by a few battered government-issue chairs. "It was pretty much of a dump," said Hulbert.

Crocker's daily routine entailed long hours and stress, in part because he was also taking part in video teleconferences with Washington that dragged on late into the night. Crocker kept military field rations, called Meals Ready to Eat, in his office so that he wouldn't have to interrupt his work to go home at dinnertime. At one point Boucher, the assistant secretary of state, got an unusual request from the embassy staff. They asked that he tell the ambassador to take a few days off so that they could get a break from their relentless schedule. "This isn't because he needs it—it's because *we* need it," one of them told Boucher.

Crocker faced a different kind of problem when, on October 8, 2005, mountainous northern Pakistan was hit with an earthquake that killed 73,000 in minutes. He argued that Washington should do all it could to help, both for humanitarian reasons and to help the tarnished American image in the country. Crocker argued so forcefully that the U.S. military commander in charge of the relief effort feared he might get in trouble. Ryan "put his career on the line to stress this was a great opportunity," said retired Navy vice admiral Michael A. LeFever, who coordinated the U.S. military's relief efforts. Washington went along and approved a program involving 1,200 personnel and 24 helicopters—the largest U.S. airlift since the 1948 effort to sustain surrounded Berlin. Crocker argued that the lumbering Chinook helicopters bringing relief should be emblazoned with large American flag decals to show average Pakistanis that the United States had an interest in their country beyond killing militants. The commander of the U.S. helicopter unit protested that the flags would attract enemy fire. "Are you completely crazy?" he said. "Why don't we just paint a big bull's-eye on them?" "No, no, trust us," Crocker said. "It'll work." It did, and Pakistani public support for the United States spiked, though only briefly. The Chinooks became symbols of the relief effort, and tiny replicas were sold in Pakistani stores.

Another of Crocker's tasks was ensuring that senior officials of the two governments got along. President Bush had gone to lengths to strengthen his relationship with Musharraf, receiving him repeatedly at the White House and praising him publicly as a reformer. The administration muted, in the first years after 9/11, any criticism of Musharraf's more dubious political maneuvers. After a disputed referendum on Musharraf's presidency in 2002, the White House prevented the State Department from voicing even mild criticism of suspected vote-rigging. "They wouldn't sign off on anything that in any way questioned Musharraf," said former ambassador Gerald Feierstein, who was then helping oversee the region at State Department headquarters. "They had a lot invested in him. . . . They were all in for him for a long time." Bush's view was that the relationship with Musharraf was a strategic necessity that assured help on counterterrorism that they could get from no one else in Pakistani politics. He believed "there really wasn't a good alternative that involved moving away from Musharraf," Crocker said. Even so, the relationship came under strain, not only over the counterterror campaign, but also over Pakistani domestic issues and the administration's desire to strengthen ties to India, Pakistan's archrival.

In early March 2006, Bush visited Islamabad after a two-day trip to India, where he had sealed an important agreement to provide New Delhi American nuclear technology for nonmilitary purposes. The trip was jarring to the Pakistanis, who were uneasy with the idea that the president was drawing nearer to their mortal rival. Crocker decided Bush needed to stay overnight in Islamabad, too, to demonstrate that the Pakistani relationship was also a high priority.

The Secret Service was reluctant. The country was seething over cartoons of the Prophet Muhammad that had appeared in a Danish newspaper, and protesters, in large demonstrations, were denouncing Musharraf's pro-Bush policies. One day before, a suicide bombing at the U.S. consulate in Karachi had killed an American diplomat and three Pakistanis. The Secret Service didn't allow Bush to travel through Islamabad in a motorcade but sent a decoy limousine through the capital while the president and Laura Bush flew secretly in a Black Hawk helicopter to Crocker's heavily guarded residence. But Crocker won the argument on the overnight stay. Bush remained, attended a state dinner with Musharraf, and took practice whacks with a cricket bat in the embassy courtyard, to the delight of a group of local schoolchildren. "I wanted to signal that I valued our relationship," Bush wrote.[3]

Despite this, the visit to India proved a turning point in Pakistani attitudes toward the counterterror campaign. Many in the Pakistani military and intelligence agencies saw the India nuclear deal as evidence Washington was willing to offer New Delhi deals they could never hope for. They concluded they needed to strengthen their own position by secretly supporting some of the militant groups battling Kabul.

Meanwhile, Bush administration officials in Washington were pushing the Pakistanis harder to pursue not only Al Qaeda but also the expanding array of other militant groups in the tribal lands who were fighting the Americans, the Afghan government, and allied forces. Crocker's in-box was filled with demands "that were always focused on the immediate and the tactical. Get that group! Get those leaders!" he said.[4]

This was more than the Pakistanis thought they had signed up for after 9/11. "We would kind of keep changing our position," said Boucher, the former assistant secretary. "It became, 'You have to go after Al Qaeda, you have to go after the Quetta Shura, the Taliban, the Haqqani network; you have to go after militants in this place and that.'"

As time passed, U.S. officials saw signs that Pakistan's military and its intelligence service were not pursuing some groups, as Washington was asking, and were tipping off others that the United States was about to attack. "They were all out against some, half out against others, and suspected of collaborating with others," Boucher said. "It got to be messy."

Washington demanded that Pakistan step up efforts against Lashkar-e-Taiba, a militant group that was focused on trying to free Kashmir, the province that had been disputed with the Indians for decades. Most Pakistanis saw the group as heroic freedom fighters. Musharraf pushed back on American demands, saying, "I cannot take them on frontally. It would not only destroy me, it would destroy the nation."

Pakistan, meanwhile, began taking steps that made U.S. officials wonder about their agenda. One was a September 5, 2006, peace agreement with pro-Taliban tribal leaders in the border region of North Waziristan. Under the deal, the Pakistani military would pull out of the area, and tribal leaders would assume responsibility for controlling insurgents and enforcing the law. U.S. officials initially withheld public criticism, giving Musharraf the benefit of the doubt. But when Musharraf visited Washington two weeks after the deal was announced, Bush, Crocker, and other U.S. officials shared their skepticism of the deal behind closed doors.

In the next few weeks Crocker began sending Washington cables detailing how the tribal authorities were failing to live up to their promises to control militants. Militants were killing Pakistanis they believed were American spies, he wrote, and sending suicide bombers to blow up local police stations. "The security situation in the tribal areas remains unstable," he wrote in a December 2006 cable. "There remains little evidence of the assertion of government authority."[5]

Crocker also pointed out to Washington the limits on how much Musharraf did against militants in other parts of the country. Following a July 7, 2005, bombing by Islamists that killed fifty-two people in London, Musharraf came under strong international pressure to crack down on extremist groups. He announced tough steps "to much public fanfare," Crocker wrote in a March 2006 cable. But his arrest of "the usual suspects"—conservative clerics and Islamist politicians—brought a backlash from Pakistanis, who didn't like to see their government knuckling under to foreigners, Crocker wrote. Musharraf quietly changed course, releasing most of the detainees and watering down rules intended to require a new transparency on Islamist schools, or madrassas, that taught fundamentalist values. "We will have to reserve judgment on whether the president has the will to hold the line against Pakistan's extremist elements in the long run," Crocker cabled Washington.[6]

Washington was eager to find out whatever the embassy could tell about Pakistan's nuclear weapons program. It was then believed to have between eighty and one hundred nuclear weapons, and U.S. officials had long worried the complex might be penetrated by terrorists or their sympathizers in the government. Crocker did what he could to gather more information but got nowhere. "I could never find the damn things," he said later.[7] Crocker also tried many times to engage the Pakistanis in a dialogue about restraining their nuclear program, the fastest growing in the world. He "couldn't even get a discussion," said Boucher.

As Crocker's years in Pakistan neared an end, Musharraf's commitment to democracy seemed ever more tenuous. After taking power in a 1999 military coup, Musharraf had taken some steps to make the government more democratic, even while making other moves that concentrated more power in his hands. The Bush

administration endorsed his program and always praised him publicly as a "Western-oriented modernizer." Under the Pakistani constitution, Musharraf was required to stop serving as both president and chief of the Pakistani army and to run in new elections in early 2007. But as the date approached, Musharraf gave off conflicting signals about what he intended to do. He became deeply worried that the powerful chief justice of the supreme court, Iftikhar Muhammad Chaudhry, might rule that Musharraf could not remain both army chief and president. "My uniform is my second skin," he said. "How can I even think of taking it off?"

On March 9, Musharraf shocked his country by suspending Chief Justice Chaudhry on unspecified corruption charges, setting off a public outcry and threatening a constitutional crisis. Thousands of Pakistan's black-robed lawyers and activists milled in the streets, some with signs that read, "Go, Musharraf, Go!" Pakistani and Western audiences were horrified when police stormed the studio of Geo TV to halt its critical coverage of the crisis. A few days later Musharraf confided to Crocker at a dinner that he had been planning the move against the chief justice for six months. Crocker was taken aback. "It took you six months to figure out how to screw it up this badly?" Crocker asked Musharraf.

Crocker had a farewell meeting with Musharraf at his residence, Army House, on March 24, 2007. The meeting got front-page coverage in the local papers, with glowing comment about the strength of the U.S.-Pakistani relationship. But the private conversation between the two men was not celebratory. Crocker asked Musharraf to meet with him alone so he could be fully candid in asking about Musharraf's recent moves. When they sat down, Crocker put the question to him again: What were you thinking? Musharraf acknowledged that "he had made a mess of corruption charges against the chief justice," Crocker reported to Washington. Chaudhry's refusal to resign caught him by surprise Musharraf conceded; it never occurred to him that might happen And he had no fallback plan.

Musharraf's political troubles were a disappointment to Crock

in part because Pakistan seemed poised for a historic breakthrough in its dispute with India. The two countries had been carrying on secret negotiations for three years on their sixty-year dispute over control of Kashmir. The issue was a core reason for the countries' animosity and a potential trigger for a nuclear war.

By the spring of 2007, as Crocker prepared to leave, they had mapped out a detailed agreement for settling the dispute. Plans had been laid for Manmohan Singh, India's prime minister, to come to Pakistan to announce the deal.

But Musharraf's collapsing political position brought the talks to a halt and left him without the influence he would have needed to sell an agreement to the Pakistani public and powerful military. If Musharraf hadn't taken on Chaudhry, "we probably would have gotten a deal," Crocker said.

# Talent Hunt

R obert Ford's work in Bahrain resumed smoothly when he
returned from Iraq in December 2003. With his ambassador,
Ron Neumann, on a temporary posting in Iraq, Ford was in
charge of the embassy. He was spending his time thinking about
an economic agreement rather than social collapse, militias, and
assassins. Ford worked out plans to move in a few months to the
embassy in Saudi Arabia, where he would be reunited with his
wife, Alison, who had been working at the U.S. embassy branch
office in Abu Dhabi.

But in three months Ford's phone rang again. It was James
Larocco, the number two in Near Eastern Affairs at State Department headquarters, calling to tell Ford they wanted him back in Iraq.
The occupation government, the Coalition Provisional Authority,
was going out of business in June, to be replaced by an interim
Iraqi government. Now the U.S. civilian effort would be led from
a reopened U.S. embassy under the new ambassador, the veteran
diplomat John Negroponte. Negroponte wanted Ford to be political
counselor, the number three embassy post, Larocco said.

"No, no, no: I've done that," Ford said. The American effort
was halfhearted and hopeless, he said, and he wanted nothing to do
with it. Larocco explained that the issue was settled: Negroponte
had already asked Secretary of State Colin Powell for permission
to give Ford the job.

In 2003 the top State Department officials in Washington had
been getting no direct information about developments in Iraq from

the foreign service staff on the ground, because Defense Secretary Rumsfeld had forbidden it. But it turned out that Ron Neumann had forwarded to headquarters the dozens of emails Ford had been sending about conditions in Najaf. They had won Ford a reputation among the brass, including Powell, in part because of his insights about the growing threat from Sunni insurgents and Shia militias. While officials of CPA and Pentagon portrayed the insurgency as manageable, Ford had painted a more ominous picture.

"The precise quote I got from the secretary was: 'He's the only one who understood what was coming,'" Larocco told Ford. He told Ford that Powell would call his wife if necessary to try to talk her into allowing the move.

Alison was not impressed. "Tell them you've done your time," she told Ford.

"I can't say no," he said. "They're really serious."

She was so angry, she hung up on him for the only time in their marriage. Later she called back and said she would agree to him going, but only if the State Department could find her a job there, too. "That way I won't worry so much about you," she said.

Ford arrived back in Iraq in June 2004, six months after he had left. He could see the grim new reality of Iraq even before his military plane had taxied to the hangar. The airport and the six-lane highway to central Baghdad were now studded with barriers, armored vehicles, and military checkpoints. Fourteen months after the invasion, Iraq was arming for civil war. When he had left, the trip from the airport to the protected international area, called the Green Zone, was a routine shuttle ride. Now travelers could risk the journey only in armored vehicles with bulletproof glass, barreling at top speed. Even so, they weren't fully safe from snipers. From time to time they heard the crump of mortar shells falling nearby.

The Bush administration's goal, with a U.S. presidential election ahead, was to accelerate the creation of a stable and democratic Iraqi government so that the United States could step aside. The administration signaled its eagerness to depart by handing control from the occupation government to interim president Ayad Allawi two days ahead of schedule. When the moment came, Secretary of State Condoleezza Rice, in Istanbul with President Bush, slipped him a note: "Mr. President, Iraq is sovereign." In truth, its sovereignty was more aspirational than real.

The administration's move to make the State Department an equal of the Pentagon in Iraq was also more hope than reality. Army General George W. Casey Jr., who took over as head of the coalition forces in June 2004, had several times more people on his personal staff than Negroponte had in his embassy.

Even so, Powell had chosen Negroponte in hopes of improving morale among the demoralized diplomats. Negroponte, British-born and with a slight patrician air, was a diplomat's diplomat. He had spent thirty-seven years in the Foreign Service, including eight posts in Latin America, Europe, and East Asia. He had never worked in the Middle East and didn't speak Arabic. But he was eager to learn from the Mideast hands.

On one of Ford's first visits to Negroponte's office, a red phone behind the ambassador rang. Negroponte picked it up and began to explain to the caller that the recent shelling of the embassy was routine—not worth worrying about. Then he began describing the conversation he'd been having with Ford about how to contain the militia leader Sadr, whose Mahdi Army had just had a bloody three-week confrontation with U.S. and Iraqi government forces. When he hung up, Negroponte turned to Ford and told him, "Colin really likes your ideas." It had been the secretary of state on the other end of the line. This was a new day, Ford thought as he returned to the trailer where he was living. Now he had input. Maybe he could make a difference. Maybe he should stay for a year.

Bush administration officials had worked out a series of steps the Iraqis were to take toward democracy. They were to choose a transitional parliament, draft and approve a constitution, and elect a permanent government under its provisions. Ford's mission was to help the Iraqis work through the politics of these steps.

It took him only a few days to see how difficult the job would be. He traveled to Fallujah, a Sunni-dominated city forty miles west of Baghdad that was a center of the insurgency, to see if he could begin talks to reduce the frictions between the U.S. military and local leaders. But such talks, he discovered, were impossible. City leaders were bitterly angry over the U.S offensive that had followed the brutal killing of four American contractors in March 2004. The city was largely in the control of insurgents, and a no-go zone for the Americans.

The battle over Fallujah was also a searing memory for the American commanders. Ford and Ron Neumann, who was then in charge of political-military affairs at the embassy, met Marine General Jim Mattis in the nearby city of Ramadi. Mattis, who later became Donald Trump's first defense secretary, launched into bitter complaints about how he had been whipsawed by orders from the White House during the First Battle of Fallujah in April 2004.

Mattis had worked out plans to gradually reclaim the city from insurgent control, using a targeted approach to limit destruction. Then, in late March, the contractors were killed and their bodies strung up from a bridge and mutilated. Amid a public outcry in the United States, the White House overruled Mattis's plans and ordered a massive military response within seventy-two hours. The result was bloody block-by-block fighting that flattened swaths of the city, killing hundreds of civilians as well as U.S. troops. And then, just before the battle was over, the White House reversed course and ordered the U.S. troops to withdraw, fearing that growing international outrage could cause Iraqi officials to quit and U.S. allies to pull their troops from the country. The result was that the insurgents, close to a defeat, had regained control of the city. "Any other general wouldn't speak to us, thinking we might tattle on him to Washington," Ford said. "Mattis was just pissed off."

The biggest challenge for Ford, as it had been for Ryan Crocker a year earlier, was finding respected, credible Sunnis who could persuade their alienated community to take part in the country's new electoral politics. The Sunnis had a long list of grievances. They had been stripped of the dominance they enjoyed under Saddam. They were being driven out of mixed Shia-Sunni neighborhoods and attacked by Shia gangs and police. The Americans didn't protect them, they complained, but raided their homes searching for weapons, sometimes arresting or injuring the wrong people.

It was Ford's job to recruit Sunnis to take public office, a task that became more and more difficult as the months passed. U.S. officials set January 2005 for the historic first election in Iraq, when the public would pick 275 representatives to a transitional legislature. But soon many of the Iraqis who stepped forward to take positions in the new government were being shot, kidnapped, and killed in bombings. Their family members, too, were targets. As the date of election drew closer, the insurgents stepped up efforts to target candidates and discourage ordinary Sunnis from voting. Abu Musab al-Zarqawi, the Jordanian extremist who headed Al Qaeda in Iraq, broadcast warnings: any Sunni who runs for office will be killed.

One of the saddest stories was that of Karim al-Burjas, the governor of Sunni-dominated Anbar Province, the epicenter of the country's violence. Burjas, one of the first officials Ford met in this tour, confided to him that he planned to give up his post because of the dangers. Five days later, on July 28, gunmen loyal to Zarqawi attacked his house and kidnapped his three sons. The Iraqi police who were supposed to be guarding the house "were either ineffectual in defending the family or complicit in the commission of the crime," Ford wrote in a cable to Washington. Burjas quit his post to win his sons' freedom. His departure left provincial government at a standstill, with grave questions about the reliability of the Iraqi police and national forces who were supposed to be protecting it.

Anbar's government "is in a state of crisis," Ford wrote in his cable.[1]

Ford spent many days trying to win the cooperation of Tariq al-Hashimi, a former army colonel who was head of the Iraqi Islamic Party. The party was the leading Sunni organization and an affiliate of the Muslim Brotherhood. Hashimi was a caustic critic of the American occupation and often a headache for American officials.

But he shared the American goals of persuading the Sunnis to compete for their share of political power in the new Iraq, and he and Ford gradually became friends.

As the election approached, it appeared the Iraqi Islamic Party would field a slate of candidates. But on December 26, a month before the election, party leaders announced that they were withdrawing the slate because of surging violence in the Sunni areas north and west of Baghdad. "I am fully with the idea of elections, but the security situation does not make it possible for Sunnis to vote," said Mohsen Abdel Hamid, a lawyer and party leader. They asked the elections be postponed for up to six months.

Ford visited Hashimi and asked him to reconsider, but he got nowhere. He was hearing the same arguments from other Sunni contacts as well: if the voting went ahead, the Sunnis wouldn't show up. In their absence, the Shia and Kurdish voters would gain an overwhelming share of power, further alienating the Sunnis.

Ford began sending cables with similar warnings to Washington. "Our Sunni contacts were very upfront about it," Ford said. "If there was an election and they voted, they would be killed. And if they didn't vote, Sunnis wouldn't be there to help write the constitution, and they would feel even more left out."

But President Bush insisted on holding to the schedule. A postponement would anger the Shia, and the administration was facing a U.S. election and under pressure to show progress toward winding down American involvement in the country.

Officials in Washington brainstormed to find ways to enable the Sunnis to vote without exposing them to danger. They called a videoconference meeting in late November with officials in Baghdad. "We've been reading your reporting, and we understand you don't think people are going to vote," Meghan O'Sullivan, a deputy national security adviser, told Ford. "We've got some other ideas."

One was to have the Sunnis vote from home with their computers. Even assuming they had computers, Ford pointed out, "there's no electricity in Ramadi, or in Fallujah, and often not even in Baghdad." A second idea was to have voters use their cell phones to cast ballots. They could scroll down to the party they wanted and click on it. Too complicated, Ford said. "How can we assume that people in Ramadi and Mosul can use a system that's more sophisticated than the one used by people in California?"

That idea died, too, and not without some damage to Ford's reputation in Washington. The following day he got a call from Richard G. Olson, then director of the Iraq desk at the State Department.

"Your attitude is unappreciated," Olson told him. "We spent a lot of time working on these ideas, and we go into this meeting, and you shoot them all down right away."

"I remember thinking, 'You guys don't begin to understand what we're dealing with out here,'" Ford said. "It was all unreal." Years later, Negroponte was still citing the voting suggestions as examples of Washington's worst ideas.

When election day came, 8.4 million Iraqis—58 percent of eligible voters—went to the polls. The Bush administration described the voting as a historic step for democracy, and the news media carried pictures of Iraqis holding up thumbs stained with purple ink, proof they had voted. Insurgents killed forty-five in about one hundred attacks but failed to stop the elections. It was "a powerful demonstration of what the path to democracy could look like in the Middle East," Condoleezza Rice, Bush's national security adviser, wrote later.[2]

But the Sunnis had stayed away. Only 2 percent voted in Anbar Province. And as Iraqi officials began writing the constitution and making choices about the distribution of the country's wealth and power, Sunnis were absent. The Shia and Kurds also used their victory to gain control over the country's police and security agencies and began using them to settle scores with the Sunnis.

The effect was to deepen their alienation from the new system and give further impetus to the insurgency. "The election made everything worse," Ford said. "It let the insurgents say, 'We need to attack any moderate who says we should play within the system.'"

In a videoconference with the White House's national security staff on February 5, Ford said the election meant that the Sunnis were now "really on the outside looking in." But he said that he intended to begin a new push to convince the Sunni leaders to join the scrum of the new Iraqi politics. With the bleak reality of their situation sinking in, he said, they might have a change of heart.

Ford also reported that the dangers from the insurgency had reached the point where it was no longer safe for him to leave the Green Zone for the personal contacts that were the heart of his job. He had gotten out in the past, at some risk to himself, but now, he told the officials in Washington, the dangers had become over-whelming. "We are trapped in the Green Zone," he said.[3]

Ford's efforts did help convince Tariq al-Hashimi, the Sunni party chief, to enter politics. He joined the fray after the election and, in April 2006, became vice president. He remained one of the most visible leaders of Iraq's Sunnis for the next six years, even as insurgents killed two of his brothers and a sister.

In the aftermath of the January 2005 election, Iraqi lawmakers began a prolonged debate about who should be interim prime min-ister. The Iraqis were working under rules that had been shaped to prevent the rise of a new strongman and required supermajority support for a candidate to become prime minister. In Iraq's frac-tured politics, that became a prescription for deadlock. The par-ties maneuvered for three months after the election trying to find an acceptable choice. It began to appear that the job would go by default to Ibrahim al-Jaafari, a physician who led the Dawa Party, a small Shia faction that had fought against Saddam Hussein.

Little about Jaafari suggested he would be able to restore a country near collapse. He was a bookish man with a scruffy beard who loved to ruminate about history and philosophy and reflex-ively sidestepped difficult decisions. "He was an odd man with the bearing of a humanities professor," Condoleezza Rice wrote later.

As the final decision grew near, Ford and Negroponte decided to sit in on a meeting where Shia leaders were debating the choice. As they approached the meeting site in an armored SUV, Negro-ponte reminded Ford that President Bush didn't want U.S. officials trying to influence the choice: this was to be entirely an Iraqi decision. If that was the case, "we should pray they don't pick Jaafari. He will talk, he won't listen, and he won't make decisions," Ford said. "If Jaafari is elected, he'll sink our boat."

Jaafari was finally chosen prime minister on April 7, precisely because of his weakness. The stronger Shia religious parties, the Sadrists and the Supreme Council for the Islamic Revolution in Iraq (SCIRI), wanted him because they didn't consider him a threat. Over the next year President Bush came to share Ford's misgivings about him.

Jaafari swept in with a new cast of Shia officials who intended to strengthen their grip on the country's security agencies and to use their power against Sunni rivals. In a cable to Washington, Ford told how the departing minister of the interior, a secular Sunni named Falah al-Naqib, had approached him to warn that Shia hard-liners were quietly consolidating power in a way that threatened the new democratic framework. In the Shia heartland of southern Iraq, SCIRI officials now held governorships and provincial councils. They were dismissing police chiefs he had appointed, Naqib said, and replacing them with members of the Shia militia, the Badr Corps. He told General George W. Casey, who was now the coalition military commander, that the Shia goal was to create an autonomous region in the southern Shia heartland and link it to Iran. A civil war was coming, he predicted. "We either stop them or give Iraq to Iran," he said.[4]

As Naqib forecast, the insurgency exploded. Killings skyrocketed as Sunni and Shia began using campaigns of killings and terror to drive their rivals out of mixed neighborhoods in Baghdad. Shia hard-liners used their control of state security agencies to wage war. U.S. troops discovered that hard-line Shia officials in the interior ministry were running a secret special interrogations unit that tortured and killed Sunni suspects in an old prison in Baghdad's Jadriyah neighborhood.

U.S. forces stepped up arrests and killings of militants and mobilized infantry in bloody efforts to retake cities like Ramadi and Fallujah that had been seized by insurgents. Despite the efforts,

Iraqi casualties rose by one-third in 2005. U.S. officials became desperate to find a way to open channels to the insurgents. They began looking for figures in the Sunni community who might have influence over them.

Ford, after some effort, found a way to reach some of the insurgents' political allies. The senior Bahraini diplomat in Iraq, a contact from Ford's posting in the Gulf kingdom, reached out to some of these Sunnis and set up a meeting in April 2005 at his home. When Ford and a young American military aide showed up at the home, in the prosperous Mansour neighborhood west of the Green Zone, he was met by an odd assortment of Iraqi men, some in coats and ties, others in tribal and traditional garb. They weren't the Iraqis the Americans usually had to tea. Among them were Salafi Muslims, with views just short of Al Qaeda, and unreconstructed members of Saddam's Baath Party. They brimmed with anger, conspiracy theories, threats, and resentments of their ethnic rivals.

"You Americans have to get out of our country," one announced. "You have damaged it, and nobody wants you here."

"We want to leave," Ford told them. "But first we have to set up a stable government. And you're impeding the effort. Why don't you help?" He told them that if they agreed to take part in the new politics, they could join the parliament, possibly take seats in the cabinet and have a say in the country's course. The conversation raged on for three hours with taunts, threats, and denunciations.

Among those in the group were two Salafis, Sheik Abdel Nasser al-Janabi and Mahmoud al-Mashhadani, a physician who had already been imprisoned because of suspected ties to insurgents. A third was Saleh al-Mutlaq, an agronomist with strong Baathist ties.

Mashhadani lectured Ford on how the Sunnis couldn't be expected to ever work with the Shia. "You have to understand, Mr. Ford," Mashhadani said in a low conspiratorial tone. "The Shia preach to you, they get into your schools and mosques, and they get inside your head. They get inside your children's heads. And they start to change you." It sounded to Ford like a racist rant from 1930s Germany.

The session ended after three hours with no agreement. As they departed, Ford joked to his colleague that the world might be better off if they had the U.S. military call in air strikes on the house.

Yet Ford's arguments convinced the angry Sunnis to take part in the government and to try to persuade others to vote in upcoming elections. Within a few weeks Mutlaq and Janabi were part of a new group of twenty-five Sunnis who took part in the debate over a draft constitution. Janabi became a parliamentarian, Mutlaq a deputy prime minister, and Mashhadani the speaker of the parliament. The three were never easy for the Americans to get along with, but Ford had succeeded in expanding the tent of Iraqi politics. His efforts to bring in the Sunnis had also been noticed by their rivals, the Shia. They grumbled that Ford had become "the Sunnis' lawyer."

Negroponte was replaced as ambassador in June 2005 by Zalmay Khalilzad, the Afghan-born American diplomat who had already served as White House envoy to Iraq in early 2003. Khalilzad was a garrulous man who spoke some Arabic, bantered with Shia clerics in Farsi, and generally had good chemistry with the Iraqis. He pushed for a further expansion of contacts with alienated Sunnis and wanted the U.S. team to take an active role in mediating between the Iraqi groups.

Ford spent much of 2005 helping Iraqi lawmakers assemble a draft constitution that would be put to a vote in a referendum in October. Day after day, often from dawn until midnight, Ford sat in on meetings on the document at the cavernous Baghdad convention center. Sometimes the process stalled and Ford and his American colleagues pitched in to give it a push. Ford and Jeffrey Beals, an Arabist and former CIA analyst who had joined the embassy's political team, suggested the terms by which the Iraqi parliament could overcome a veto of legislation by the prime minister. The Iraqis accepted the language, and it eventually became part of the constitution.

At the same time Ford was struggling to keep the Sunni bloc cooperating in the effort to form a new government. Every few days

U.S. troops would arrest prominent Sunnis, setting off an uproar in their community and building new pressure on the Sunni leadership to break off cooperation with the Americans. Regularly, Ford would be awakened in the middle of the night by irate Sunni leaders calling to complain about an arrest and demanding that the Iraqi be released. Ford argued with U.S. military officers about whether they could release Sunnis that the military believed had attacked American soldiers. Sometimes he persuaded them and sometimes he didn't.

One night Ford was told the troops had picked up Naseer al-Ani, a tall affable Sunni who was then vice president of the parliament. It appeared he had been mistaken for another Iraqi. Ford put in a call to General George Casey, commander of the coalition forces. "This cannot stand: you have to release him," Ford said.

Ford remembers the period as the most exhausting of his career. Every few months he and his wife, Alison, who was then helping organize logistics at the embassy, would take a few days off to travel to Amman, Jordan. They would check into the InterContinental hotel and hole up in a room. They would order their meals by room service and sleep the time away.

The next major step on the political timeline was an election on December 15, 2005. This time Sunnis turned out in large numbers, including in cities like Ramadi with a heavy insurgent presence, and in Saddam Hussein's hometown of Tikrit. Some 70 percent of eligible voters cast ballots in Sunni-dominated Anbar Province. Some insurgent groups declared a cease-fire for the day to encourage Sunnis to vote. "We had expected blood and mayhem, and it didn't turn out that bad," Ford said.

A Sunni bloc won 44 of 275 seats in the first permanent parliament, giving them for the first time a solid share of power. The Shia, Sunnis, and Kurds had taken an important step in coming to an agreement on a constitution in October, and they seemed to be within reach of an equitable division of power. Yet, in the first two months of talks, the Iraqis again seemed stalemated in forming a new government.

Then disaster struck. On February 22, 2006, Al Qaeda in Iraq blew up the Golden Mosque in Samarra, an 1,100-year-old structure that was one of the holiest sites in the Shia world. The bombing set off a convulsion of Sunni-Shia sectarian violence that led to the deaths of hundreds a day. Sectarian conflict was ripening into all-out civil war.

President Bush, nearly despondent over the sectarian fighting, had now lost patience with Jaafari. The prime minister was resisting pressure for action to quell the conflict, telling Khalilzad that Iraqis were only "letting off steam." Jaafari had also resisted American pressure for steps to stop Shia officials in the security agencies from imprisoning and torturing Sunnis. His cabinet meetings would drift on for as long as nine hours without agreeing on any action to counter the insurgency or restore public services.

After insisting earlier that the Iraqis should be free to pick their own leader, Bush changed his mind about the Iraqi prime minister. "Bush sent us clear marching orders: Get him out of there," said Ford. American officials continued to insist publicly, as they always did, that Washington was not choosing Iraq's leaders, but they were now public in demanding that the Iraqis find a leader who could finally form a government.

It was not easy. Jaafari had narrowly won balloting by the Shia political coalition, edging out Adel Abdul-Mahdi, an economist and vice president, by one vote. Khalilzad, accompanied by Ford, visited Jaafari at his home, a villa in a Baghdad neighborhood laced with canals, sometimes called Little Venice. Washington, Khalilzad told Jaafari, could no longer support his leadership. But Jaafari simply ignored Khalilzad's ultimatum. The meeting dragged on for two uncomfortable hours as Jaafari rambled between topics.

Finally Khalilzad broke in: "You don't understand: We can't work with you anymore. You've got to step down."

"Oh, no, I have the votes in the parliament," Jaafari countered. "I'm not going." It was the most agonizing meeting Ford had ever been part of. At midnight Khalilzad and Ford left and returned to Khalilzad's office. Khalilzad sat at his desk and fumed.

He smashed his fist down. "I have 150,000 troops in this country," he said. "How can this man say no to me?"

Khalilzad sought help from other influential players. He had President Bush write a letter to Grand Ayatollah Sistani, urging him to find another leader for the country. Sistani soon issued a statement saying the country needed a leader to unify the country—signaling that he, too, wanted a change. The Iranians, a powerful influence with their Iraqi Shia brethren, had come to the same conclusion.

Khalilzad found an alternative in Nouri al-Maliki, a man the ambassador had been introduced to by Ford. Maliki was a longtime Shia dissident who had fled Saddam's Iraq in 1979 and lived in Iran and Damascus. Although a top official of the small Dawa Party, he was not prominent in the Iraqi political class. "Who can we get?" Khalilzad asked Ford. "There's this one guy," Ford told him. "He's a tough cookie. He's dependable. And he's not Iran's guy." At the time, he wasn't.

When Khalilzad approached other Iraqi Shia and Kurdish leaders, he found many willing to accept Maliki. With some American help, Maliki was able to muster majority support in parliament. On May 20, he took over as prime minister and named a new government.

Jaafari ended his time in office with a lavish farewell luncheon that offered a glimpse into the state of Iraqi politics. The entire Iraqi political world turned out for the event, held at a fashionable private club, Ford wrote Washington in a confidential cable. Yet "all those present barely acknowledged their guest of honor, consumed with the ongoing cabinet formation negotiations and jockeying over prime cabinet positions." No one stood to toast Jaafari's accomplishments, nor did they invite the prime minister to list his contributions. Most of Jaafari's former cabinet officials didn't even sit with him.

The dramatic climax of the gathering came when Safia Taleb al-Suhail, a prominent female member of the Iraqiya Party, stood up to loudly denounce Ahmad Chalabi, the controversial expatriate financier who had worked with American neoconservatives to lobby for the 2003 U.S. invasion. Chalabi had defamed her sister, she said, by leaking to a Shia newspaper pictures of the sister dancing at her own wedding. Suhail accused Chalabi of being corrupt, dishonest, and treacherous, Ford wrote. "Don't call me crazy! I've known you since you were 18 years old," Suhail cried. "I know every trick of yours!" She collared Bayan Jabr Solagh, Iraq's interior minister, and demanded that he investigate Chalabi.[5]

As the new government took shape, Ford wound down his tour and prepared to leave his post in Iraq for Algeria, where he had been chosen to serve as ambassador. He had served on this tour for twice as long as he expected. As on his first tour, he had lost friends to the violence.

One of his worst days in the posting was in January 2005 when insurgents from Al Qaeda in Iraq, the country's deadliest terror group, assassinated one of his closest Iraqi friends, Ali Radhi al-Haidary, the governor of Baghdad Province. A businessman and farmer, Haidary had worked his way up the ranks of the provincial government. He had been committed to a better Iraq and unafraid. It was the eighth attempt on his life since he took office in June 2004, Ford wrote Washington in a cable. This time, attackers in one of Baghdad's poorest neighborhoods swarmed Haidary in his unarmored BMW, killing him along with six of his bodyguards. After an attack in September 2004 had destroyed his armored vehicle, Ford had urged him to put off traveling until a new armored car arrived. Haidari refused. "He would say, 'I will not let these bastards beat us. I will not,'" Ford recalled afterward.

Haidary's killing was the latest in a convulsion of assassinations. Over the past fourteen months, insurgents had killed the deputy governor of the province, the deputy mayor of Baghdad, and twenty-six members of the provincial council, Ford wrote. The killing was meant by the terrorists to demonstrate that "even the most heavily protected local official is not safe . . . that anyone is within the insurgents' reach," he wrote.[6]

Ford and his wife slipped out of town at night. The trip to the airport, as always a quick measure of life in Iraq, was now so dangerous that no one drove it during daylight hours. Ford had been discouraged when he left Iraq at the end of his first tour, in 2003. This time, as his armored vehicle raced along the road, skirting the charred husks of burned vehicles, his mood was even grimmer. Nothing the U.S. team tried seemed to work.

Ford's new life was going to be different. From a cramped shoe box in a Green Zone trailer park, he was moving into one of the State Department's most spectacular residences. The Villa Montfeld was a pearl-white Moorish estate on a five-acre property in the coastal hills overlooking Algiers. In a symbolic act, he tossed out the threadbare clothes he had been wearing in Iraq and bought an entire new wardrobe. Iraq, he hoped, was behind him.

CHAPTER 7

# From Enemies, Friends

For J. Christopher Stevens, diplomacy was about listening. When he met new contacts in the Middle East, he would sit patiently, sipping tea and offering pleasant silences that beckoned his companions to share. Many times they came expecting a bustling American functionary with a list of rat-a-tat bullet points. Instead they found a sandy-haired man with a toothy smile who was happy to linger, at the pace of the Arab world, to hear them out. Often they left feeling they had found a friend.

Chris Stevens's approach was well suited to his diplomatic postings in Libya, where he was sent three times. It was a place where America needed friends. For most of the forty-two years that the country was led by the flamboyant strongman Muammar el-Qaddafi, the United States and Libya had been bitter enemies. Ronald Reagan had denounced Qaddafi for his terrorism as the "mad dog of the Middle East." Qaddafi, in return, made a strident anti-Americanism the justification for his rule.

In 2003, Libya took the first steps toward ending its pariah status and thawing relations with Washington. Under American pressure, it surrendered its rudimentary nuclear weapons program, renounced terrorism, and declared that it would reform its government. Stevens arrived for his first posting in July 2007, just thirteen months after the U.S. embassy in Tripoli was formally reopened. He was nominally the embassy's number two, although for most of his assignment he ran the mission as acting ambassador. His instructions were simple: Make friends and try to nudge Qaddafi toward reform.

In making friends, Stevens had a lot to overcome. Libyans "had been taught Americans were devils," said Bubaker Habib, a teacher from Benghazi who served as Stevens's fixer. "Everyone was suspicious." Stevens's approach was to win them over one by one. He hung out in cafés, engaging young Libyans in Arabic. He ate goat meat off a spit at Bedouin campfires and learned to tell jokes in local dialect.

Libya was a thinly populated country the size of Alaska that Italian colonizers had tried to assemble from three mismatched regions. Its erratic leader and government were viewed with scorn by most Arab leaders. But Stevens felt, from the start, an attraction to the country's people and its whitewashed villas, luminous desert landscapes, and rose-scented souks. "There's something special here," Stevens told a colleague in Washington soon after he arrived.

He even tried to make friends with the secret police who shadowed him. On a trip to the Greco-Roman ruins in Cyrene, Stevens was trailed at a few feet by plainclothesmen. They carried cameras and continually shot pictures of him. When he saw this was alarming tourists, Stevens turned the tables on them, seizing a policeman's camera and laughingly shooting pictures of them. "Hey, you're scaring people," Stevens told the agents. "What do you want to know? Have some coffee and talk to me." The goons, abashed, agreed.

Qaddafi and his government were ambivalent about the new relationship with America. When Stevens met with government officials, they were friendly, eager to talk about the weapons, aid, and new ties to the outside world they hoped the Americans could provide. After decades on the margins, the regime yearned to be taken seriously by America. But an uneasiness lurked, a shadow of suspicion that Washington might have secret agendas—like regime change.

Stevens saw in his first face-to-face encounter with Qaddafi that the old anti-Americanism lingered. In July 2007, two weeks after he arrived, Stevens was invited to a state dinner at Bab al-Aziziyah, Qaddafi's fortress residence in Tripoli, to mark a visit by French president Nicolas Sarkozy.

Qaddafi, a dashing figure when he seized power in 1969, was still striking at sixty-five. The leader "looked great in a white suit with a black shirt, a large pin of Africa on his lapel, and a pair of very cool looking black-framed shades," Stevens emailed friends. Introduced to Stevens in the receiving line, Qaddafi gave the diplomat a bemused look and moved on without comment. But the evening said a great deal about the leader's feelings toward Americans.

The dinner was held on a sweeping outdoor patio against the jarring backdrop of a scarred building that Reagan had bombed in 1986 in retaliation for a Libyan terrorist attack at a Berlin nightclub that killed two U.S. soldiers. The building had been converted after the attack into a memorial to what an explanatory plaque described as "the failed American aggression." Qaddafi and Sarkozy sat at a head table near a sculpture depicting a huge gold fist crushing a U.S. fighter jet. As the dinner began, the band swung into Lionel Richie's teary soft-rock classic "Hello." Then it turned to a peppy patriotic anthem recalling Libya's heroic defense against the 1986 American strike. "Unreal," Stevens wrote friends.

Stevens went to Libya as one of the Foreign Service's rising stars. An athletic-looking Northern Californian, Stevens had during his twenty-six years in the diplomatic service traveled the circuit of the State Department's important Mideast posts: Egypt, Saudi Arabia, Syria, Israel. He was the second-ranking U.S. liaison with the Palestinians in Jerusalem from 2002 to 2007, during the uprising called the second intifada. He had the idealism of the Peace Corps volunteer he had been, and believed that engaging adversary countries could help resolve long-running conflicts. When he worked on the Iran desk in Washington in the late 1990s, he designed the Clinton administration's effort to open a dialogue with a newly elected Iranian president, Mohammad Khatami. When the Palestinian Islamist group Hamas unexpectedly took control of the Gaza Strip in a 2006 election, Stevens wrote friends that he hoped Washington would work with the group to moderate its approach rather than try to undermine it. "Islamist doesn't necessarily translate to extremist," he wrote. "He displayed the quintessential sunny optimism of Americans," Roya Hakakian, an Iranian-American writer who became Stevens's friend, wrote later.[1]

But Stevens had a more nuanced view of the world and its dangers than was sometimes remembered after he was made famous by his death in a terrorist attack. While he was political counselor in Jerusalem, he toned down cables written by his subordinates if he thought they were too critical of Bush administration policy or Israel. At one point three junior officers who worked for him became dissatisfied with the administration's approach to Israeli treatment of Palestinians and drafted a cable for submission to the State Department's "dissent channel," a forum for registering objections to policy. When they asked Stevens to join their dissent, he declined, telling them good-naturedly that it was the wrong approach. A head-on challenge to the policy was fruitless, he said. Instead they should try to gather the facts and present them as vividly as they could in hopes it would persuade higher-ups to change course. "That was not an easy argument for us to hear because we were all pretty idealistic first tour foreign service officers," said Prem Kumar, who was part of the team and later became a top adviser to President Obama on the Middle East.

Stevens embraced the State Department's Arabist tradition. Stevens showed colleagues a photo of a relative who had traveled alone in the Middle East in the nineteenth century and was captive to its charms and mysteries. In the photo, Stevens's relative is wearing an Arab robe and burnoose, in the style of British adventurers like T. E. Lawrence and Sir Richard Francis Burton. "It's a family gene—maybe a slightly defective one," he joked to friends. He told them that one of the books that most shaped his life was *The Arabists: The Romance of an American Elite*, a 1993 work by Robert D. Kaplan that profiled the State Department's old guard of Mideast specialists.

But Stevens parted company with some Mideast hands, such as his friend Ryan Crocker, who believed foreign service officers in Iraq should be willing to pitch in. Stevens thought the war a disastrous foreign policy blunder and didn't want to work in a military occupation with suffocating security rules, his friends recalled. Prem Kumar, of Stevens's staff in Jerusalem, asked him if any administration policy made him so uncomfortable that he might file a dissent or quit. The Iraq invasion might fall into that category, Stevens told him. He was convinced, from what he had heard from colleagues, that American diplomats were being sent out with little regard for their safety. "You could get killed out there," he cautioned a colleague who was considering an Iraq assignment. He made fatalistic jokes to family members that he might get transferred any day to Baghdad.

Robert Ford, then the longest-serving foreign service officer in Iraq, called Stevens twice from Baghdad to try to recruit him, and twice Stevens made clear "he wanted nothing to do with it," said Ford. Stevens's effort to stay out of Iraq "was unusual for somebody with his seniority in the Foreign Service who wanted to become an ambassador," said Kumar. "It was considered almost a required duty." Instead, Stevens went, at the height of the U.S. buildup in Iraq, to Libya. At the time it seemed safer.

Stevens, though a believer in U.S. engagement with adversary regimes, had no illusions about Qaddafi's rule. Washington was eager to see signs of reform and wanted Stevens to encourage it if possible. As it turned out, he spent his three years chronicling the government's brutality, corruption, and laughable incompetence.

A month after Stevens arrived, the regime raised hopes for reform by announcing that it was beginning the process of writing a constitution that would provide for a free media, an independent central bank, and new civic institutions. The drafting was to be done by a twenty-member committee that would include Libyan intellectuals, political scientists, and legal scholars, including foreign academics. Qaddafi had put his son and presumed heir, Seif al-Islam el-Qaddafi, in charge, and it appeared the effort might strengthen popular support for the government. But nine months later Stevens was cabling Washington to explain why the initiative had slowed down and dropped entirely from public view. The hopeful explanation, Stevens wrote, was that Qaddafi was keeping the deliberations secret to protect the project from attack by hard-line old guard opponents. But committee members worried that it was disappearing from sight so that "it could be abandoned altogether if Qaddafi changed his mind."[2]

Stevens passed along signs that Qaddafi, who regularly meddled in African power politics, was trying to accelerate the proxy war between Chad and Sudan by sending rebel forces some 130,000 Kalashnikov rifles. The Libyan government wouldn't explain the secret shipments, but Stevens noted the quantity was far more than needed for Qaddafi's 60,000 ground troops.[3]

And he reported that Qaddafi was bullying the Greek embassy by refusing to deliver supplies from abroad, including alcoholic beverages, unless the embassy issued travel visas for well-connected Libyans who wanted to vacation in Europe. It was part of a larger pattern where the government "has essentially blackmailed foreign embassies," Stevens noted.[4]

In another cable, Stevens told the alarming story of a two-meter diameter sewage pipe that was dumping one million liters of raw sewage a day into the Mediterranean next to the busiest swimming beach in Tripoli. The Libyan authorities were desperate to halt the flow, not because of the risk to swimmers, but because it was giving off an odor near Qaddafi's residence in the city center. "The focus on mitigating the stench near Qaddafi's compound, as opposed to protecting the broader public health, is telling," Stevens cabled Washington.[5]

Stevens helped prepare Secretary of State Condoleezza Rice for a September 2008 visit to Tripoli, which was the first time a U.S. chief diplomat had been to the country since a visit by John Foster Dulles in 1953. The Libyans were anticipating the trip as a signature event in Libya's efforts to be reintegrated into the world community, he wrote in a cable to Rice, and a "grand opening" of U.S.-Libya relations.

Qaddafi was fascinated by Rice and had been demanding to know why the "African princess" hadn't visited him already. Stevens's cable cautioned that an encounter with Qaddafi could be a strange event. Qaddafi followed the news closely, he said, and could be at moments "an engaging and charming interlocutor." But he was also "notoriously mercurial," Stevens wrote. "He often avoids making eye contact during the initial portion of meetings, and there may be long, uncomfortable periods of silence."

As expected, the meeting took strange turns. Qaddafi left Rice waiting for hours before beginning the meeting. When it did start, he carried on a reasonable conversation with Rice about African issues but then abruptly demanded that President Bush stop pushing for the creation of a separate Palestinian state. Both peoples should occupy one state, to be called "Israelstine," he barked. He insisted that Rice dine alone with him in his private kitchen, an idea that made the Secret Service uneasy. Qaddafi gave Rice a video of her and world leaders, set to a tune he had commissioned called "Black Flower in the White House." He presented her a necklace but inexplicably declined to shake hands with her. "Was it a deliberate slight?" Stevens wrote friends. "Was it a gesture of Ramadan modesty? Who knows?" The meeting, Stevens concluded, was "unforgettable." Rice left that night convinced that Qaddafi was dangerously deluded and that it was for the best that he had surrendered his nuclear, chemical, and germ warfare weapons. "There in his bunker, making his last stand, I have no doubt he would have used them," she wrote in her memoir.[6]

Stevens left Tripoli in 2009 to return to Washington for an assignment there. He stayed in touch with his Libyan contacts, including Ali Aujali, the genial Libyan ambassador to the United States. Stevens, an accomplished tennis player, played regularly with the ambassador, in part to keep current on developments in Tripoli. Stevens made sure to lose his matches with the older, slighter ambassador. It was part of the diplomat's job. "One never beats the ambassador," Stevens explained to his friend Austin Tichenor.

U.S. relations with Qaddafi's government didn't improve as hoped but instead deteriorated. One blow came in November 2010 when the anti-secrecy group Wikileaks released 251,000 American diplomatic cables. Among them were reports, signed by Ambassador Gene Cretz, enumerating Qaddafi's eccentricities. The cables described Qaddafi's reliance on a Ukrainian nurse, Galyna Kolotnytskaya, who was described as a "voluptuous blonde." They told how Qaddafi hated to be on the top floors of high buildings and refused to fly over water. Cretz had had good relations with the regime and was in regular contact with Seif el-Qaddafi, the dictator's son. The Wikileaks disclosures changed all that.

Cretz, a veteran foreign service officer and old friend of Stevens's, was called in by Libyan officials for questioning and began to be harassed when he ventured out in public. When he went out for a run, he was jostled; angry mobs showed up when he went on a picnic or to play tennis. The regime insisted the harassers were just ordinary Libyans. But there were telltale signs. Cretz noticed the same thug at every one—a man wearing a pair of fancy and blindingly white Nike sneakers. Qaddafi and his team "were unhappy, obviously, about the whole situation," said Cretz. Soon the foreign minister and intelligence chief were telling Jeffrey Feltman, the top State Department official for the Middle East, that it would be better if Cretz left. "People get killed here for writing things like that," a Qaddafi henchman told U.S. officials.[7] In January 2011, Cretz returned to Washington. U.S. relations with Libya seemed headed for more trouble.

CHAPTER 8

———

# Not Peace but More Peaceful

P resident Bush got right to the point. He was taking the struggling American effort in Iraq in a new direction and wanted
Ryan Crocker to lead a new civilian team as ambassador. It
was a crucial assignment, he said, and Crocker was just the man to
take it on.

In that late-night call to Islamabad in November 2006, Bush
did not say that the fate of an American war, and possibly a presidency, might hang on the new team's effort. He didn't bring up its
long odds of success. All that was understood. Bush "just asked me
to do it," Crocker said. "And I thought, *Oh, somebody shoot me
now.*" But the words that came out of his mouth were, "Yes, sir,
thank you, sir."

Crocker had left Iraq in August 2003, discouraged at the chaotic American occupation and hoping Iraq's problems would never
again be his. He spent three years as ambassador to Pakistan, dealing with a twilight war against militants, political crises, and an
earthquake. Now, at fifty-seven, he was contemplating retirement
from the Foreign Service. But it was the code of the Foreign Service that you go where you're needed—especially, of course, when
the request comes from the president.

Bush's new approach, which became known as the surge, sent
another 30,000 U.S. troops to Iraq in an attempt to halt the insurgency and sectarian fighting that had turned the country into a char-
nel house. The ultimate goal was not military but political. The U.S.
troops flooded battleground neighborhoods to reduce the fighting

and Iraqis' fears of each other. Officials hoped that would open a window for the country's three dominant groups—Sunnis, Shias, and Kurds—to settle their disputes and restore order. Crocker, as an Arabic-speaking four-time ambassador, was formally in charge of the toughest and most important part of the mission, the search for political reconciliation. As part of the job he also helped oversee the largest nation-building effort since World War II.

In the new job he was half of a power pair. He shared leadership for eighteen months with Army General David Petraeus, whom Bush had installed in February 2007 as the new commander of coalition forces in Iraq. In influence and star power, the general and the diplomat were not equals. While Crocker was by law the leader of the U.S. team in Iraq, Petraeus commanded 170,000 U.S. coalition troops and 154,000 contract employees,[1] with personal control of billions of dollars. Petraeus was the most celebrated military man of his generation and a pop-cultural hero, described in newsmagazine cover stories with such phrases as "the oracle of Mesopotamia." The ambassador, in contrast, was revered within his small diplomatic tribe and in the fusty world of Washington foreign policy insiders.

But they agreed to work as a team. While Crocker was still in Islamabad, Petraeus called him from Fort Leavenworth, Kansas, and they agreed to try to coordinate their work as closely as possible. "If we don't work together, failure's a certainty," Crocker told him. Since the 2003 invasion, the U.S. military and civilian leaders had often squabbled over turf, sometimes in full view of the Iraqi leaders they were supposed to be guiding. Crocker had seen the damage that caused. Now they were going to row in the same direction.

Petraeus set up a second office just twenty feet from Crocker's in the presidential palace, on the edge of a large common space. They met almost daily and traveled together for almost all meetings with Iraqi prime minister Nouri al-Maliki. They each had veto power over major decisions. Each time Petraeus planned a nighttime raid into Sadr City, a violent Shia slum in eastern Baghdad, he checked to see that Crocker had no objection. Every Sunday,

Crocker would helicopter to Camp Victory, the military hub next to the airport, so that he and Petraeus could run a six-mile course together to chew over their plans. "We could solve everything rhetorically in the course of six miles," Petraeus said. In their year and a half together, they became so closely in sync that, when they briefed presidents and lawmakers, they knew without prompting who should speak.

Petraeus was a can-do leader of troops, always optimistic and full of ideas on an infinitely broad range of subjects. He was always ready to make a case that the mission could be accomplished, sometimes when success seemed a long shot. Crocker was skeptical by nature and quicker to acknowledge doubts. Sometimes, if he thought Petraeus was too sanguine, he would try to ratchet down Iraqis' expectations. His staff thought he was sometimes too willing to let the military take the lead in managing Iraqi political processes and public relations. But Crocker picked his battles carefully. Harmony was essential.

Crocker did not seem to mind that the world saw Petraeus as the big dog. Three years later, when Petraeus worked with former ambassador Richard Holbrooke, who was then overseeing the U.S. mission in Afghanistan and Pakistan, Holbrooke bridled when Petraeus referred to him as his "wingman." Civilians, and not military officers, were supposed to be lead pilots, in Holbrooke's view. Crocker raised no objection to the term and showed no sign of yearning for more recognition. "You never felt Crocker needed to be in the picture," said British Mideast expert Emma Sky, who served as political adviser to the American military commanders. "If you've got a big ego, you'd have a hard time dealing with the fact that the generals have so much more than you. Crocker didn't have that." Petraeus agreed: "He didn't feel threatened by a fairly high-profile general, as some of the other ambassadors did, frankly," he said later. Petraeus also valued Crocker. The four-star general usually knew more than anyone else in the room. But with Ryan Crocker in the room, Petraeus understood, the sum of knowledge was expanded.

The other key inside player was President Bush. Bush had sub-contracted the war to others in its early stages and had come to regret it. Now he was in direct control, following developments hour by hour, as if he were the desk officer for Iraq. He opened lines to Petraeus and Crocker that bypassed much of the bureaucracy, in a consolidation of authority like few in the foreign policy annals. The general and the ambassador had the principal speaking roles in weekly videoconference meetings held every Monday morning at 7:30 a.m. with the president and his full national security team. Bush started these sessions by asking them asking for the facts and their personal takes. "How's it going?" Bush would begin. Most of the time he deferred to their judgment, even on some of the most politically sensitive calls.

Bush had been considering sending Crocker to Iraq for months before he offered him the job. In a series of visits to the embassy in Pakistan, he spent hours with Crocker, drawing him into his inner circle and discussing a range of topics, including domestic issues. Crocker realized this was building up to something, and guessed Bush was sizing him up for the big job in Iraq.[2]

When it came time on March 29, 2007, for Crocker to assume the ambassador's position, he did not fly to Washington for the usual formal swearing in within the pink-columned grandeur of the State Department's Benjamin Franklin State Dining Room. The White House wanted not even a day's gap between the departure of his predecessor, Zalmay Khalilzad, and Crocker's assumption of the job. He flew from Islamabad directly to Baghdad and was given the oath of office, without flourishes, by a junior foreign ser-vice officer.

Crocker brought a far different style from Khalilzad's. The Afghanistan-born Khalilzad was a schmoozer who got along eas-ily with Iraqi politicians, teasing and cajoling them and instinc-tually understanding their horse-trading politics. When he met resistance, he could turn fiery. He sometimes crossed swords with the U.S. military commander, General George Casey, in front of Iraqi officials.

Crocker was formal and respectful with Iraqi officials. He pressed them with demands but never exploded. When he got angry or frustrated, he became quieter and his face became expressionless, drained of color. The meetings he ran were sometimes more stilted than free flowing. But the Iraqis knew he had juice with Washington and they appreciated that he understood their country. "He got the Arabs and they got him," said former ambassador Gordon Gray III, who became Crocker's adviser on Shia southern Iraq.

Crocker inherited a gold-accented French Empire–style desk that had become a symbol of authority for the senior American civilians in the country. It had been built, with three contrasting shades of wood, for Saddam Hussein, then passed between occupation chief Paul Bremer and ambassadors John Negroponte, Khalilzad, and Crocker when they took over. The desk was an incongruous spot of luxury in an office that was otherwise stripped-down utilitarian. When the office was Khalilzad's, he adorned it with photos: shots of him in the White House, in the cockpit of an F-16 fighter jet, with Vice President Cheney. During Crocker's stay, the office revealed little about its occupant. The walls were blank except for a few maps, the furnishings well-worn government issue. The office once had a window view and streaming sunlight. But when the insurgents began lobbing rockets at that corner of the palace, the window was hastily covered with an oversized armored plate and the curtains were yanked closed for good.

In his residence, a three-story limestone villa once occupied by Saddam's mother-in-law, Crocker hung a poster of a favorite heavy-rock song, Iron Maiden's *2 Minutes to Midnight*. It depicted a post-apocalyptic scene with a row of flags, including those of the United States and Iraq, fluttering on tall poles over a shattered landscape.

When Crocker arrived, parts of Baghdad looked like the poster. Almost 2,000 Iraqis were dying each month from the fighting between Sunnis and Shia, and militias were expelling Sunnis from mixed neighborhoods. On the night that he disembarked into a bath of steamy air at the Baghdad airport, Crocker felt like he was again in Lebanon in 1983, with the Syrians and Iranians mobilizing proxy militant groups in hopes of inflicting enough pain that they could drive out the Western invaders. The Iranians and Syrians had thought after the U.S. invasion of Iraq in 2003 they would be the next target. Now the United States was in a quagmire and they were helping militants bleed the Americans. "I felt like I had stepped back a quarter century," he said.

The new American team's arrival had been trumpeted in worldwide news coverage, and expectations were high. A week after Crocker got to Baghdad, a group of Iraqi journalists pressed the ambassador on how long it would take him to bring the insurgency under control. He had been there only a week, Crocker joked in Arabic, and would need at least two.[3]

In his first week in Baghdad, Crocker went with Petraeus to visit the city's embattled Dora neighborhood, in the city's southern end. When Crocker had ended his last tour in Baghdad four years earlier, the Sunni neighborhood was a bustling commercial hub with hundreds of shops and tidy parks, an advertisement for the country's once-comfortable middle class. Now the shops were closed, the streets heaped with trash and marinating in black pools of sewage. Insurgents hid bombs in the rubble and dead animals. There was an average of fifty attacks and three car bombs each day in Baghdad.

"We're just trying to survive," a Sunni resident told him. "We pray that no one gets hurt because if they do there is absolutely no chance of treatment. There is not a doctor in the district." When Crocker pointed out that there was a medical complex, Medical City, just across the river, they looked at him like he was stupid. "No Sunni would reach that facility alive," they told him, because they would be stopped at Shia checkpoints.[4]

Crocker returned from the outing in despair. "I put my head on my desk and said to myself, 'How did I get into this and how am I going to get out of it?'" he recalled. Petraeus felt the same way.

Crocker's first round of meetings with Iraqi officials was jarring. Since the beginning of 2005 the Iraqis had begun conducting

elections and installing national leaders from the three principal groups. But they were gridlocked on the compromises they needed to make to divide power and make the government a shared enterprise with popular support.

Iraqi politics was "a zero-sum equation," Crocker said. "The Kurds wanted theirs, the Shia wanted theirs, and the Sunni wanted theirs. The spirit of compromise was nowhere evident." The reason for this was the bloody, brutal past, in which "compromise meant concession, concession meant defeat, and defeat meant death. It was clear to me in my first weeks in Iraq that if anything good was going to happen, we would have to be the essential middlemen."[5]

And the Iraqis weren't all on board with Bush's new strategy. Iraqi prime minister Maliki sent word to Petraeus before Crocker arrived that he did not accept the new surge plan. He didn't want U.S. troops flooding the neighborhoods again but instead accelerating their handover of military control to the Iraqis. Petraeus threatened to quit to shut him up.[6]

The pair's weekly video teleconference meetings with President Bush and the National Security Council were grim. The sessions began each Monday with a report on the political developments from Crocker and one on the security situation from Petraeus. In one of the first sessions, Crocker riffed on Voltaire's line that the Holy Roman Empire was neither holy, Roman, nor an empire. "Sir, we call this a national unity government," Crocker told Bush. "My initial impression leads me to believe it is by no means national. I is certainly not unified and meets no test that I can think of bein an actual government."

Crocker's presentations were a dose of castor oil, not at all lik the optimism that Bush had usually heard in the past four years Iraq briefings. After a couple of them Bush came up with a nic name. "What have you got for me today, Sunshine?" Bush joke On other days Bush teased that Crocker was the "glass half empt man.[7] But somehow the bad-news ambassador became a presid tial favorite.

Crocker strengthened and expanded the embassy team. Con

leezza Rice promised him he could have the staff he wanted in order to make the embassy the biggest and most capable in the world. He replaced some section chiefs with foreign service veterans who had risen to ambassadorships. He brought in Charles Ries, ambassador to Greece, as economic counselor; his wife, Marcie Ries, ambassador to Albania, as political-military counselor; Adam Ereli, ambassador to Bahrain, as the senior public affairs official. Patricia Butenis, who had been ambassador to Bangladesh and his number two in Islamabad, returned as his second-in-command to manage the operation. Robert Ford, then ambassador to Algeria, returned for his fifth Iraq tour as head of the political section. "He took some of the best talent in the Foreign Service out of their own castles, their embassies, and brought them in," said Ali Khedery, an Iraqi-American who had been a senior aide to a succession of top U.S. officials since 2003 and was now special assistant to Crocker. "It was a team of all-stars." It may have been the only time in foreign service history that one embassy had seven ambassador-level officials under its roof.

Marcie Ries had been finishing up her tour in Albania and planning to move to Athens to live with her husband. The ambassador's residence in Greece was one of the nicest in the system, in a spacious old house on three acres, surrounded by tall trees, a swimming pool, and a tennis court. In place of that, the couple moved into one of the twenty-two-foot-by-eight-foot aluminum-sided "containerized housing units" in the Baghdad embassy's cramped trailer park. In thirty years in the Foreign Service, "it was the first time anyone had come to me and said, 'You need to do this for your country,'" Charlies Ries said. "I felt I couldn't say no." Later he discovered that others had said no and some had gone to great lengths to avoid Baghdad duty.

The Rieses lived in a corner of the trailer park also inhabited by the embassy's number two, Pat Butenis, and Philip Reeker, the embassy spokesman. They called their corner of the park Georgetown, after the tony Washington neighborhood. Crocker, dropping by one day for a party, mused that the coziness might be too much

of a good thing. "One rocket could wipe out the senior staff," he told them.

But even though many of the top talent had answered his call, Crocker believed he needed more. Four years after the invasion, many top foreign service officers were reluctant to risk their lives for what they viewed as a catastrophic blunder, and some were saying so openly. Many of those who did go weren't the most accomplished but the young and inexperienced, or officers drawn by the war-zone pay supplements that could double their compensation. Crocker had raised the number of political officers from 15 to 26, and the economic staff from 9 to 21. In all, the embassy, with a $1 billion budget, included 1,000 Americans and 4,000 Iraqis and other foreign nationals.[8] But the foreign service generalists numbered 140 at their peak, while Petraeus had thousands of officers on his staff.

In May, Crocker cabled Rice for reinforcements. "Simply put, we cannot do the nation's most important work if we do not have the department's best people," he wrote. He urged her to pressure her assistant secretaries to locate and send the most skilled candidates. Rice warned that if there weren't enough volunteers, she would make Iraq assignments mandatory, a step that hadn't been taken since the Vietnam War. The department was offering not only pay supplements but special sweeteners, including expanded vacation time and special consideration on future assignments. Officials joked that they were nearly at the point where they would be offering volunteers Porsches in the color of their choice. Even so, recruitment remained a challenge. Former ambassador Tom Krajeski, who was in charge of recruitment for Iraq posts for part of 2007, said the assignment made some in the Foreign Service treat him like the Grim Reaper. When he walked down the halls of State Department headquarters, they dove out of sight.

The unhappiness of some foreign service staffers burst into public view on October 30, 2007, when management held a meeting at the State Department's largest auditorium to discuss Iraq staffing. A few days earlier, officials had sent emails to 250 candidates for Iraq duty, saying that if volunteers didn't fill 48 spots by the following summer, the department would require some to go.

Jack Croddy, a thirty-six-year foreign service officer who had spent much of his career in Europe, rose to complain. An assignment in Iraq was "basically a potential death sentence, and you know it," he said. "Who will raise our children if we are dead or seriously wounded?" The line drew noisy applause from the audience of three hundred, and the event degenerated into a shouting match. A woman who had recently returned from Iraq tearfully described how she suffered from post-traumatic stress disorder after seeing a bloody terrorist attack but had been unable to get the department to pay for treatment. Harry K. Thomas Jr., the director general of the Foreign Service, snapped at the audience over their criticism. When the criticism continued, he closed the meeting abruptly. Details of the meeting appeared in the *Washington Post* the next day, "conjuring an image of disloyal, cowardly diplomats, which stood in stark contrast to that of the brave soldiers protecting the United States abroad," wrote J. Anthony Holmes, president of the Foreign Service's union.[9] It was a public relations debacle. Palmer Rosselli, a foreign service officer who served in Iraq and Afghanistan, emailed a journalist to point out that, contrary to the general impression, 2,000 diplomats had already done tours in Baghdad, many at great risk. "So we are not all a bunch of cocktail-sipping, pinstripe-wearing, European-capital-serving whiners," he wrote.[10] Despite the furor, volunteers gradually stepped up and eventually filled all the slots. No one was forced to go.

Crocker took an uncompromising position in the debate over security, arguing inside the administration that service amid danger was just part of the job. The department had gone too far in shielding diplomats from risks since the 1983 Beirut embassy bombing, he argued, to the point that the staff were barred from places they needed to be, including some major cities in Iraq. If the State Department's security standards were fully applied, "we would have no diplomatic presence in Iraq," he wrote in his May cable to

Rice. If the military's security standards are good enough for the troops, "they should be good enough for us," he wrote. [11]

When President Bush gave Crocker the job, the White House sent along a customary official letter outlining the new ambassador's goals. At the top of the priority list was ensuring the safety of the staff. Crocker thought it was absurd to have security the top priority in a war, and said if that was the administration's foremost concern, they would need to find someone else to run the embassy. The White House took the language out.

Crocker made it a personal mission to make sure the military as well as the embassy's civilians understood the basics of how the world and the war looked through Iraqi eyes. The country wouldn't be stabilized unless some core political and social issues were resolved, in his view, and everyone in the U.S. mission had to help with that. In his 2003 tour in Iraq, he found many of the commanders focused on deploying, pointing, and shooting. In staff meetings Crocker talked about Iraq's history and the factions' struggles and goals. He speculated about ways they might find compromises that the Iraqis, with their fraught history, could live with. Bush administration officials usually talked about the war as part of an evolution toward a more American-style government, a narrative Iraqis didn't follow. "When we went into Iraq we had all this make-believe about democracy and freedom; it was all that sort of talk," said Emma Sky, the political adviser. "Crocker wasn't using that language at all." The U.S. team, who had to sit through detailed reports daily, found Crocker's broad analyses memorable. When he began talking in his quiet, halting manner, many would pick up pencils and take notes.

Many on the military and foreign service staffs were working more closely with each other than they ever had, and sometimes their new partners seemed like an alien species. Robert Ford found the Iraqis easier to understand at times than his military peers. Crocker and Petraeus told their teams there would be no complaining about the other side. A few were caught squabbling and were sent home.[12]

Crocker's job became an endless round of meetings with Iraqi officials to try to convince them to give ground to sectarian rivals. The White House and Congress were pressing the Iraqis for fast legislative action on a series of issues that defined the balance of power: the distribution of oil profits, the powers of provinces, the conduct of elections, and the treatment of former members of Saddam's Baath Party. Crocker and the embassy team rode herd on the deliberations in the Iraqi parliament, lobbied officials until late at night, and sometimes proposed to sell compromises.

Crocker and Petraeus sometimes used the good-cop, bad-cop routine with Iraqi politicians. Crocker had a diplomat's skill at laying out Washington's position in neutral language that sought to avoid inflaming passions. Crocker sometimes started meetings with Prime Minister Nouri al-Maliki by telling jokes in Arabic or recalling Arab proverbs. "Maliki was a very stiff character," said former ambassador Charles Ries, the economic counselor. "Ryan could loosen him up."

Petraeus added another dimension, becoming more emotional at times and occasionally punctuating his arguments with a few choice profanities. Petraeus said these displays of anger were calculated for effect but also acknowledged that sometimes he could get carried away because the stakes were high.

Crocker and Petraeus sometimes used an approach they called "preemptive praise." They would burst into Maliki's office complimenting him effusively for his decision to work with his rivals to resolve their latest conflict. This was all news to Maliki, but if they were lucky he would be flattered and do as they suggested.

Crocker was more attuned to the Iraqis' sensitivities than most of the U.S. military leaders. As time passed, the Iraqi leaders increasingly resisted what seemed like orders from the Americans, especially when they came from the military. They wanted to feel that they were running a normal government in a normal country, although in truth Iraq was anything but that. They dressed in suits and ties and resented that the U.S. military officers showed up for meetings in camouflage combat fatigues, helmets, and body armor, and roared around the city in convoys with their weapons loaded. Crocker and his senior staff always changed into suits and ties before meetings with the senior Iraqi leadership. He barred the staff from wearing lace-up desert boots with their suits, the signature look of the former occupation chief, Paul Bremer. "You're diplomats," he told them. "I ruined some good wingtips," said former ambassador Tom Krajeski, who was Crocker's point man with the Kurds.

When the American team needed to ask the Iraqi leadership for an important concession, they would often have Crocker or other embassy civilians do the asking. The requests grated less coming from a diplomat than from an officer of an occupying army. "Ryan had much better relations with the Iraqis than the military did," said former ambassador Ries, the economic counselor. "Petraeus really needed him."

Crocker noticed that the administration was failing to help some of the Iraqis who most needed their help. He realized the U.S. government was keeping tight limits on the Iraqis admitted to the United States as refugees—only 1,600 in fiscal 2008, a year when tiny Sweden admitted 40,000. Crocker wrote cables to Washington complaining that U.S. officials were failing their moral obligation to the country, including the families of translators who risked their lives working with U.S. troops. He left the cables unclassified so that they would reach an audience of thousands in the government, making it likely they would be picked up by the press. "I did everything but give them to Karen DeYoung," he said, referring to a *Washington Post* foreign affairs reporter. The cables were publicized and the State Department raised the Iraqi refugee ceiling to 17,000 for fiscal 2009.[13]

The relationship with Maliki remained one of the most trying. A longtime backbencher, he had been chosen by other Iraqi politicians in 2006, with U.S. support, because he was presumed to be too weak to threaten the dominant parties. Maliki turned out to be craftier than expected and far less malleable. Since he was in his teens Maliki had been a member of the Dawa Party, a secret fifty-year-old Islamist faction that had been persecuted by Saddam Hussein and had, in turn, plotted against him from exile. Maliki had fled Iraq after being sentenced to death, and members of his family had been hunted down and killed by Saddam.

Crocker spent his first meetings with Maliki simply trying to understand his personal history and building trust. Maliki saw coup and assassination plots everywhere, and it made him suspicious of other Iraqi leaders and unwilling to compromise. Crocker was frequently exasperated with Maliki, but he also acknowledged that his attitudes were understandable, given his personal history. Maliki was paranoid, yes. It was also true that a lot of people wanted him dead.

Maliki yielded on some issues and stayed stubbornly dug in on others. He permitted the U.S. troops to pursue the Shia militias, who were becoming a greater threat than the Sunni militants. But for years he resisted strong American pressure to incorporate cooperative Sunni tribal fighters from a movement against insurgents, known as the "Awakening," into the Iraqi security forces to make them an inclusive national institution. Petraeus was forced to keep 100,000 Sunni fighters on the American payroll at $300 apiece each month.

Crocker and Petraeus had a long-running battle with Maliki over Major General Mahdi Gharawi, a hulking Shia police division commander accused of personally torturing and killing Sunni prisoners in secret prisons. An investigative unit had accumulated detailed evidence of Gharawi's alleged crimes when he ran the Interior Ministry's Public Order Special Police Division in 2005 and 2006. The American team pressed for his arrest, arguing that for sectarian tensions to cool, Sunnis had to see that top-level Shia officials like Gharawi were not above the law. Crocker's personal view was that he deserved to be hanged. But Maliki, who was trying to consolidate Shia control over the security services, shielded Gharawi from prosecution.

The argument reached a climax in June 2008. Petraeus and Crocker headed to Maliki's office with a plan: if Maliki continued to resist, Petraeus would raise his voice and show some emotion. In the opening round, Maliki wouldn't budge. Petraeus erupted with blunt warnings and a few swear words. The conversation devolved into a near shouting match, and Maliki began to look rattled. Crocker touched Petraeus's arm. "Dave, calm down," Crocker told him. "It did not end well," said Ali Khedery, Crocker's aide, who was present. But Maliki held tight to Gharawi. He made him a special adviser to the interior ministry, and in 2011 promoted him to top Iraqi officer in Mosul, Iraq's largest majority-Sunni city, over the objections of U.S. officials and Sunnis. "One of my greatest regrets was not getting that sorry-assed failure," Crocker said later.[14]

As the American team wrestled with Iraq leaders, in the first few months of the surge the security picture only got worse. The American death toll rose steadily for the first four months, from 81 in February to a peak of 126 in May. Crocker prepared himself to acknowledge that the president's "new way forward" had cost hundreds of additional lives yet failed. But then the violence began to subside, and American deaths started to edge downward. They fell from 101 in June to 84 in August.

The American effort had been given a crucial boost in late 2006 by the decision of tribal sheikhs in Sunni-dominated Anbar Province to join forces against the insurgents as part of the Awakening. They had grown fed up with the harsh rule of the Al Qaeda fighters, who beheaded children and doused women in acid for failing to cover their heads. These Sunnis were eager to have the American troops back them up and were willing to stand publicly with the Americans. As the surge reduced attacks, it diminished public pressure on politicians to take a hard line against the opposing communities.

Hopeful signs began to appear. The bombing of the al-Askari mosque in Samarra in February 2006 had set off a convulsion of ethnic killing that launched the country into a full-blown civil war. On June 13, 2007, insurgents attacked the Shia shrine again, toppling its two remaining ten-story minarets. American and Iraqi officials both feared the attack might set off a new spike in violence.

Crocker was in his office when word came of the bombing. As he picked up his phone to call Petraeus, the general burst into his office. They both had the same idea at the same time: they needed to meet with Maliki to discuss how to prevent an ethnic explosion. In minutes they were there, suggesting a series of steps to prevent another conflagration. The most important was to ask Grand Ayatollah Ali al-Sistani, the country's foremost Shia religious leader, to issue a statement calling for calm. Another was to invite the leading Sunni politician, Vice President Tariq al-Hashimi, to the premier's office to work out a joint statement.

Maliki didn't need to be threatened or cajoled to take these steps. He was ready to reach out to the Sunni leader, although he and Hashimi loathed each other. "What you had was three very worried men, Maliki even more than us," Crocker said. "He required no threats; he got it. On the Hashimi meeting, he didn't quibble for a second."

Maliki and Hashimi made a joint statement decrying the bombing as "an instigation," Crocker recalled. "We cannot rise to it. Sunni and Shia must stand together," they declared. Crocker cabled Washington: "Maliki has said and done the right things."[15] There were some retaliatory attacks, but nothing like the all-out convulsion of violence the leaders feared. "It may well have been the turning point of the surge," Crocker said.

Another important step came in early September, when Maliki was persuaded to write a check of $120 million for reconstruction in Anbar Province, the Sunni heartland. The money was a signal of encouragement to anti-insurgent militias that had been looking for support from the central government. The press was told that the commitment was Maliki's idea. That wasn't entirely true. Crocker had been pushing for weeks, badgering Maliki to make the gesture as a sign that there could be progress toward Sunni-Shia political reconciliation. Maliki had resisted stubbornly, arguing that he couldn't provide such a grant to the Sunnis before he had done so for Shia-dominated provinces. Crocker persisted. "I basically had to sit on his head to get him to do it," Crocker said.

When Maliki yielded, Crocker went to Ramadi with other top Iraqi officials to announce the step in an exuberant gathering with Sunni sheikhs and provincial and national officials in the city's government center. Earlier in the year the center had a been a battleground heaped with rubble. By the time of the meeting, buildings in the complex had been rebuilt and painted in bright colors. Officials could come and go without body armor or helmets. At ground zero of the insurgency, it almost felt like peace. The Sunni bloc in parliament, which had walked out earlier in the year in protest, returned to the legislature.

Crocker and Petraeus's first half year in Iraq had been building up to a joint appearance before Congress to provide a public assessment of whether the surge strategy had worked. Congressional critics of the war wanted proof that it had been worth its cost and were threatening to cut funds and force a military withdrawal. The event was going to be a televised spectacle on the scale of General William C. Westmoreland's appearances before Congress at the height of the Vietnam War. With support for the war in the tank, White House officials were hoping that the general and the diplomat would have credibility other administration officials did not possess.

Before the two testified, President Bush met personally with Crocker to feel out the ambassador's views on the long-term prospects for Iraq. In a meeting at the Al Asad Air Base in the desert wastes of western Iraq, Bush probed Crocker about how much effort it would take to overcome Iraq's internal division. Was Iraq's trauma akin to America's civil rights struggle? he asked. Far worse, Crocker told him. Saddam had "deconstructed" the country in his thirty-five-year rule, dismantling national institutions and killing the most talented leaders—the potential Nelson Mandelas—who could have led it back from the brink. Crocker argued that the U.S. invasion had compounded the damage, inflicting harm that went far beyond a simple change of leaders. "This is winnable, but it will take a U.S. commitment and a long time," Crocker said.[16]

Petraeus and Crocker had spent months assembling the arguments they would use in the congressional testimony. When September 10 arrived, they sat down under hot lights in jammed committee rooms for two days and twenty-one hours of testimony. The TV networks broke into their programming to carry it live, and other events in official Washington came to a halt.

Petraeus, addressing the security issues, had the easier case to make. The numbers were on his side: American deaths had declined nearly a third from their peak, and Iraqi deaths and suicide bombings were down by almost half. "The military objectives of the surge are in large measure being met," he testified.

On the political front, Crocker's responsibility, evidence of progress was far harder to see. While there were some encouraging developments, the political deals and ethnic reconciliation that had been the administration's goal remained a distant hope. Crocker offered no guarantees. "The process will not be quick, it will be uneven, punctuated by setbacks as well as achievements, and it will require substantial U.S. resolve and commitment," he testified. But he warned that the outcome of a troop pullback would be even worse: an ethnic slaughter, an influx of terrorist groups, and an expansion of the influence of Iran and other dangerous neighbors. "Our current course is hard," he told them. "The alternatives would be far worse." The diplomat who had warned about getting into Iraq was now warning about getting out too quickly. "He was, in State Department-ese, as gloomy as you could be," assessed an analysis from the Council on Foreign Relations.[17]

Senators of both parties, including five presidential aspirants, poured out their frustrations on Crocker and Petraeus. "You have been made the de facto spokesmen for what many of us believed to be a failed policy," said Senator Hillary Rodham Clinton (D-N.Y.). "The reports you provide to us really require a willing suspension of disbelief." Senator Barack Obama (D-Ill.) weighed in with an insightful question that took so long to unspool that the chairman had to move on to the next senator before Petraeus had a chance to answer. When Senator John McCain (R-Ariz.) asked Crocker whether the Iraqis would actually take the steps toward reconciliation the Americans were urging, Crocker did not spin. "My level of confidence is under control," he said.

The long hours of testimony were an endurance contest. The lawmakers dropped in to the hearing room for only a few minutes and often asked the same questions that colleagues had put many times before. If they could land a zinger, they might make it onto cable news. Crocker's patience was not infinite, as was apparent by the final hearing, in the Senate Foreign Relations Committee. He pointed out to Obama that he had responded to one of the Illinois senator's questions before Obama had reached the committee room.

As the round continued, "I was about to say, 'Gee, senator, that was a very interesting question the first eight times I heard it,'" Crocker recalled later.[18] Petraeus noticed that Crocker was at the end of his patience, scrawled a note on a scrap of paper, and passed it to Crocker. The ambassador unfolded it and saw, in block letters, a single word: CALM.

But Petraeus in his sober Army green, and Crocker in funereal gray, struck the right note. Their "quiet competence and honesty had a big impact," Secretary of Defense Robert M. Gates wrote.[19] The White House had already disclosed that it was planning to draw down all of the surge troops by July, taking some of the edge off the demands for withdrawal. Now the debate was not about whether to stay in Iraq but the pace of withdrawal. When Crocker and Petraeus left Washington, the deep divisions over the war remained, but it was clear that the critics did not have the votes to force an end to the mission. The joint appearances had bought time.

The political success in Washington did not ease the burden in Baghdad. Three days after the testimony in Washington, the U.S. team lost one of its most important Iraqi allies, Sheikh Abdul Sattar Abu Risha. Abu Risha, a dashing figure in aviator sunglasses and gold-trimmed robes, was the charismatic tribal leader who had become a founder of the Awakening movement after militants killed his father and two brothers. At a time when the U.S. team was in despair over corrupt, sectarian, and erratic Iraqi leaders, Abu Risha had impressed all with his steady leadership. A few days before Crocker headed to Washington, he had Abu Risha to his residence to drink tea and plan the next steps in their anti-insurgency fight. "This guy is the real deal," Crocker's aide, Ali Khedery, gushed to him at the end of the meeting. "We need to protect him, because the bad guys are going to kill him." About a week later Khedery's hunch was proved right. Abu Risha was killed by a bomb hidden near the horse stables at his home in Ramadi.

Crocker's grinding schedule was taking its toll. He suffered increasingly from the effects of dystonia, a movement disorder that was worsened by stress and made it difficult to walk. The doctors had never seen a case like his and began trying various drugs, none of which were exactly right. Finding the right treatment would have required much more time with doctors than he had. He had to get by as best he could. Sometimes his security detail had to brace him so he could make it up and down the long stairways of the presidential palace. When his mother died in July 2008, Crocker was immersed in negotiations with the Iraqis and had to delay his return to Spokane for her memorial service.

Secretary of State Rice and President Bush were both alarmed, in visits to Iraq, to see the effects of his illness. "I was worried about him, and the president was worried about him," said Rice. "You could see that he struggled sometimes to walk."[20] When they asked how he was doing, he said he was fine.

Crocker's dystonia made it impossible for him to continue his running routine, depriving him of his favorite way to relax. Crocker at times reduced his workload by asking subordinates to handle routine phone calls and other tasks. He never asked to leave Baghdad.

When he was not in meetings, he was buried in paperwork. He was impatient with interruptions. Ali Khedery recalled how other U.S. officials riding along in Crocker's armored Suburban would sometimes try to engage him in small talk. "How's it going, Ambassador?" they would ask. "He'd respond with a one-word answer," Khedery said. If the official didn't grasp that Crocker didn't want to talk, Khedery would shoot a dirty look to restore silence.

Crocker had little tolerance for poor staff work. His aides would see flashes of anger, and occasionally he would call out the offender in front of others. "He didn't have the time to do it any other way," said one former colleague. Occasionally, especially when he was tired, he would rely on translators during meetings with Iraqis. But if he was unsatisfied with the translators, he would dismiss them on the spot and take over himself.

On one occasion a security aide's blunder caused a major blowup with Maliki. Maliki would visit a top secret videoconference room on the top floor of the presidential palace almost every week to take part in secure sessions with President Bush. But one day Maliki and his party couldn't get through the palace's entrance checkpoint because an American security aide assigned to oversee the process had wandered away from his office and couldn't be reached. As a consequence, the troops at the checkpoint had examined Maliki's vehicle with explosive-sniffing dogs—a grave affront, because Iraqis consider dogs unclean. Maliki and his team, outraged, turned around and returned to Maliki's villa.

When Crocker heard of the foul-up, he was white with anger. "Whatever son of a bitch was responsible for this, I want him gone by the end of today," he said. When it came time for the Bush-Maliki videoconference, Crocker apologized to Bush and offered his resignation. Bush shrugged it off. "Stuff happens," he said. "We'll sort it out." The security aide was on the next flight home.

With his team, Crocker was economical with praise. Many subordinates saw him as remote and intimidating. Sometimes Pat Butenis, his efficient deputy, would step in with reassurance for staffers who felt underappreciated and needed pats of encouragement. "That's just Ryan's way," she would tell them. "He appreciates what you're doing."

He sometimes needed coaxing to take part in social events at the embassy. But he could work a roomful of Arabs. Krajeski, then the embassy's point man with the Kurds, saw Crocker come alive with jokes and banter when Masoud Barzani, the Kurdish president, threw a dinner party in Erbil. Crocker understood the job required schmoozing but "he also had a genuine interest in Barzani and his guys," Krajeski said.

As months passed, Maliki veered from crisis to crisis with the Americans. He squabbled with the Kurds over disputed territories and with the Sunnis over their demands to be fully a part of the military and the economy. He was becoming more authoritarian and more resistant to steps the U.S. team thought were needed to overcome the country's sectarian divisions.

In December 2007, rival leaders of the three communities approached the U.S. leadership to disclose that they were talking about engineering a no-confidence vote on Maliki in the parliament and trying to replace him. The anti-Maliki group that met with the Americans to discuss this was broad: it included not only Iraq's president, Jalal Talabani, but two vice presidents and two deputy prime ministers.

In their videoconferences with Bush, Crocker and Petraeus had repeatedly floated the question of whether Washington needed to intervene to replace Maliki. As 2007 ended, Crocker and Petraeus were leaning in the same direction as Maliki's rivals. In a videoconference they began to make the case that only with a different leader could Iraq become the inclusive, integrated state that Washington wanted. Before they reached their conclusions, though, Bush cut them off. Switching out Maliki for another candidate would only create new problems, he said. There was no alternative candidate with the skills and political support to replace him, he said, and it would likely take at least five months, as it had the last time, to get the Iraqis to agree on a new government. "We're going to make it work with Maliki," Crocker remembered him saying. "There's no other alternative." If this was frustrating, messy, unsatisfying, it was democracy, Bush told them. "Welcome to my world." Crocker came to the view later that the president was right.

As the Sunni insurgency receded as a threat, dangers from the Iranian-backed Shia militias were growing. In their determination to drive out the Americans, the Iranians were becoming ever more brazen in mobilizing Shia militias to attack U.S. forces. The Iranians were training some fighters in Iran and sending into Iraq units of the Quds Force, the special forces unit of the Iranian Revolutionary Guard Corps responsible for operations abroad.

In May 2007, at the Iraqis' urging, Crocker began a series of three meetings with Iranian officials to discuss the two countries' face-off in the country. The first was held in a conference room in Prime Minister Maliki's offices, with the two delegations facing each other across a polished oak conference table. Crocker had a long history negotiating with Iranians and had usually gotten along well with them. This round was different. There was no joking or discussion of American college football. A top American military intelligence officer ran through a series of slides showing Iranian weapons that had been captured at different spots in Iraq, some with Persian script on them. Crocker brought up, too, growing evidence that the Iranians were even helping Al Qaeda. The Iranian ambassador to Iraq, Hassan Kazemi Qomi, insisted Iran had no military presence in the country and responded to each slide with a flat denial. "That's fake," he said. "You made that up. This is your propaganda." The two men went back and forth for two hours. "Ryan was like a beagle: he wouldn't let go," said Robert Ford, who was part of the U.S. team that day.

Crocker finally rose abruptly and announced he was leaving. "Mr. Ambassador, I'm sure you have a busy schedule today," he said. "I know I do. This meeting is getting nowhere." He and the rest of the U.S. team hastily gathered up their papers and headed out the door. As the team crossed the threshold, the Iranian called out to Crocker to ask him to stay. "Mr. Ambassador, it is true we have a certain influence here," he conceded. "Let us continue to discuss." Crocker and the team went back. After half an hour, there was still no progress and the American got up again and left.

The U.S. team went back for two more meetings. Crocker noticed that the Iranian ambassador often called a halt to the talks to leave the room. Crocker figured Qomi had a weak bladder. Later he learned the ambassador had been calling Tehran to ask for instructions. Qomi would tell his superiors, "The Americans said this. How do I respond?" "He was on a very tight leash," Crocker said.[21] The talks produced no progress and petered out.

Within the administration, Crocker was arguing not for an end to the talks but for more and broader ones. Top administration officials viewed talks as a reward for Tehran and barred wide-ranging discussions until the Iranians stopped enriching uranium as part of their effort to develop nuclear weapons. Crocker had a different view. He argued that broader talks that recognized Iran's interests in the region and tried to begin cooperation on areas of common interest could have advanced U.S. interests, as they had after 9/11 in the U.S.-Iranian talks about Afghanistan. But top administration officials weren't persuaded.

One of the gravest crises for the U.S. mission came in March 2008 over the Iranian-backed Shia militias, controlled by Moktada Sadr, that had taken control of the southern city of Basra. After months of anger over the militias' domination of the region, Maliki abruptly notified the U.S. military that the Iraqi army would be attacking them in less than a day. The news terrified U.S. officials, who feared that Maliki's poorly trained and ill-equipped forces could be routed and his government might fall.

In a videoconference with the White House, Crocker and Petraeus, both ashen, warned that the consequences could be dire. "The general and the ambassador each took turns excoriating the prime minister for his incompetence and recklessness," Condoleezza Rice wrote in her memoir.[22] But Bush had a different view than his subordinates. He was pleased with Maliki's move, which he saw as a gutsy if risky attempt to finally assert the government's writ. "This could be a truly decisive moment for Iraq," Bush said.

Petraeus and Crocker flipped off the microphones in front of them and turned to each other for a word in confidence. Yes, decisive—but maybe not decisive in the way he thought, they grimly agreed.

In the first major clash between Maliki's troops and the Sadrists, hundreds of troops from an Iraqi brigade stripped off their uniforms, abandoned their American Humvees, and disappeared into the heart of Basra. Soon the large entourage that Maliki had brought with him to Saddam's former palace in Basra came under deadly artillery fire that killed his chief of security and almost killed Maliki himself. The prime minister's operation, grandly named "the Charge of the Knights," began to be mocked as "the Charge of the Mice."

Maliki's offensive put the Americans in Baghdad at risk, too. Shia militiamen in the impoverished Shia neighborhood of Sadr City, about six miles from the embassy, lobbed hundreds of 107-millimeter rockets and mortar shells from trash-strewn lots into the Green Zone. In the middle of one meeting, an aide brought Crocker a note: "Your house was just rocketed, but wife is OK." The bombardment had blown out every window on the second floor of the ambassador's house. But Christine was unhurt, and decided, as she had after the attack on the ambassador's house in Damascus, that she would stay.

As the days passed, Petraeus's forces rushed to Basra, bringing military advisers and airpower, including fighter jets, Apache attack helicopters, and AC-130 gunships. Sadr realized that the U.S. and Iraqi force was only going to get bigger, and on March 30 called for a ceasefire.

While U.S. troops mobilized, Crocker was working in Baghdad to head off a political disaster. Maliki's Sunni, Shia, and Kurdish political rivals, sensing in the offensive's opening days that the battle could be a major blow to Maliki's political fortunes, began talking again about calling a no-confidence vote in parliament that could topple the government. Crocker got in touch to argue such a move would badly weaken the entire government, and not just Maliki. They held off.

In the end, the campaign bolstered Maliki's standing. By taking on his fellow Shia, he looked for once like a national leader rather than a sectarian politician. Vice President Tariq Hashimi, the ranking Sunni in the government, put out a statement praising Maliki, and Sunni officials who were boycotting the government decided again to rejoin it.

Maliki's success made it seem that victory had been inevitable. In fact, the outcome had been in doubt throughout, and key decisions were made on the fly, based on partial information, said Crocker. "It's hard to convey how often you're flying by the seat of your pants," he said.

While southern Iraq was in turmoil, in Iraq's north the Kurds were struggling with Arab Iraqis over territorial disputes. In September 2008 it appeared the Iraqi army was close to an all-out battle with the Kurdish forces over Kurdish units' presence in the east-central province of Diyala, dozens of miles south of the designated Kurdish region. Troops on both sides had exchanged gunfire and neither side was yielding to U.S. pressure to pull back. Krajeski, the embassy's point man in the north, met with Kurdish president Masoud Barzani and asked him to pull back the Kurdish forces as the Iraqi army withdrew. Barzani, furious, made no promises. "I don't believe a word you're saying. And I don't trust you. You're a diplomat and I don't trust diplomats, except Crocker," Barzani stormed. Crocker soon arrived from Baghdad for a one-on-one and "the whole atmosphere changed," Krajeski said. The Kurds withdrew and the Iraqis stood down.

During his final year in office, President Bush was increasingly focused on getting written agreements with the Iraqis that would authorize the continued presence of U.S. troops and define the future relationship between the two countries. The goal was essentially to lay out a dignified exit strategy to make it more likely that the next American president didn't order an abrupt troop withdrawal that threatened the gains of the past two years. At the beginning of 2008 it appeared the deal was in hand. Then it became clear that, five years after the invasion, Iraqis were not eager to sign up for what looked to many of them as more occupation.

The administration dispatched a team of specialists to Baghdad in March 2008 to begin negotiations for a status of forces agreement, or SOFA. U.S. administrations work out such detailed agreements with countries around the world to set the terms of the U.S. military presence and to ensure U.S. troops aren't at risk of harsh penalties from local courts. On a separate track, U.S. officials began thinking about a strategic framework agreement, an understanding that would plan U.S.-Iraqi cooperation on national security, education, trade, and technology. U.S. officials hoped that the rich benefits of such an agreement would be a sweetener that would help win Iraqi public support for the agreement on troops.

Many top Iraqi officials saw the benefits of a continued U.S. presence: it could protect them from their domestic rivals and the predations of aggressive neighbors. But no politician was eager to be seen publicly defending an extension of the U.S. troop presence. The most resistant were the allies of Shia leader Moktada al-Sadr, who, with strong support from Iran, were campaigning all out against any such deal.

The first version of a troop agreement was written with the strong language the Pentagon favored. It gave Washington wide latitude in using its forces and strong legal protections for troops and for the thousands of U.S. defense contractors in the country as well.

The proposal set off alarm bells for Crocker. He worried that the deal would be seen by Iraqis as a repeat of the Portsmouth Treaty of 1948, a British agreement with the Iraqis that was supposed to pave with the way for British withdrawal. The pact left control of Iraqi foreign affairs in British hands for twenty-five years, igniting such outrage in Iraq that it toppled Iraq's first Shia prime minister, Saleh Jabr. This troop agreement, Crocker understood, would sell only if it looked like a win for the Iraqis. And indeed, when the initial American proposal began to circulate, it drew fire from Sunnis and Kurds as well as Shias. It prompted Tariq Hashimi, the Sunni vice president, to raise publicly for the first time the idea that the Americans would need to set a firm departure date for their troops.[23]

Bush and others in the administration had fought hard for years to avoid committing to a specific departure date, arguing that it would only allow the government's enemies to wait out the Americans. But as the talks bogged down in May on the major issues, Crocker said the administration needed to find a way to finesse the issue. Even if it avoided setting a firm departure date, the Americans should offer a formulation that would signal the Americans were on the way out, he argued in a National Security Council meeting on June 30. President Bush, in a sign of his deference to Crocker, agreed to consider it. "Ryan really had an unusual position," said Robert Loftis, an experienced SOFA negotiator who had been sent to Iraq in March to help arrange the deal. "More than any other ambassador I've seen, he really had the lead role in determining our relationship with Iraq."

Resistance to the first American offer hardened as negotiations continued. Maliki refused to yield on point after point. In some cases when he won an argument, he would come back to demand even more. American officials complained privately that he was becoming bullying and erratic.

The Iranians, determined to move the Americans far from their borders, were stepping up their pressure. Major General Qassim Suleimani, the feared head of Iran's Quds Force, insisted to Iraqi president Jalal Talabani that the Iraqis should not sign any such agreement with the Americans. Behind the scenes, the Iranians were using every lever of influence. An Iranian brigadier general was arrested for offering Iraqi legislators $250,000 each to vote against the SOFA, Petraeus reported to Defense Secretary Gates.[24]

As talks continued, Crocker assigned staff members to reach out to various Iraqi officials in hopes of persuading them on key points. But it was a frustrating process. The U.S. team would reach agreement with one Iraqi faction on a disputed point, only to find that another group was refusing to sign on because of a different issue. In a staff meeting Crocker compared the scene to the circus act where a group of clowns are trying but failing to all ride their motorbikes in a circle. As soon as one clown gets mounted and moving, another falls off. "The good news is that we got the Sunnis to sign on last night," Crocker told the team. "The bad news is the Kurds just fell off."

The pressure on Crocker grew steadily. Officials in Washington made clear that the U.S. team could not fail to complete the agreements. We sent you there to get this done, they would tell Crocker in teleconferences. Get it done.

In one staff meeting Crocker and the team discussed how to get enough votes in the parliament that Grand Ayatollah Ali al-Sistani, the supreme Shia leader, would not try to kill the deal with a fatwa. Emma Sky, the British adviser, recalled in her memoir how an intelligence official interjected that Sistani had no votes in the parliament. Of course, Sistani had considerable sway over the lawmakers. Crocker stared at the official. "Sweet Jesus, do you think I'm fucking stupid?" Crocker shot back. "I looked down at my toes," Sky wrote. "I had never seen Crocker so stressed."[25]

The U.S. team found a way to finesse the issue of legal protections for U.S. troops. The Iraqis wouldn't accept any use of the word "immunity"—to many Iraqis, it meant Americans slaughtering civilians and then escaping punishment. Instead, the U.S. team decided to define the issue as one of jurisdiction. They proposed to give Iraqi courts jurisdiction over crimes committed by U.S. troops who were off base and off duty. "No member of the U.S. military in Iraq was ever off duty: you're never off duty in a war," Crocker said. "The Iraqis understood that, and we never had a case."

In October 2008, with time running out, the Americans still had to deal with the final issue of the departure deadline for U.S. troops. The Americans wanted the language kept vague so that the troops could stay longer if a security threat emerged. But the Iraqis hated that idea. Maliki had decided that, without a specific exit date, the agreement would indeed look to Iraqis like another Portsmouth Treaty, and it would force the ouster of the second Shia prime minister, as it had the first. "We have got to take the occupation argument away from our opponents," he told the Americans.[26] Crocker decided there was no way around it. They had to agree to a specified departure date and then hope the next administration could open new negotiations to extend the troops' stay if that were needed.

Crocker called Lieutenant General Douglas Lute, the White House czar for Iraq policy, and told him he wanted Bush's approval to include a firm departure date of December 31, 2011, for all U.S.

troops. Lute and his boss, National Security Adviser Stephen Hadley, tracked Bush down in the White House gym, where he was on an exercise bicycle, and told him what Crocker wanted. Bush didn't delay. "Okay, I agree with it," Bush said. "If Ryan needs it, that's what we're doing."[27] Aides, and Crocker himself, were surprised by Bush's quick assent. The president didn't need further discussion or a meeting with top national security officials.

After more debate and a few more American concessions, the Iraqi parliament ratified the agreement on November 27, Thanksgiving Day. The vote was 149 in favor and 35 opposed. Afterward, critics inside and outside the administration contended the American side had given up too much in the negotiations. Ed Gillespie, counselor to the president, called it "an eviction notice."[28] But it had to be judged by what Iraqis were willing to accept after five years of American occupation.

With Obama elected and his departure close, Bush planned a final trip to Iraq. He would sign the agreements and affirm the continuing U.S.-Iraqi relationship in a way he hoped would draw international attention and build support for a continuation of the mission under the new president.

A week before the trip, a mysterious delegation of U.S. officials in black raincoats showed up Baghdad. They were from the Secret Service, sent to begin planning the presidential visit in deepest secrecy. The plan was to have a ceremonial signing of the agreements, followed by a short press conference and then a final dinner with top Iraqis and top Bush administration officials. The Secret Service, nervous about security, wanted only the American press allowed in to ask questions. "Obviously that was not going to fly with the Iraqis," said Ali Khedery, Crocker's aide, who helped plan the event. "The prime minister's office wanted the Iraqi media, too." It turned out to be a fateful decision.

At the appointed moment, Bush and Maliki took their place at podiums in front of Iraqi and American flags. But before they could sign the documents, an Iraqi television journalist, Muntader al-Zaidi, jumped from his seat and threw one of his shoes at Bush. "This is a farewell gift from the Iraqi people, you dog!" he yelled. Bush gamely ducked the first shoe. He and Maliki both tried to deflect the second one. The room erupted in pandemonium, with journalists and then Iraqi security officials trying to wrestle Zaidi to the ground. White House press secretary Dana Perino was bumped by a microphone in the confusion and left with a black eye.

Bush seemed unfazed by the attack. Within a few seconds he was joking, shrugging, and playing down the incident. "It doesn't bother me," he told the reporters. "If you want the facts, it was a size 10 shoe." But Maliki was upset and angry, viewing the attack as a personal humiliation on his home turf. He pounded his hand with his fist and barked orders for his aides to seize the journalist. They dragged Zaidi out of the room, beating him and drawing blood. The Secret Service, fearing Iraqi security might kill him, intervened to stop the beating. Later, Ali Khedery noticed that the Air Force physician traveling with Bush had a brown stain on his camouflage uniform. The doctor had tried to halt the beating and had gotten an imprint of Zaidi's face, in Zaidi's blood, on the uniform.

It appeared the attack might spoil the rest of the day's planned events, if not force their cancellation. That was Crocker's cue to intervene. Speaking in Arabic, he told Maliki that while Bush understood his anger, the president found the incident amusing, especially since the assailant couldn't throw straight. Bush hoped they could continue plans for dinner and discuss a few more points of substance, Crocker told him. The prime minister calmed down.

Bush departed office with Iraq more stable if not fully peaceful. U.S. and Iraqi troops were battling the remnants of Al Qaeda more than a real insurgency, and violence was at a post-invasion low. Oil exports were generating more than a billion dollars in revenue weekly for the government. "That period 2007 to 2009 was the only time in the whole war when we had the right strategy, leadership, and resources," said Emma Sky, the generals' political adviser. Even Democratic critics of the war no longer disputed that the violence had dropped.

The last surge troops had left Iraq in July, and Petraeus gave up his post and left Iraq in mid-September to become regional military commander for the Middle East and Central Asia. Crocker, drained by his illness, planned to follow him out soon after Barack Obama became president. But he remained concerned about the unanswered question of what was next for the Iraq effort. Crocker believed the gains were fragile and the Sunnis had not been knit into the country's fabric. Washington needed to maintain some forces and continue an active role as political go-between, he thought, if those gains were to be preserved.

In a visit to Iraq on July 21, 2008, as the presumptive Democratic presidential nominee, Obama had met with Crocker and Petraeus in a conference room at the presidential palace to discuss the future of the mission. Crocker and Petraeus had set up storyboard charts on easels and briefed Obama on their plans to gradually shift U.S. troops to a noncombat "overwatch" role, with no firm dates specified. Obama argued for a continued drawdown of troops, saying the United States needed to deal with an economic crisis at home and to bolster the under-resourced U.S. military effort in Afghanistan. A president needed to assess what the United States could do in Iraq based on America's limited resources, he told the team.

Crocker took some reassurance from the meeting. While Obama was clearly leaning toward the exit, he was prepared to listen to their arguments, and he didn't tell them he was committed to the sixteen-month timeline for departure that he had described in his campaign. He seemed thoughtful and open to debate. "He didn't foreclose, really, anything," Crocker said.

After Obama's election, the U.S. team in Baghdad waited anxiously for word on what the new president wanted to do. For the first month there was no communication at all. Then the White House called: it wanted a report on the status of the Iraq campaign. The senior military staff jumped into action and produced a glossy document filled with PowerPoint slides. The images were the Pentagon's favored means of communication, and a bane of the diplomats. Four days after it was forwarded to the White House, Crocker showed up for the morning senior staff meeting looking more chipper than usual. The White House, he said, had sent back word that they wanted no more PowerPoint reports. No more bullet points. Reports were henceforth to be in complete sentences and paragraphs. "The universe has been restored to equilibrium," Crocker announced. The embassy staff tittered appreciatively and the military team looked stricken.

Just before Obama's inauguration, Crocker got word that the new president wanted to discuss Iraq on his first full day in office. During his campaign Obama had promised that he was going to summon the military leadership on his first day in office and order the end of the Iraq war.

As Crocker prepared for the videoconference with Obama, he sent word to the White House asking for instructions on how the meeting should be held. The new team said they didn't have any special instructions; he should do it just as he had with Bush.

Crocker began with his usual report on the political and economic landscape, and General Raymond Odierno, Petraeus's successor, offered an overview of the military situation. Before they had gotten deep in discussion, Obama held up his hand. "Before we start, there's one thing I want to tell you guys," he said. "I do not want to screw this up." Crocker and Odierno took it as a signal that the new president would not order an abrupt departure that would risk the gains of the past two years. "We refrained from bursting into cheers, but we thought, *Damn, this is going to work*," Crocker said.

Crocker again offered his advice on relations with Iraq in one of his last cables when he assessed troubling signs that Maliki was becoming ever more authoritarian and sectarian. "A key question posed by Maliki's evolving hold on the levers of political and security power is whether the PM is becoming a dictator bent on subordinating all authority to his hand, or whether Maliki is attempting to rebalance political and security authority" that had been shifting from the central government to tribal and provincial leaders. He gave Maliki the benefit of the doubt. "We believe the answer lies closer to the latter than to the former," he wrote. But to ensure the right outcome, he wrote, Washington needed to continue to use all of its levers of influence to keep Iraq closely bound to the United States.[29]

One of his last tasks as ambassador was to visit Ramadi to see Ahmed Abu Risha, the head of the Anbar Awakening Council, the Sunni anti-insurgency movement, and the older brother of the assassinated sheikh Abdul Sattar Abu Risha. Ramadi had been the site of some of the American military's bloodiest fights in Iraq. But now the city was safe enough that Crocker and Abu Risha decided to go for a walk, an idea that two years earlier would have been unthinkable because of the insurgency threat. "My security guy said, 'Why not?'" Crocker said.

Another sign of the changing mission had come in January 2009 when the State Department opened a $750 million embassy complex of 27 buildings on 104 acres at the southern end of Baghdad's walled-off government section, or Green Zone. Crocker had been pushing U.S. officials to get out of the presidential palace as soon as possible to end the perception that Washington was an occupying power. The new complex, as large as Vatican City, had six hundred blast-resistant apartments. Tenants had a view of the Tigris, access to an Olympic-size pool and tennis court, free gym memberships, free dry cleaning, and of course round-the-clock security. "If it had been in New York my apartment would have gone for millions of dollars," said former ambassador Gordon Gray, who was then Crocker's adviser on the southern Iraq region. In Manhattan, of course, there was no threat of incoming rockets or mortar rounds, he acknowledged.[30]

On Friday, February 13, Crocker flew out of Baghdad for the last time as ambassador, with his wife and Afghan-born dog, March, on a C-12 Huron military turboprop plane. Before he left, every U.S. general in Iraq had flown to Baghdad to show their respect at a goodbye dinner. "He had provided the strategic direction and guidance the military so craved from civilian leaders, and so rarely received," wrote Emma Sky.[31] Now Crocker was headed for Spokane and a seminar on retirement. His next job, beginning in January 2010, would be as dean of the Bush School of Government and Public Service at Texas A&M University.

Two weeks later Obama announced a new strategy for Iraq, in a speech at Camp Lejeune, North Carolina. His timetable called for withdrawing the last combat troops by August 31, 2010, a date that was within the range that Crocker and Odierno had suggested in a policy memo.

But the new administration didn't share Crocker's view that America needed to continue to provide top-level attention and play a central mediating role in Iraq. Obama halted the regular presidential videoconferences with Maliki. Instead of choosing a Mideast hand as Crocker's successor, the surprise choice was veteran diplomat Christopher R. Hill, who had made his name negotiating with the North Koreans and Serbs. Hill had no experience in the Middle East and spoke no Arabic but had the support of Secretary of State Hillary Clinton and the veteran diplomat Richard Holbrooke, who had been Hill's boss in the Balkans. Arriving in March, Hill told his staff he was going to shift gears into a more traditional diplomatic relationship with the host country, allowing the Iraqis to make more decisions by themselves. Hill believed there were limits to how the United States could engineer change in troubled countries like Iraq. The Americans had been acting too much in loco parentis, he told the staff, and that was going to stop. He would be the "un-Crocker" and would "break Crockery," he joked to aides.[32]

Hill's relationship with the U.S. military commander, General Ray Odierno, was not like Crocker's with Petraeus but a reversion to earlier days when generals and ambassadors had different ideas and maneuvered for control. Hill believed Odierno was trying to exert too much influence over Iraqi affairs, while Odierno thought Hill was not trying nearly hard enough to build relationships and push the rivalrous groups to compromise. Hill also had frictions with Robert Ford, who was now number two in the embassy. Hill wasn't interested in Ford's in-depth reporting on Iraqi politics and wanted him instead devoted to the managerial tasks that were the customary focus of an embassy's deputy chief of mission. Ford also thought Hill was damaging relationships with the Iraqis, became dissatisfied, and left in April 2010. Before Ford left, Hill made him move out of the deputy ambassador's residence so that his replacement, former Holbrooke aide Cameron Munter, could move in. Others at the embassy thought it was harsh treatment for a diplomat who had spent more time than any other foreign service officer dealing with Washington's worst Middle East mess.

In the spring of 2010, Odierno took his complaints about Hill to Gates and Secretary of State Hillary Clinton. Gates turned for answers to Crocker, asking him to a round of consultations in Washington about the U.S. team's problems. He convened a high-level meeting that included former secretary of state Condoleezza Rice, national security adviser General James L. Jones, and CIA director Leon Panetta. The meeting didn't allow time for an in-depth exploration of the strained relationship. Vice President Biden, who wasn't scheduled to be part of the session, wandered in and launched into a monologue that took up a large chunk of the group's limited time.

In the remaining minutes Crocker told them he was not alarmed. "Don't panic," he told them. He made another pitch for his view that the Americans needed to keep playing an active role in bro-kering agreements between the Iraqis. He urged them to rely on U.S. officials who had already proven themselves in Iraq and didn't need to be brought up to speed.

Hill left Baghdad and ended his foreign service career in August 2010 with sour relations with Iraqi leaders and a continuing stale-mate over the formation of a new Iraqi government. He later wrote a bitter take on his tour, complaining that no one at the Clinton State Department looked out for the Baghdad embassy's interests or even read the weekly memos he had been asked to write. In the new administration Iraq had acquired "the bureaucratic reputation as a loser, something to stay away from," he wrote in 2014.[33]

On December 18, 2011, Obama ordered the final troops from Iraq as scheduled and celebrated an end to the mission. The Iraqis, he said, should be taking control of their affairs. Prime Minister Maliki agreed with him on that. One day after the last troops left, Maliki cracked down. He issued an arrest warrant for Tariq al-Hashimi, the Sunni vice president, causing Hashimi to flee the country and bringing the coalition government to the edge of collapse. Maliki inaugurated a tougher approach toward the Sunnis, especially in their home turf of Anbar Province, leading to new ethnic fighting. He strengthened ties to the Iranians. While Crocker was in Iraq, the prime minister was "the good Maliki," said Sky. "When Crocker left he became the bad Maliki."

The negotiations that the Bush administration officials and Crocker hoped would further extend the troop presence broke down in a legal dispute. A debate raged for years afterward about whether it was the Iraqis or the American side who were most to blame for the failure. The debate flared anew in 2014 when Sunni militants from an ascendant jihadist group, the Islamic State, seized huge tracts of territory in northern Iraq, forcing Obama to resume a limited U.S. military effort in the country with special forces and warplanes.

In hindsight, it looked like the U.S. leadership had stepped back from its role in Iraq too abruptly. The Obama administration had decided the fragile Iraqi government needed to be free to make its own mistakes. While that idea had merit, "in retrospect, it was too much, too soon," said Charles Ries, the former ambassador who had been the embassy's economic counselor during the surge period.

To Crocker, the Obama team had sent the wrong signal by curtailing top-level involvement. Obama took no trips as president to Iraq. Clinton took one and handed off the Iraq portfolio to Vice President Biden. On Obama's first day in office, Crocker had been reassured by Obama's promises that he wouldn't casually surrender the hard-won progress. In hindsight it looked to Crocker like he'd done just that. "He did screw it up," Crocker said.

# CHAPTER 9

# Lost in Translation

O n her third night at the U.S. embassy in Islamabad, Pakistan, Anne Patterson was jolted awake by explosions and gunfire coming from half a mile away. It was still two hours before dawn, but the gun battle splashed the sky with red and blanketed the city center in inky smoke. Pakistani commandos had begun an assault on radical Islamist clerics and students barricaded in the landmark Lal Masjid, the Red Mosque. The militants had been there all year, building an arsenal and digging tunnels and bunkers in preparation for a confrontation with the government. The compound in the capital's heart had become a symbol of militants' growing numbers and influence in the country, and their determination to challenge the state. "We could hear everything, and you could smell the cordite," Patterson said.

The battle, which began July 3, 2007, raged for eight days, with militants firing at the encircling government troops from the minarets and lobbing homemade bombs and rocket-propelled grenades. On the final day the commandos overwhelmed them with an assault that destroyed the mosque in a fiery conflagration and killed 102. Instead of snuffing out the threat of jihadism, the attack united extremist factions against the government and spurred them to begin a campaign of bombings and attacks that continued for years in the country's biggest cities. More than 5,000 Pakistanis were killed in the three years that Patterson was ambassador.[1]

Patterson, watching this grisly drama, realized that her previous assignment—in Colombia, the murder capital of the world—would seem simple compared to Pakistan. "I could see this was going to be on a totally different scale," she said.

She took over as ambassador at a pivotal moment. America's relationship with Pakistan had been relatively strong after the 9/11 attacks. It came under new strain in the following years, during Ryan Crocker's posting as ambassador, as Washington stepped up a counterterror campaign that became controversial with Pakistanis. During her three-year tour, the antiterror fight reached its violent peak and the relationship became steadily more difficult. At the same time, Pakistan was buffeted by domestic political crises that threatened to topple its weak civilian government. Patterson's priorities were ensuring the terrorism cooperation continued and the government continued its wobbly journey toward democracy. Her mission was as important as any assigned an American ambassador: America could allow some nations to go to hell, U.S. officials knew, but not this one. It was, President Obama said later, "the most dangerous country in the world."

Before she left for Islamabad, Secretary of State Condoleezza Rice brought Patterson to the Oval Office to hear firsthand the concerns of President Bush and Vice President Cheney. Patterson had met the president before, but she knew the weight Bush attached to the assignment, and she was nervous. Bush spoke of his worries about the growing threat of the extremists inside Pakistan and about the country's future leadership. He saw that President Pervez Musharraf's political position was unraveling and worried the new leader might be former prime minister Nawaz Sharif, who Bush feared had sympathies for the militants.

Cheney wanted to talk about the dangers of the Pakistani nuclear program. U.S. officials had been helping the Pakistanis improve the security of the nuclear complex and always insisted in public appearances that it posed little risk. Privately they worried militants could get hold of a bomb, or at least bomb components, perhaps with the help of sympathetic government insiders. Cheney spoke about the uncertainties of the program: U.S. officials did not know how much inventory and bomb-building capacity the Pakistanis had or even where the key elements were located. The Pakistanis prohibited U.S. aircraft from flying near Pakistani nuclear facilities, fearing the Americans were gathering information that would enable them to seize weapons in a crisis. "That was his concern," Patterson said. "It was a sensible one."

Pakistan was as close a partner as America had in the fight against extremist groups. But Islamabad wanted to battle some jihadist groups and collaborate with others as allies against their Indian and Afghan rivals. So the U.S.-Pakistani relationship became a marriage in which the partners were both cheating but had no choice but to stay together. "The relationship is one of co-dependency, we grudgingly admit," Patterson cabled Washington at a later moment of crisis.[2] "Pakistan knows the U.S. cannot walk away; the U.S. knows Pakistan cannot survive without our support." In that situation, an ambassador expected crises and worked to prevent them from exploding into disaster.

On political matters, Patterson's mission was a preventive one. She needed to help keep the country's politics from becoming so chaotic or dangerous that the army, Pakistan's most powerful institution, felt the need to install new leaders to restore order. Pakistan had been through three military coups and many near coups in its sixty-year history. "The role of the American ambassador to Pakistan is to talk to the president, to talk to the military, and to try to prevent them from doing something stupid," she said. "You've got to walk them back from the ledge."

In her three years as ambassador Patterson often played the role of political counselor to the leadership. She was also military adviser, banker, and sometimes psychotherapist. In moments of crisis her black armored Mercedes would glide up to the presidential palace or army headquarters and the diminutive blond ambassador would emerge to offer her counsel. Her message was polite but direct. If she needed to say the same thing day after day, she would do it.

The Pakistanis' treatment of the U.S. ambassador ran hot and cold to comic extremes. Opposition lawmakers rose regularly in parliament to accuse Patterson and the Bush administration of siding with the country's Indian rival or violating Pakistani sovereignty with the counterterror campaign. The Pakistani press swirled with accusations that U.S. forces were operating illegally in the frontier area and plotting to seize the nuclear weapons. When Patterson visited leaders, she often went under cover of night in order to avoid a new round of stories in the press accusing Washington of trying to run the government.

Yet Patterson got a far different reception from the country's politicians in private. The same leaders who condemned America in the morning trooped through her office in the afternoon asking for money, help with their careers, or advice in running the country. They assumed America was all-powerful and treated the ambassador with the deference accorded a colonial viceroy. They desperately wanted her on their side.

Soon after she arrived in Pakistan, Patterson was invited out for a jovial meal with Maulana Fazlur Rehman, the luxuriantly whiskered leader of a pro-Taliban Islamist party. He wanted her backing, it turned out, for his bid to become prime minister.[3] "Nothing would mean more to me than the ambassador's support," he beseeched Patterson in a letter.

Nawaz Sharif, a center-right politician who has been prime minister three times since the 1990s, built his popularity in part on defiance of America. But in the privacy of her office, he sought to convince Patterson he didn't deserve his reputation as a political Islamist. He was fully behind American goals, he insisted. He even thanked Patterson for installing General Ashfaq Parvez Kayani as army chief—a decision she had no role in. In a cable to Washington, Patterson cited Sharif's comments as a laughable example of how Pakistanis always imagined America had limitless power.[4]

Patterson decided soon after her arrival in Islamabad that Pakistanis simply saw the world differently. She had spent years as a diplomat in Latin America and the Middle East. But she was perplexed by Pakistanis' way of thinking when she arrived, and still baffled three years later when she left. There was always a complexity, a mystery, about the Pakistanis' thinking that wasn't there in her postings in other parts of the world. The country's politics were awash in intrigue, double-dealing, and conspiracy theories that seemed to follow the physics of a different reality.

At a reception in Islamabad, Patterson met an accomplished Pakistani, a man who had earned a doctorate at one of the best American universities. When the two began talking about the tragic assassination of former prime minister Benazir Bhutto, the conversation began along conventional lines. Then the man confided that he knew exactly how it happened. Bhutto, he said, had been struck by a deadly ray from outer space. Patterson didn't know quite how to respond.

Pakistani politicians were often equally perplexing. After one visit with President Asif Ali Zardari, Patterson was asked to look over a press announcement the Pakistanis were issuing to describe the meeting. "This doesn't say a thing about what we actually discussed," Patterson pointed out. "Why would you want to say what we talked about?" countered Zardari. "It was hard to answer that," she said later.

Part of Patterson's job was to explain Pakistan's ways to Washington. It wasn't always easy. One night in 2010, Patterson joined a videoconference call with Washington and found President Obama and his team struggling to understand how the Pakistanis were pressing for U.S. help with disastrous flooding but were rejecting visa applications from U.S. officials who needed to enter the country to assist. "OK, let me get this straight," Obama said. "Pakistan is asking for our support but they're not letting us provide it. Can someone explain this to me?" "They're nonlinear thinkers," Patterson told him.

The ambassadorship in Islamabad was Patterson's first assignment in South Asia. But her superiors didn't hesitate to give her the post, because she had proved herself in some of the State Department's most challenging assignments. She had made her reputation as ambassador to Colombia from 2000 to 2003, at the height of the American "war on drugs," when the threat to Bogotá from an insurgency had made it a top priority for Washington. The government was under siege by leftist guerrilla groups that enriched themselves in the drug trade, and there were fears that the government itself could collapse, leaving a failed state. Washington was trying to deal with the threat with a multibillion-dollar U.S. aid program called Plan Colombia that gave the Colombians helicopters, arms, and training to strengthen their military and enable them to reclaim the vast tracts of territory held by the insurgents. The ambassador's job involved overseeing a small army of 4,500 U.S. employees from 40 agencies at what was then the largest U.S. embassy in the world. The job appeared to intimidate a lot of other foreign service officers, because few applied for it.

Colombia was then the most violent country in the world, with ordinary criminal gangs as well as insurgents and private militias. Patterson had repeated brushes with danger. On a trip to the countryside, her limousine was almost blown up by a roadside bomb. She came under fire when rebels bombarded the inauguration of Colombian president Álvaro Uribe with homemade mortars, killing twenty-one.

She repeatedly clashed with the Colombian military over some officers' ties to drug cartels and the country's brutal right-wing paramilitaries. Under U.S. law, Colombian military units couldn't receive U.S. aid if any officers had records of human rights abuses. The tensest confrontation was over an elite air force unit that dropped a cluster bomb on a tiny town near the Venezuelan border, killing seventeen and injuring thirty. Patterson pushed for four years for a full investigation, then successfully argued that the State Department should cut off aid to the unit. Six months later, when the unit's commander continued to stonewall, Patterson convinced President Uribe to force his resignation. José Miguel Vivanco, of Human Rights Watch, said Patterson's approach was to avoid provocative statements in public while pushing in private for action. "She didn't have an easy time with the Colombian military," said Vivanco, who focused on Colombia for his organization for a quarter century.

When Patterson left Colombia in 2003, Plan Colombia had succeeded like few U.S. aid programs. The Colombian military recaptured with ease territory that had been lost to the insurgency. Between 2002 and 2009, the country's death toll fell by half and kidnappings by 90 percent.[5] Patterson shared the credit for the plan's success.

After six months as acting U.S. ambassador to the United Nations in 2005, Patterson took on a grueling job leading the State Department's Bureau of International Narcotics and Law Enforcement Affairs. The bureau, known to insiders as "drugs and thugs," oversaw and funded counter-drug, police training, and other law enforcement programs in more than ninety countries. Its $5 billion budget was the biggest of any bureau in the State Department, and its complex, expensive programs generated controversy and drew congressional scrutiny. Secretary of State Condoleezza Rice, who had decided that the bureau's previous manager had lost control of spending, brought in Patterson to take charge. "There was no stronger manager and leader in the Foreign Service than Anne," she wrote in her memoir.[6]

Among the bureau's toughest missions were training police in Afghanistan and Iraq and trying to halt the flow of drugs from Afghanistan. In both Iraq and Afghanistan, U.S. officials working on police training struggled with corruption, dysfunctional government ministries, and constant staff turnover. The drug business in Afghanistan was exploding, and administration officials were deeply divided on how best to fight it. Patterson's introduction to the job was sobering. On December 1, 2005, when she started the job, Patterson went to a briefing on the outlook for narcotics in Afghanistan and was told that the 2006 opium crop was expected to be the biggest in history—60 percent bigger than in 2005. She turned to her deputy, Thomas Schweich, and asked him, still smiling, "What have we gotten ourselves into?"[7]

The Pentagon, she learned, was too busy to help. A few weeks after she took the job, Patterson met with Lieutenant General Karl Eikenberry, then the U.S. military commander in Afghanistan.

Eikenberry told Patterson that the drug mission simply wasn't the military's priority. Instead, the military intended to clear the country of insurgents, then leave it to others later to try to clean up the drug trade. Patterson tried to change his mind, warning that Afghanistan could become like Colombia, where drugs generated cash for the insurgency and made it a far more dangerous force. Eikenberry was unpersuaded. But by the end of the year U.S. officials were seeing evidence that the jihadists were financing their war with drug money—"just as Patterson had predicted," Schweich wrote later.[8]

In the spring of 2007, Rice came to Patterson again to ask if she would take an even harder job, as ambassador to Pakistan. Ryan Crocker, the current ambassador in Islamabad, was being rushed off to lead the embassy in Baghdad so that he could help General David Petraeus in a last attempt to end the country's ethnic civil war. There were two other candidates for the Pakistan job, both of whom had served in high-priority frontline ambassadorships. But one was in trouble with the FBI because of allegations he had failed to protect classified information. The other had a wife who refused to let him go to a post that didn't allow spouses. "I didn't have a good excuse, so I accepted," she said.

In the spring of 2007, as Crocker prepared to leave Islamabad, the Pakistani government stumbled into crisis. President Pervez Musharraf had suspended Iftikhar Muhammad Chaudhry, the chief justice of Pakistan's highest court, who he feared threatened his power, igniting huge protests in the streets.

Musharraf's political troubles only deepened in the first weeks after Patterson's arrival. Amid his battles with the lawyers and militants, his public support was evaporating, while backing for his political rivals was increasing. Bush administration officials had growing anxieties that the country might end up under the control of a government with much less interest in pursuing extremists. Their answer was to try to broker a power-sharing agreement between Musharraf and his strongest rival, Benazir Bhutto, a former prime minister who led the huge left-leaning Pakistan Peoples Party. Bhutto had fled abroad to escape corruption charges, but she retained broad popular support, and her party's political agenda was relatively progressive. U.S. officials hoped joint leadership would stabilize Musharraf's rule while giving it a more democratic face. Richard Boucher, the assistant secretary of state for South and Central Asia, shuttled between Musharraf and Bhutto to seal the deal.

On August 8, U.S. intelligence picked up alarming news: Musharraf was about to declare a state of emergency, take steps to consolidate power, and move against his rivals. Patterson, sitting in the embassy at 3:00 a.m. with the CIA station chief, put in a call to Musharraf. "Mr. President, don't do it," she said. Such a step could deepen the turmoil in Pakistan and only compound his political troubles, Patterson warned him. But Musharraf was noncommittal. Patterson's next call was to Secretary of State Rice. "Anne was always cool as a cucumber," Rice wrote. "But I could hear the concern in her voice."[9] Patterson warned Rice about what Musharraf was planning and said she would meet with him the following morning to try again to talk him out of it. Rice headed to the White House for a meeting with President Bush, where they agreed that they needed to do all they could to prevent Musharraf from making such a blunder.

In the middle of that night, Patterson awakened Rice with a phone call to report that Musharraf had told her in a meeting that he planned to announce his move later that day. "You've got to talk to him now," Patterson told her. When Musharraf said he didn't want to take a call from Rice, Patterson insisted. If he didn't speak to her now, Patterson warned him, Rice might never talk to him again.[10]

At 2:00 a.m. Washington time, Rice called Musharraf and argued that steps to increase his power would lead to more violence, not less, and would reduce his chances of winning reelection the following year. "You will have no credibility," Rice told him. In a few hours Musharraf did an about-face, announcing he was sticking to plans for the elections and saying nothing about his moves to consolidate power.

But as Rice and Patterson suspected, the crisis was not the last. Musharraf was growing ever more fearful of the protests in the streets and the risk that he might be charged with treason for seeking to remain president while he was also the army chief. On November 3, Musharraf defied Washington by imposing measures that gave him nearly absolute power. He suspended the constitution, fired the chief justice, arrested human rights advocates, and closed private TV stations. In a rambling televised defense of his action, Musharraf insisted the move was necessary to end the country's disorder. He spoke for a few minutes in English, saying he wanted to address the United States and the West. "I cannot allow this country to commit suicide," he said.

In Washington, President Bush told top administration officials that he didn't want anyone "trashing" Musharraf. "The United States isn't going to be in a position of bringing him down."[11] But U.S. officials condemned the power grab. Patterson lodged protests with top Pakistani officials and cabled Washington, urging that senior U.S. officials do the same.

When the Pakistani foreign minister invited diplomats to the ministry for an explanation of Musharraf's moves, Patterson stood up to complain that implementation of the law was "thuggish and heavy handed." She sent a cable urging top officials in Washington to condemn Musharraf's action publicly as well as privately. The administration "should issue public and private condemnations to deter further restrictions of civil liberties," she wrote.[12] Musharraf responded angrily, summoning Patterson to dress her down about America's "abandonment" of him.

Patterson was also trying to restrain the increasingly dangerous maneuvering between Bhutto and Musharraf. Bhutto's trump card was her ability to bring crowds of hundreds of thousands of her political supporters into the streets. The rallies carried huge risks for her: intelligence was picking up information that multiple terror groups were preparing to attack the rallies and kill Bhutto. Musharraf feared the crowds could overthrow the government, and he threatened to arrest Bhutto to prevent the rallies from taking place.

Patterson repeatedly urged Bhutto not to risk her life at rallies, even as she entreated Musharraf and his aides not to arrest Bhutto or halt her campaign. It was all leading, she feared, to the worst outcome: an escalating battle in the streets, then another army coup. "This is a dangerous game that could trigger serious popular unrest and an even stronger reaction from Musharraf," Patterson cabled Washington.[13] Meanwhile, Musharraf's national security adviser, Tariq Aziz, was appealing to Patterson to use her influence to restrain Bhutto.

Bhutto returned from her decade of exile to a massive home-coming rally in Karachi on October 18. For eight hours she rode atop a truck, inside a plexiglass chamber, waving and speaking to a crowd of one million. Then, as feared, she was attacked. At nearly midnight, two car bombs exploded only feet from her vehicle, killing 139 and narrowly missing her. A few days later Bhutto asked Patterson to provide a team of American security personnel to protect her. Patterson declined. She feared that U.S. security wouldn't be able to prevent Bhutto from continuing to take risks but would take the blame if an attack did occur. In addition, she worried that a visible American presence would further anger militants and increase the risks of attack. Instead, Patterson offered to provide security advice from U.S. experts and to recommend Pakistani companies qualified to handle her protection.

Pressure continued building on Musharraf. President Bush, determined to see Pakistan back on track, called Musharraf personally to urge him to end the emergency law, schedule elections, and commit to stepping down as army chief. Soon the Pakistani army joined the chorus telling Musharraf he needed to give up the uniform and end emergency law. And on December 15, Musharraf yielded, ending the emergency and designating General Ashfaq Kayani the new military chief. Eight months later, with the coalition government threatening to impeach him, Musharraf gave up the presidency, too. "I hope the nation and the people will forgive my mistakes," he said in an hour-long national radio address. "Musharraf's resignation is a sad yet familiar story of hubris, this time in a soldier who never became a good politician," Patterson cabled Washington.[14]

His exit had taken a year, becoming "another huge drama because Musharraf just didn't want to leave power," said Patterson. "We had to coax him out. And finally we got him out."

Even this wasn't the final act. One night in late 2008, Patterson went to a Pakistani friend's home in Islamabad for a casual get-together and found Musharraf sitting on a sofa, waiting for her. He had decided, he told her, to put the new prime minister in jail and take back power. His supporters, including some business leaders, were insisting that he return to leadership for the sake of the country, Musharraf said. Patterson rushed to the embassy and convened a secure video teleconference with Washington. "Guess what—he's coming back," she told them. But Musharraf's plan was soon snuffed by the military. General Kayani, who had sources all over Islamabad, learned of his former boss's intentions. He got on the phone with Musharraf and made clear there would be no second act.

Behind the scenes, Patterson had been pushing Musharraf's political rivals to promise they would not put him on trial after he stepped down. That might mobilize Musharraf's military supporters and lead to a new upheaval and potentially a coup, she told them. They agreed.

In Patterson's view, Musharraf was another in a long line of authoritarian leaders who give up power, then find life outside the palace a lot less fun. "They think they're going to play golf, write, and lecture at universities," she said. Once they're out, they regret it and want power back. "Mostly," she said, "they just cause a huge amount of trouble."

Bhutto and her party appeared headed for a victory in February parliamentary elections and probably in the upcoming presidential elections as well. But on December 27, Bhutto was assassinated during a rally at a park in Rawalpindi. At the close of the gathering, as her armored Toyota Land Cruiser nosed through the crowds toward the park exit, Bhutto poked her head through the sunroof one last time to wave. A young man wearing a black vest and sunglasses approached the vehicle, fired three shots at her, then set off a suicide vest stuffed with ball bearings. Bhutto and twenty-four others were killed.

Bhutto's death left the country in mourning. Pakistan had lost a charismatic leader who many had hoped could restore a credible civilian government after a decade of military rule. It was also a body blow to American hopes. The new leader of the party was likely to be her politically inexperienced husband, Asif Ali Zardari. A tycoon with a sly grin and brilliantined hair, Zardari was seen by most in Pakistan as a hustler rather than the deserving heir of the Bhutto political dynasty.

In their first meeting Zardari acknowledged to Patterson that he didn't have his wife's skills or charisma. "I'm not Benazir and I know it," he confided. "I need help, especially from the U.S." America was Pakistan's "security blanket," Zardari said.[15] Support from Patterson and the Americans, he believed, would get him what he wanted. What he could do for the Americans was less clear.

# CHAPTER 10

# The Lid Stays On

M onsoon rains in the summer of 2010 brought Pakistan its worst flooding in eighty years. The Indus River swelled until it burst its banks, killing 1,700 and threatening 20 million across a thousand-mile stretch. For weeks TV screens were filled with pictures of dikes crumbling, homes collapsing, and helicopters plucking victims from angry waters.

A second, lesser drama was also riveting the public. Each day Pakistan's news stations covered the progress of the country's president on a five-star tour of Western Europe that became known as "Zardari's joyride." While villagers struggled, President Asif Ali Zardari toured his family's sixteenth-century chateau in Normandy, reposed in the comforts of the Churchill hotel in London, and dined in the English countryside with British prime minister David Cameron. As days passed, criticism of Zardari grew, sharpened by his government's sluggish response to the disaster. Outside Zardari's West End hotel, protesters howled. When he appeared at a rally of his party's British chapter, an elderly Pakistani Briton threw his shoes at him. "President Zardari seems to have badly miscalculated the impact this untimely visit will have on his image," wrote *Dawn*, the Pakistani newspaper.

At home in Islamabad, one of Zardari's most important political advisers watched the spectacle with growing alarm. Anne W. Patterson, the American ambassador to Pakistan, worried that the public outrage threatened Zardari's shaky political standing and perhaps Pakistan's fragile democracy itself. She called Zardari with blunt advice. "This is not what a president does," she told him. "You really need to be back here."

Zardari heard her. He returned and began to make rounds of stricken communities in Sindh and Punjab Provinces, as she had suggested. Patterson met with Zardari on August 13 "and urged him to continue his public engagements on the flooding crisis," Huma Abedin, Hillary Clinton's personal aide, emailed the secretary of state after hearing from Patterson. "She believes he is getting the message."[1]

Guiding Zardari was a central part of Patterson's job for most of her ambassadorship in Islamabad. After vaulting improbably to the presidency after the assassination of his wife, former prime minister Benazir Bhutto, Zardari hung precariously to power for five years. He collided again and again with rivals, including three-time prime minister Nawaz Sharif, and the chief of army staff, General Ashfaq Kayani, the country's most powerful figure. Patterson offered advice, acted as a go-between with other leaders, and urged restraint from all sides. She helped Zardari sidestep calamity.

Her first meeting with Zardari came one month after Bhutto's assassination, at Bilawal House, the family home in Karachi. Looking like a prosperous Westerner in blue blazer and slacks, Zardari told Patterson that he and his wife had both been strongly committed to American goals for the country. He supported democratic reform and the joint fight against terrorism. His wife had returned to Pakistan after a long self-imposed exile, he said, only because of American "clearance." Zardari pulled out a photocopy of a handwritten note from Bhutto that he said was proof that his wife had bequeathed the party's leadership to him. It was clear what he wanted: a pledge that Washington would support him if he ran for president or sought to lead his party, the Pakistan Peoples Party. Patterson heard him out but stopped short of any commitment. She would say only that Washington continued to support the PPP in "our shared struggle against extremism and in favor of the democratic process in Pakistan."[2] Afterward, in a cable to Washington, she gave him credit for new signs of political savvy. Zardari had talked up the American agenda, she said, and avoided the familiar dramatics and conspiracy theories. He "knew what his audience wanted to hear," she wrote.

A month later, swept along by a wave of public sympathy, the Pakistan Peoples Party won the most seats in the parliamentary election. The party joined in a ruling coalition, and in six months Zardari had become president. Along the way, he drew Patterson into his circle, asking her advice on politics and financial and security issues. In one session he confided his thoughts on possible prime ministers. He told her that one candidate, veteran PPP official Amin Faheem, was simply "too lazy to be prime minister." Faheem hadn't even taken part in the campaign, instead enjoying himself in Dubai with his new twenty-two-year-old wife, Zardari said.[3]

Zardari wanted to solve Pakistan's perennial problems with more aid from America. His requests were incessant. Zardari argued to Patterson and other U.S. officials that Pakistan was at least as important to American security as AIG, the New York–based insurance giant that was bailed out by Washington during the financial crisis of 2008. "You gave AIG one hundred billion," he told a U.S. delegation in June 2009. "You should give Pakistan the same!"[4] Patterson made no promises.

Zardari's gravest crisis came in early 2009, when he drifted into a confrontation with former prime minister Nawaz Sharif that came close to triggering violence in the streets and a military coup. The crisis began in a dispute over Zardari's refusal to reinstate the maverick chief justice of the supreme court, Iftikhar Muhammad Chaudhry, who had Sharif's backing. It deepened when the other judges of the supreme court, made up of Zardari allies, ruled that Sharif and his brother, Shahbaz, the chief official in powerful Punjab Province, were unqualified to hold office. The move was widely seen as a Zardari maneuver to marginalize his chief rival. Sharif mobilized his followers for a four-day march from Lahore to Islamabad that threatened a climactic street battle just outside the capital.

When the chief political players failed to find a way to resolve the fight, they turned again to Patterson for help. Genera Kayani, Sharif's brother, and officials of several smaller parties all appealed to Patterson to broker a deal and then use her influence with Zardari to make sure that he followed through. These appeals represented "the abandonment of all pretense that the U.S. should not intervene in Pakistani internal affairs," Patterson cabled Washington. "Ambassador has been careful to keep the U.S. out of the political souk. However, it is in our interest to ease Zardari off the ledge he has walked onto, and avoid the kind of violence that will force the army to restore law and order."[5]

Over the next few days Patterson met with all sides and passed messages between the principal players to nudge them toward a compromise. The negotiations showed once more how the Pakistanis assumed Washington held supreme power. One important party leader, Chaudhry Shujaat Hussain, told Patterson he would agree to follow U.S. wishes—if the Americans arranged for him to lead the Pakistani senate. Zardari confided to her that he feared he would soon be assassinated, and told her he wanted his sister, Faryal Talpur, to be given his post if that happened.[6]

General Kayani was, as always, at the center of the drama. The son of a low-ranking soldier from Punjab, Kayani surveyed his country from beneath a gold-braided officer's cap with hooded eyes, looking like a perched bird of prey. He wanted to avoid having to try to restore order with Pakistan's fourth military coup but feared Zardari's government might be close to collapse.

General Kayani confided to Patterson that he was, in fact, thinking of easing Zardari out. In their fourth meeting in a week, the army chief said he was considering replacing Zardari with an official of a smaller party in a way that would keep much of the existing government in place without a coup or new elections. Kayani's goal wasn't to intervene, Patterson reported to Washington, but to "lay down a clear marker" in hopes that the Americans could then arrange a political compromise. "Kayani is trying to leverage what he considers predominate American influence over Zardari," she wrote.[7] She speculated that the army chief hadn't told Zardari this directly for fear that the president would panic and make a "disastrous" decision to try to oust Kayani. Instead, he was turning to Patterson to pass on his message.

Three days later, after quiet conversations with Kayani and Secretary of State Hillary Clinton, Zardari backed down, allowing the chief justice to regain his post and ending the crisis.

In Washington, the State Department congratulated Pakistan for coming back "from the brink." Following the usual practice, American officials denied U.S. officials had played any consequential role in the outcome. "This was basically a decision made by Pakistanis for Pakistanis," said State Department spokesman Robert Wood. "They deserve all the credit."

After demonstrating her diplomatic skills with the Pakistanis, Patterson showed her touch in dealing with superiors in Washington. In a cable to Washington a week later, she attributed the successful resolution of the crisis entirely to Clinton and her new boss, Richard Holbrooke, the veteran U.S. diplomat who, in January 2009, had been given an oversight role for the region as special representative for Afghanistan and Pakistan (SRAP). "The Secretary and SRAP Holbrooke are wisely and positively credited with pressuring both Zardari and Nawaz Sharif to compromise and avoid further street violence," she wrote.[8]

As she worked to sort the political conflicts, Patterson was also helping keep the counterterrorism program on track at a time of growing frictions between the governments. On July 7, 2008, one year after she arrived in Pakistan, a twenty-two-year-old Pakistani suicide bomber detonated two hundred pounds of explosives at the entrance to the Indian embassy in Kabul, Afghanistan, killing fifty-eight. U.S. intelligence picked up evidence that Inter-Services Intelligence (ISI), the Pakistani intelligence organization, working with militants in the Haqqani network, had directed the bomber. The bombing hardened President Bush's attitudes about the ISI and led him to send a new message to Islamabad: The ISI needs an overhaul. Patterson led a delegation of Americans, including top military and intelligence officials, to convey Bush's message to

Kayani, intelligence chief Nadeem Taj, Zardari, and Prime Minister Yousaf Raza Gilani.

Kayani, chain-smoking Dunhill cigarettes from a holder, accepted no blame for the deaths but didn't deny that Pakistani officials maintained contact with even the worst of the militants. "You see, any intelligence agency, if they're going to do their job, they have to have contacts," he told them.[9]

Bush also approved more aggressive rules governing drone strikes. With U.S. officials increasingly convinced that Pakistan was tipping off militants of impending strikes, Bush decided the CIA didn't need to provide Islamabad with advance notice of attacks. The CIA was also cleared to target militants based on what appeared to be threatening actions even if they didn't know definitively who the attackers were. Drone strikes leaped from four in 2007 to thirty-six in 2008.[10]

Washington's more aggressive approach widened the breach between the governments. And Patterson was always first to hear the Pakistanis' complaints. In January 2008, soon after the new policy began, General Tariq Majid, chairman of the Pakistani joint chiefs of staff, summoned Patterson. He complained that the U.S. strikes were inflaming anti-American sentiment in Pakistan and said Pakistan was considering unspecified retaliation. "It has got to the point where we are looking at our own contingencies," Majid announced. He was hinting, without saying so, that Pakistan might use its allied militant groups in Afghanistan to strike back at U.S. forces. Patterson told Majid that "his statement was astonishing," she reported afterward to Washington.[11] If the government wanted to tamp down anti-American public reaction in Pakistan, she told Majid, it should stop government-owned broadcasters from airing "absurd conspiracy theories and drivel that feed anti-American and anti-[Pakistani] sentiments."

Sometimes the Pakistani foreign ministry called in Patterson to complain about drone strikes that the Pakistani military had already been told about and approved. The dressing downs were a bit of theater, intended to show the public the government was as out-

raged as they were. "The foreign ministry would call me to complain and I would say, 'This is a big waste of time for all of us,'"
she said. "'Your military knows all about this. Talk to them.'"

Patterson spent hours reviewing planned strikes with CIA officials, who had a staff of hundreds in Islamabad gathering and sift-
ing information on targets. She was the first ambassador given
authority to challenge plans for a strike if she objected. She did so
rarely. But sometimes she objected if she thought a strike could set
off a public backlash, or if she and her team had information suggesting the targets were not militants, or if civilians would be at
risk. Sometimes the CIA knew little more than that the targets were
military-age males, while embassy experts knew enough to suggest
the targets weren't a threat.

Patterson convinced the CIA to hold off on strikes in early 2008,
when a new civilian Pakistani government was getting organized
and she wanted to avoid publicity over a drone attack that could
cause embarrassment at a sensitive moment. She did the same in
early 2009, when the Obama administration was new and still trying to decide its approach to the Pakistan mission.

She intervened in October 2008 when she learned some Pentagon
officials were thinking about striking close to crowded camps for
Afghan and Pakistani refugees near the border. The U.S. military's
Special Operations Command and its contractors had been asking
the embassy for information gathered by U.N. agencies about the
location and population of the camps and the aid groups working
in them. Their questions suggested they were considering a strike
that might inflict huge civilian casualties. "We are concerned about
providing information gained from humanitarian organizations for
military personnel, especially for reasons that remain unclear," she
wrote.[12] Senior officials in the Pentagon shared her concerns, and
the plan was dropped.

Patterson also helped convince the Pakistani military in the fall
of 2009 to allow twelve U.S. special forces troops to secretly join
Pakistani troops on the ground in the tribal areas to feed them live
battlefield intelligence. Pakistan had publicly insisted it would not

allow U.S. troops on the ground, a step many Pakistanis saw as a violation of their sovereignty. But because of "patient relationship building with the military" by U.S. officials, the Pakistanis had agreed twice that fall to such American help, Patterson wrote in a cable. It seemed to mark a "sea change in their thinking," she wrote. She predicted the military would halt the practice if the U.S. troops' presence ever became public.[13]

Like Crocker before her, Patterson regularly had to deliver tough messages to the Pakistani leadership. The duty was sometimes painful for her as well as them. Patterson visited Kayani at army headquarters in Rawalpindi in December 2009, just after militants had attacked a mosque near the headquarters, killing forty, including women and children. Before their meeting, Kayani had been trying to comfort parents, some of whom had lost more than one child in the attack. As Patterson told Kayani what Washington wanted of him, she realized he was struggling to pay attention. He had been shaken by the day. "I felt badly about it," she said. "Here was a guy who had real problems."

Like other war-zone ambassadors, Patterson became involved in detail on defense issues. She urged the Pentagon in 2009 to step up its personal contacts with the Pakistani military to strengthen personal ties and ease the strains between the governments. She and her aides pushed for an overhaul of the system by which Washington reimbursed the Pakistanis for what they spent in the counterterror effort. Washington had given Pakistan $5.6 billion in reimbursements in the program's first five years, but it appeared Pakistani officials were overcharging and seeking compensation for items that had little or nothing to do with the joint effort against terrorism. In a cable to military and intelligence officials in the end of 2007, Patterson pointed out that the Pakistanis had asked in one year for $26 million for barbed wire and $70 million for repair of air defense radars—even though the militants, of course, were not using any aircraft.[14] The U.S. money went into Pakistan's general treasury, and from there Washington had no way of knowing in whose hands it ended up, she pointed out.

Patterson also weighed in on broader U.S. strategy during President Obama's long deliberations in his first year over how to fight the war in Afghanistan. She sat in on nine long videoconference meetings in which Obama and his war council debated their approach. Obama stepped up drone strikes sharply during Patterson's years in Islamabad, from 4 in 2007 to a peak of 122 in her final year of 2010.[15] Patterson supported the drone campaign as a necessary way to kill the militant leadership and throw their operations into disarray. But she pointed out that the program could reach a point of diminishing returns, when it would undermine U.S. goals. "Increased unilateral operations in these areas risk destabilizing the Pakistani state, alienating both the civilian and military leadership, and provoking a broader governing crisis in Pakistan without finally achieving the goal," she wrote in a September 2009 cable.[16] "You can't kill your way out of this," she told an interviewer in August 2009.[17] The only way to deal with the threat from the region was a years-long effort to stabilize Afghanistan's government, extend the Pakistani government's control over the independent tribal areas, and reduce its fears about the threat it faced from India, she wrote.

She thought Obama had undermined the purpose of his surge of troops into Afghanistan by announcing at the start that he would begin withdrawing them in eighteen months. And she had reservations about a 2009 U.S. law, the Kerry-Lugar-Berman Act, that would pump billions in new civil aid for Pakistan in hopes of strengthening public support for U.S. efforts. Many of the bill's supporters hoped money for domestic projects would ultimately help convince Pakistan to cut its ties with militant groups. Patterson argued that the Pakistanis couldn't be bought off this way: they believed they needed ties with those militant groups to deal with the Indian threat and to help them pursue their interests in Afghanistan in the future when American troops left. "A grand bargain that promises development or military assistance in exchange for severing ties will be insufficient to wean Pakistan from policies that reflect accurately its own most deep-seated fears," she wrote.

In a striking dissent, she also called for the administration to rethink its moves to strengthen U.S. ties with India, a top strategic goal for both the Bush and Obama administrations. Such steps "feed Pakistani establishment paranoia and pushes them closer to both Afghan and Kashmir-focused terrorist groups," she wrote.[18]

With the arrival of the Obama administration, Patterson had to adjust to a new boss, Richard Holbrooke, who had been made special representative for the region in hopes he could find a way to end the war. Holbrooke had ambitions to negotiate a peace as he had ended the war in Bosnia in 1995. He built a bureaucracy of almost one hundred in a warren of first-floor offices in the State Department and began replacing diplomats in the region with his own choices.[19] He removed William B. Wood, the ambassador to Afghanistan, and let it be known that he wanted to replace Patterson as well. His impatience with Patterson was visible at embassy meetings, where he showed little interest in her views and would sometimes cut her off abruptly, staff members noticed. On a trip to Islamabad soon after his appointment, Holbrooke gathered the embassy staff and announced that things would now be done a lot differently. Holbrooke was not specific, but the implication was clear: the embassy team didn't know what they were doing.

But when Holbrooke pressed Washington to give him a replacement, he got nowhere. Patterson, it became clear, had support from Vice President Biden, Secretary Clinton, the military, intelligence officials, lawmakers, and the Pakistanis themselves. Holbrooke "pushed it, and got slapped down," said former ambassador Gerald Feierstein, who was then her deputy. "Her reputation was such that Clinton and the president and Biden weren't going to have any of it. . . . Anne was pretty much untouchable." As months passed, it was Holbrooke who gradually became marginalized because of his bad chemistry and policy differences with Obama.

Patterson agreed with Holbrooke on the value of opening talks with the Taliban, but was skeptical that talks could lead to a deal that would have any political support in the United States. The Taliban would be unlikely to agree to a deal unless it allowed them to keep the large areas it then controlled—a demand likely to set off a political outcry in the United States. Others in the administration, including Clinton and General David Petraeus, then the regional military commander, opposed negotiations until the United States and its allies had a stronger military position. "It was clear to me, this wasn't going anywhere fast," she said.

Holbrooke's plans and brusque manner worried the Pakistanis, who feared he might cut a secret deal with the Afghans that would weaken Islamabad's influence over its neighbor. Holbrooke visited Islamabad often and pushed the Pakistanis with demands. But the approach he had used against beleaguered Slobodan Milosevic in the Balkans didn't work in Islamabad. "If you come in and bully them, they will simply shut down and won't do anything for you," said Feierstein. After Holbrooke's visits, Patterson would reach out to the Pakistanis to try to keep relations on track.

The Pakistani nuclear program was another chronic source of friction. U.S. officials said publicly they believed the growing Pakistani program was secure. Privately they worried that militants or their sympathizers within the government might be able to gradually smuggle out enough fissile material to make a bomb. The Pakistanis were reportedly moving some nuclear assets farther from areas subject to Taliban attack, and U.S. officials worried that weapons could be vulnerable while they were in transit. The Pakistani military and intelligence agencies grew increasingly agitated by Western media reports that the weapons might be seized by militants, and complained bitterly to Patterson.[20] By the spring of 2009 they halted cooperation with U.S. agencies on nuclear security and called off high-level talks on nuclear nonproliferation.[21] At the same time they were believed to be feeding fanciful stories to the Pakistani press that Washington was secretly building up a force of tanks and Marines at the embassy so that the Americans could seize the weapons.

As the rumors swirled, Patterson notified Washington in May 2009 that the Pakistanis were refusing to honor their commitment to return a stockpile of highly enriched uranium, a potential nuclear bomb fuel. The stockpile, which the United States had provided in the 1960s for peaceful nuclear research, was potentially enough to create a nuclear bomb or a couple of the irradiating weapons called "dirty bombs." The original agreement said the United States had the right to take back the bomb-grade material, which was being held at an aging research reactor in Karachi. But Pakistan told the embassy they were unable to make good on a promise they had reaffirmed as recently as 2007 because they feared a popular outcry. The local press "would certainly portray it as the United States taking Pakistan's nuclear weapons," officials told the embassy.[22]

Patterson had to worry about Abdul Qadeer Khan, the former chief of Pakistan's nuclear weapons program. Khan had led the program for twenty-five years and in the process opened a side business of selling nuclear secrets to what Washington considered the world's worst renegade regimes, including North Korea, Iran, and Libya. To Washington and Western allies, Khan was the worst proliferator of all time, creating almost single-handedly the strategic threats they faced from rogue nations. In Pakistan he was a national hero. Under international pressure to take Khan out of circulation, Pakistani authorities would not jail or even indict him, agreeing only to place him under house arrest. In 2008, Washington was alarmed to hear reports that Khan was to be freed. "Express Washington's strong opposition," Richard Boucher, the assistant secretary for South and Central Asia, cabled Patterson. Patterson protested repeatedly to Pakistani officials, insisting that Khan be confined and officially charged rather than held under informal house arrest. Islamabad backed down. But one year later Pakistan's highest court ruled that he was free to move around Pakistan as he wished, ignoring Washington's protests.

Patterson jousted regularly with the Pakistani press. They had been given new freedoms in reforms praised by Washington. But they had a taste for sensational anti-American stories, a habit encouraged, U.S. officials believed, by the Pakistani military and intelligence. In July 2010 an airliner crashed near Islamabad on a flight from Karachi, killing 152 persons, including 2 Americans. It was the country's deadliest air disaster to date. "You watch, they'll try to blame this on us," Patterson told her staff. Sure enough, one of the Pakistani papers soon published an account saying that operatives from the controversial security contractor Blackwater had been on board and had tried to fly the plane into a Pakistani nuclear weapons facility to destroy it. The pilot, a good Muslim, had resisted and flown the plane into the ground to spare the prized nuclear facility, the account said. The story was entirely fabricated.

Another story described how U.S. Army General Stanley McChrystal, then the military commander in Afghanistan, had visited Islamabad and supposedly dressed down Pakistani leaders for failing to fully crack down on militants. McChrystal had planned to come but in fact had canceled at the last moment. Patterson, irate, called up the paper's owner to point out that the visit had never happened. "It's entirely fabricated!" she told him. "Oh, what's the big deal?" he replied.

Patterson had to deal with real news when Pakistani terrorists attacked the Indian financial capital of Mumbai in late November 2008, in the closing days of the Bush administration. It led to what appeared to be one of the world's closest brushes with nuclear war. Patterson had flown to Washington for Thanksgiving, which came three weeks after Barack Obama's first presidential election victory, at a moment when few were thinking about foreign affairs. But as she arrived, she heard that terrorists had begun what became a four-day rampage that killed 174 people, including 6 Americans. She got a panicked call from Zardari, who told her that India's foreign minister, Pranab Mukherjee, had called with accusations that Pakistan had supported the terrorists. "They say they're going to attack!" Zardari told her.

The call from Mukherjee turned out to be phony, U.S. officials determined. But they remained worried that the Pakistanis might be so alarmed that they would launch a preemptive attack on India. Soon after the Mumbai killings began, U.S. intelligence found signs that it had been carried out by Lashkar-e-Taiba, a government-supported Pakistani militant group dedicated to driving India out of the disputed Kashmir Province.

Through a long weekend, tensions continued to rise in New Delhi, Islamabad, and Washington. As the governments exchanged threats, Indian fighter planes darted in and out of Pakistani airspace. Two days after she arrived in Washington, Patterson boarded a plane to hurry back to Islamabad.

Officials all the way up to President Bush, and including President-elect Obama, tried to talk the two sides down. The Pakistanis needed to acknowledge the Indian concern and to promise that they would cooperate in the investigation of the attack, Patterson told officials in her first round of calls. No one in Islamabad was ready to make the slightest conciliatory gesture. "They have their heads in the sand," Patterson told Rice.[23]

When Patterson arrived in Islamabad, she made a round of visits, to Kayani, Zardari, and Prime Minister Yousaf Gilani. She pointed them toward a charity called Jamaat-ud-Dawa that was believed to be a front for Laskhar-e-Taiba, and its leader and cofounder, Hafiz Saeed. "You've got to take action against these guys," she told them. To show Pakistani connections, she handed over stacks of "tearline information"—intelligence that has the most sensitive elements removed so that it can be passed to foreign governments considered not fully trustworthy. The papers described what Indians had learned from the surviving attacker and talked about a Pakistani company that had sold a dinghy used by the terrorists.[24]

None of Patterson's arguments, however, made the Pakistani officials more willing to acknowledge that the investigative tracks led to their country. Most Pakistanis viewed Lashkar-e-Taiba fighters as national heroes.

In early December, Secretary Rice showed up in Islamabad and did only slightly better. Kayani, while not accepting responsibility, "understood that Pakistan would have to give an accounting of what had happened. That was a start," Rice wrote later.[25] Over the next month tensions gradually eased. Zardari conceded that there were "non-state actors"—militants—in Pakistan that had to be eliminated. Indian tempers cooled.

But when U.S. officials tried to see that the Pakistanis made good on their promises, they again met only frustration. Richard Boucher and Patterson visited Pakistan's foreign minister, Shah Mahmood Qureshi, to insist that they needed to provide the CIA station all the help needed in the investigation to help track down the suspects and close the terrorist camps. Not much happened. The civilian authorities who made the promises didn't have the leverage to get the more powerful military and intelligence officials to deliver. "We got good promises from people who couldn't carry them out, and empty promises from people who could," Boucher said. The Pakistanis had again followed a familiar pattern of deflecting international pressure by making minimal promises and then failing to follow through. They believed they could weather the storm without giving ground.

Despite years of U.S. pressure on Islamabad, including sanctions and a $10 million bounty on his head, Pakistan released the founder of Lashkar-e-Taiba, Hafiz Saeed, from house arrest in November 2017. The same year Saeed formed a new political party, a signal that he wanted an active and public role in Pakistan's ruling structure.

As frictions with the Pakistanis increased during the final years of Patterson's tour, life at the embassy became ever more stressful. The embassy in Islamabad had once been seen as one of the most comfortable and family-friendly in the world. It occupied thirty-two acres in the manicured diplomatic quarter of the city and had a pool, an indoor jogging track, tennis courts, and a softball field. The schools were good and the staff could move around freely to enjoy the city's delights.

While the U.S. counterterror campaign had the official approval of civilian Pakistani officials, many in the military and intelligence agencies viewed it as a foreign power waging a war within their country's sovereign borders. They viewed the U.S. embassy as a nest of spies and a center of military plotting, and waged a campaign of pressure and harassment to make U.S. operations ever more difficult. The pressure rose sharply in the spring of 2009. The

Pakistani security agencies held up imports of armored vehicles, slowed delivery of U.S. aid for the civilian government, delayed visas the embassy wanted, and harassed embassy staff by stopping and detaining embassy vehicles.[26] They planted provocative and groundless news stories in the local press that further stoked public suspicions of the Americans.

The tensions increased when the State Department announced in 2009 that it would build a new $1 billion embassy and expand the U.S. staff from five hundred to eight hundred. The Pakistanis tried to block the embassy from acquiring the land it wanted for the expansion. The government demanded that the embassy identify who was working in the CIA station and disclose the jobs of other U.S. officials who were seeking visas, setting off another long-running dispute.

In December 2010 the name of the CIA station chief in Islamabad became public, forcing him to leave the country, in a leak that U.S. officials attributed to Pakistani intelligence. The Geo television channel and a national newspaper published photos and addresses of homes where CIA agents and Blackwater security contractors were supposedly living, as bloggers urged attacks on them.[27]

There were new restrictions on where the staff could go, so that at times the staff was almost entirely on lockdown. Once welcoming, the embassy was now off-limits to most Pakistanis. Because of the dangers, staff assignments in Islamabad were cut to one year, which meant that employees were packing to leave almost as soon as they understood their jobs.

Even during the Bush years, Patterson had worried about the toll of the stress and confinement on the embassy staff. Some embassy workers spent their limited free time drinking or in flings with colleagues. Patterson asked Boucher, her boss, to send her more so-called tandem couples who both worked for the Foreign Service. "Send me more couples who don't need to go down and get drunk at night," she told him. Some on the staff found the pressure too much and asked for transfers.

The stresses took a toll on U.S. work in the country. After greatly expanding the American aid program in Pakistan, Washington was unable to recruit the mid-grade staff they needed to carry out the mammoth assistance effort. It was another blow to a program Patterson believed had too many projects and too little focus.

The embassy staff was always keenly aware that in 1979, a mob of 15,000 Pakistanis assaulted the embassy, burning it to the ground. The attack began when the government bused in students to protest false reports that the United States had attacked a Muslim shrine in Mecca, Saudi Arabia. But the government apparently lost control of the group, and they scaled the embassy walls. Two Americans and two Pakistani embassy employees died in the attack. One hundred and thirty-eight embassy employees hid for five hours in a steel-lined safe room on the top floor of the embassy.

Other U.S. buildings in the city had been attacked from time to time going back to the 1950s. And to remind visitors of the risks, Patterson left in the guest bedroom a copy of a report on the 1979 attack. "We were all conscious of how bad things could get, and how quickly," said Boucher.

The struggles of the embassy even drew notice in Hollywood. The spy drama *Homeland*, which began on the Showtime network in 2011, featured a blond U.S. ambassador to Pakistan who struggled with duplicitous Pakistani officials, freelancing CIA operators, and an embassy under siege. The show was a favorite of President Obama and the Clintons. But its renown didn't seem to extend to the foreign service troops on the ground. Asked later about her fictional counterpart, Patterson confessed she hadn't heard of the character or the show.

Patterson left Islamabad in October 2010, more than three years after she came, to become ambassador to Egypt. She had held the job longer than was customary and been pressing Washington for a transfer for some time. But finding an exit strategy was not simple. Holbrooke's first two choices to replace her were rejected by the White House. President Zardari and others in the Pakistani leadership were uneasy about being left at the mercy of Holbrooke or a new ambassador who might be less able to manage the countries' strange relationship. "They're not going to let you go," Patterson's team joked.

When Patterson finally left, tensions were still on the rise with the Pakistanis. U.S. officials were becoming increasingly open in accusing the Pakistanis of double-dealing in their secret support for militants. But Patterson, like Crocker before her, was able to see the conflicts from Pakistani eyes. She understood, even if she didn't fully accept, the Pakistanis' arguments on why they needed to maintain ties with some militants. The view that they played a two-faced game with Washington was "the American view," she said.

At the end of her three years, the Pakistani civilian leadership remained "weak, ineffectual and corrupt," Patterson wrote in a cable briefing for FBI director Robert S. Mueller III in February 2010 in advance of a Mueller visit to Islamabad.[28] Even so, Musharraf and Zardari had each given up power peacefully, without a military coup. When Zardari surrendered the presidency to Nawaz Sharif in September 2013, it was the first democratic transition in Pakistan's history. Patterson and her team helped make that happen. The State Department, in recognition of what Patterson had done in Pakistan, gave her a prize named after her predecessor: the Ryan C. Crocker Award for Outstanding Achievement in Expeditionary Diplomacy. "Her job was to keep a lid on, to keep this very messy and rocky transition to democracy going," said Richard Boucher, the former assistant secretary. "She managed it. She got it all the way through."

# CHAPTER 11

# Flowers, and Stones, for the Ambassador

In late January 2011, Robert Ford went to see Syrian president Bashar al-Assad at his sleek marble palace on a plateau overlooking Damascus. As the new U.S. ambassador to Syria, Ford had a lot to talk about with Assad. Egyptian demonstrators were demanding the resignation of longtime president Hosni Mubarak, Tunisian president Zine el-Abidine Ben Ali had been driven from office, and it appeared that other Arab leaders might soon fall to the violent updrafts of the regional uprising that came to be known as the Arab Spring.

Tall and slightly stooped, Assad greeted him cordially as they settled into pastel-blue armchairs in a palace reception hall. His English was adequate, his manner courteous, and Ford's first impression was that the heir to the Assad dynasty would make a congenial dinner companion. But on some subjects he was touchy.

"It looks like kind of a difficult time for authoritarian regimes," Ford ventured. "How do you intend to get ahead of the problem?"

"It'll never happen here," Assad said, closing discussion of the topic before it had begun.

Ford had arrived in Damascus as the first U.S. ambassador in Syria in five years. The Bush administration had withdrawn his predecessor in 2006 to protest suspected Syrian involvement in the car-bomb assassination of Rafik Hariri, the former prime minister of neighboring Lebanon. A handful of Republican senators were trying to block Ford's confirmation, convinced that dispatching an ambassador would signal American acceptance of Damascus's bad behavior. But Barack Obama wanted to engage adversary regimes like those in Syria and Iran in hopes of solving long-standing disputes. So Washington had sent Ford, who, with five years in Iraq and fluent Arabic, was one of the department's most accomplished Mideast hands. The State Department hoped Ford would give them a clearer view of the region and might, in time, find a way to break off Assad's troubling alliance with Iran.

Ford had some misgivings about the job. He told his bosses he was worried that it could become a never-ending argument with the Syrians over their human rights abuses. But after five wearying years in Iraq, he was ready for an assignment in a new Arab country. He accepted the job and promised the Senate in a hearing that "unfiltered straight talk will be my mission priority." The staff at the embassy, which had felt leaderless and rudderless, was glad to have him.

Ford made a memorable entrance. Many ambassadors are formal and some even require their staffs to stand when they enter the room. The new boss the embassy team welcomed that day was a skinny, friendly man in an open-collared shirt with a book bag slung over his shoulder. He wanted to keep it informal. "Hi, I'm Robert," Ford told them. "Don't call me 'Ambassador.'" Ford said he was still at heart the long-haired Peace Corps volunteer he had been in his twenties.

Many ordinary Syrians were also cheered by Ford's arrival, hoping that it meant better ties with the United States and perhaps economic improvement. The regime had played up the return of the U.S. ambassador in state newspapers and television, so that when he walked the streets many Syrians recognized him. In his first days his staff took him through the crowded souks of the old city of Damascus, where merchants greeted him, chatted in Arabic, and offered tastes of their pistachios and dates.

He began rounds of meetings with local leaders. The pace was unhurried, following Arab tradition. Ford would start meetings talking about family and local life. He told his deputies not to take notes for fear that the Syrians might become self-conscious or intimidated and clam up. The meetings were to be just conversations. Ford could quote lines of Syrian poetry, and he knew, too, the songs of Fairuz, one of the most popular Lebanese singers. He would share a bit of American life. He would occasionally draw an analogy from the games of the Baltimore Orioles, his favorite baseball team since his days at Johns Hopkins University. "In my country, there is a sport I love called baseball . . . ," he would tell puzzled sheikhs.

But Ford's mission changed quickly when the first eddies of the Arab Spring reached Syria. Under the forty-year rule of the Assad family, Syria had a history of bloody repression, and many observers were skeptical that the regional protests would penetrate the country's borders. But on March 6, five weeks after Ford's arrival, a group of schoolboys ages ten to fifteen in the southern town of Dara'a spray-painted a wall with a slogan from other uprisings they had seen on satellite television. "Your turn, Doctor," they wrote, meaning that Syria's ophthalmologist turned president needed to step down, as the Egyptian and Tunisian leaders had. The boys were arrested by security police. Then were interrogated and beaten bloody, and some had fingernails pulled out. The town, outraged, marched in protest. The protesters posted pictures and videos on social media, and Syrians in other cities, who knew of similar horrors in their communities, took to the streets as well. Soon protests were swelling into the thousands and sprouting across the country. Because of social media, "in an unprecedented way, people all over knew what was happening," Ford said.

He told his bosses in Washington that the movement's gathering momentum was inspiring to watch. He had long wondered whether citizens in repressive Middle East states would risk their lives demanding freedom. He had had his doubts. Now he saw they would.

Ford sent his political staff to the streets to find out who was demonstrating and, if there was violence, which side started it.

He told them to watch from a distance, without taking part, and collect information. Early in the day he would tell members of the political team to "go out and get me nuggets." When they returned they would brainstorm about what they had found and what conclusions to draw in their cables to Washington. If Ford thought they were mistaken, he would tell them: "What you might be getting at is this . . ." Ford took time to share what he had learned in the service, as older Mideast hands had shared with him. The staff understood that he respected their opinions and it earned him fans.

They found the opposition groups were forming spontaneously without a real hierarchy. Many of the groups' most prominent members in the early days were part of the professional elite, including doctors, lawyers, and human rights advocates. The protesters had not worked out specific goals. Syrians had no independent civic institutions and they had no experience of grassroots politics.

The government's first reaction to the peaceful protests was hesitant. But by April, Assad had returned to the family playbook, dispatching snipers to pick off demonstrators and rolling tanks into public squares to intimidate them. By May, fifty or more were being killed each week and hundreds arrested.

The security services noticed that the embassy staff were watching the protests and began keeping a close eye on them. Plainclothes security men staked out the embassy staff's homes day and night. They appeared in cars with tinted windows and blacked-over license plates. They lounged against the cars, watching menacingly as the diplomats left in the morning and came home at night. It was all calculated to intimidate. The diplomats would find their drawers rummaged, their underwear on the floor and furniture dragged from room to room. The diplomats learned that the police were arresting their regular Syrian contacts, interrogating them about the Americans, and beating them up.

One young American diplomat who was spotted watching a protest was arrested, hooded, and held for hours in a cell next to one in which a Syrian was being tortured. The American was not touched, but the victim's cries were meant to scare him, and they did. He asked Ford if he could be excused for a few days from duty scouting the streets. The staff knew their phones were all bugged because security men would show up at their destinations when they ventured into the city. The embassy kept watching the protests but increasingly tried to do it out of view of the police.

As diplomats, the embassy team were not supposed to take sides in internal political conflict. They were entitled, under diplomatic agreements, to speak out in favor of the right to peaceful protest. The State Department had reciprocal agreements with the Syrians that entitled them to travel in the country.

As the uprising gathered momentum, Ford thought he needed to talk to the protesters both to find out what they were doing and to share his views. One night in late May, Ford made a furtive late-night trip to the borough of Bab Touma in the old city for a meeting with a dozen top opposition leaders at the home of a Syrian Christian activist. Ford and his aides wanted to avoid attention, so they left the armored limousine and full security detail behind and traveled in a VW Jetta owned by embassy political officer Mounir Ibrahim. They parked a distance from the meeting spot and wound their way through unlit streets. They found the apartment, in a squat building, and were shown in for three hours of conversation over tea and cake.

The group said they wanted to get rid of Assad. Ford told them he shared their goals of reform. But his advice, shaped by his years in Iraq, was that they should set their sights on achievable goals, negotiate for reforms, and avoid violence that could lead to a calamitous all-out war. "If you're trying to topple the regime, what incentive do they have to talk to you?" he asked the protesters. The opposition leaders were "shooting for the moon," said political officer Ibrahim. "Robert tried to put a dose of reality in them."

Their most passionate disagreement was on how Washington would respond to the war. The opposition leaders were convinced America, following its past pattern, would send troops once the struggle became bloody. "Don't worry, the U.S. will intervene to stop this," Walid al-Bunni, a prominent human rights activist, told him. "You'll see." Ford tried to convince them that the United States, after Iraq and Afghanistan, was no longer in a mood for more Mideast wars. "We are not bringing in the 101st Airborne," Ford told them. "The American cavalry is not going to save you." Bunni and the others didn't believe him, and the debate went back and forth. Ford kept having the same argument with the opposition for the next three years.

Ford and officials in Washington continued calling for the opposition to refrain from violence. But as the body count mounted, that advice became tougher for the opposition to bear, and sometimes they pushed back. Ford got a lecture on the issue at a late-night meeting in August with Razan Zaitouneh, a human rights lawyer who was widely considered the godmother of the nonviolent opposition. Zaitouneh, a thirty-four-year-old woman with wide-set eyes and straight brown hair, had gone into hiding after her husband was arrested. Ford's team went to great lengths to ensure that their meeting was secret. They darted through Damascus's darkened streets, making hairpin turns to try to lose the secret police who were tailing them. With some effort they did. They changed their meeting place several times in the final minutes of the trip for fear of detection. They ended up in one of the bare-bones temporary residences—"burner apartments"—that Zaitouneh's supporters shifted her to every day or two to try to ensure her safety. It was empty except for a table, chairs, and a computer with an Internet connection. The floor was littered with cigarette butts.

World powers were then focused on trying to get Assad to agree to reforms. But Ford had by this time concluded that all-out civil war was ahead and that Assad would go to any lengths to preserve his hold on power. "It will be very bloody," he told her. "We are prepared for that," Zaitouneh told him. She was never part of the violent resistance, but she did not object to it. And she told Ford the Americans should not bother with lectures about nonviolence. "We're not going to march to our death like Gandhi did," she said. "We're up against something much worse than the British."

Zaitouneh disappeared in late 2013 and is widely believed to have been kidnapped by a jihadist group.

Ford limited his own appearances at demonstrations, knowing that an ambassador's presence would draw much more attention and probably provoke a harsher government response. But he also knew that his higher profile would also bring more pressure on the government to refrain from attack, and for that reason he did venture out from time to time.

In early July, Ford decided to attend a demonstration in the west central city of Hama, 116 miles north of Damascus. Hama was the country's fourth largest city and the site of the Assad regime's most notorious attack on political opponents, a 1982 army assault on Sunni insurgents that killed tens of thousands. In early July 2011 thousands of protesters had been gathered near the city's central square for days. The embassy was hearing that the military was ringing the city, as it had in 1982, with plans to crush the protests. "Given the unhappy history, I thought I needed to go there myself," Ford said. "If there were violence, I would be an eyewitness and tell the world who started it." He had limited leverage as a diplomat, but he had the power to bear witness. Ford and the French ambassador to Syria, Éric Chevallier, agreed to meet in Hama and watch events from a distance. The night before the trip, Ford left a telephone message for his boss, assistant secretary of state Jeffrey Feltman, letting him know he intended to make the trip and warning that there could be a strong reaction from the government.

Ford set off on the day of the protest with his defense attaché and another military aide in an armored white Toyota Highlander. When they arrived at the city, they were waved through a series of army checkpoints, to their surprise. "Who are you?" they were asked. "American diplomats," they said. "Wonderful—please go through" was the response. They wandered through the city for a while, then realized they were lost and discovered they had no map. Ford asked his attaché where it was and was told he thought Ford was bringing it. "I'm the ambassador—you know I don't do anything useful," Ford told him.

They got out of the car at a café and were surrounded by a group of curious Syrians. The Syrians were at first skeptical that this ordinary-looking man could be the American ambassador. But they soon pulled up wobbly plastic chairs and launched into stories about their grievances against the government. Ford heard tales of how relatives had been arrested and never seen again and how homes and businesses had been seized. After tea, Ford's new friends tried to lead them by car to the demonstration. But the Americans got separated and once again lost. Then they made a fateful mistake. They nosed the Toyota out of a side street and found themselves in the middle of a sea of tens of thousands of demonstrators near the city's central Al-Assi Square. When the protesters realized who they were, they festooned the Toyota with roses and olive branches and began chanting and clapping. They took his presence as a sign of support. "The American ambassador's here!" they cried. It was flattering but more than a little unnerving. "My bodyguard almost had a heart attack," Ford said.

News of the diplomats' appearance was quickly picked up by Arab satellite channels and then by other international media, making headlines around the world. Ford's plan had gone awry: they looked like active supporters of the protests rather than neutral observers. The Syrian government, which Ford had notified in advance of the trip, tried to taint the protests by claiming in broadcasts that they were provoked by the Americans.

But the worldwide news coverage also made it impossible for Assad to attack the protesters. His appearance had made Ford a human shield for thousands of Syrians and turned him in minutes into an international celebrity. "Residents feel a kind of protection with the presence of the ambassador," Omar al-Habbal, an activist, told the *New York Times*. "The authorities wouldn't dare react with violence."[1]

When Ford returned to the embassy, he got a call from his boss, Jeffrey Feltman. "I don't know what you're doing out there, but it really pissed them off, so it must be good," Feltman told him. Officials in Washington had their hands full that summer with other wars and revolutions across the Muslim world, and they told Ford it would be largely up to him to figure out the path in Syria. Hillary Clinton, then secretary of state, wrote later that the Hama trip convinced senior officials Ford should be the U.S. link to the opposition, a job he held for the next two and a half years. "This was another example of an experienced diplomat taking risks to get out from behind embassy walls to do the job right," she wrote in her memoir.[2]

As Ford had suspected, the trip to Hama had enraged the Syrian government. The foreign ministry summoned Ford and French ambassador Chevallier to protest that the trip to Hama had violated the country's sovereignty.

The regime didn't limit its reaction to talk. Four days after the trip, a caravan of four buses rumbled by the embassy at midmorning and parked a block away. Burly plainclothes security police emerged carrying broom handles and two-by-fours. From his office window, Ford watched the rent-a-mob gather and prepared for a difficult day. For several hours the crowd stood in the plaza outside the embassy, shouting anti-American slogans, waving Syrian flags, and pelting the embassy with eggs, melons, and rocks. Then the police who had been separating the crowd from the embassy melted away and the protesters attacked.

The embassy complex was one of the most vulnerable in the world, located just off a busy traffic circle with only a few feet of setback. Parts of the building were draped in razor wire and some sections were sheathed in what was supposed to be climb-proof fencing. But two dozen attackers quickly scaled the fence, with some reaching the chancery roof and others descending into an outdoor parking area in the interior. The men on the roof yanked down the American flag and raised a Syrian flag in its place. Some tried to set fire to a rooftop trapdoor, while others began smashing a glass bulletproof door leading down a staircase to the center of the embassy. On the interior side of the door, two young Marines waited with M16 rifles, preparing to shoot if the attackers made it in. "If they get through, we are going to shoot," one of the Marines said. "Don't shoot unless they charge," Ford told them. When the attack began, the American diplomats assumed the regime wanted to scare but not injure them. As the attack continued, that seemed less certain.

Most of the embassy staff had been herded into the safe haven, a reinforced room in the chancery built for just such an emergency. But the attackers had made it in so quickly that the staff from other buildings in the compound were still on the outside, and at risk. In front of the building, the crowd was hanging flags and pictures of Assad, spray painting anti-American slogans, and ripping letters off the embassy sign. "Ambassador—dog," one graffiti read. The Marines fired tear gas canisters into the crowd, but the wind carried the gas back into the embassy so that it affected the staff more than the attackers.

Across town, another mob was attacking the French embassy, smashing the ambassador's car and using a battering ram to try to break into an entrance. The crowd injured three French soldiers before the troops fired live ammunition over their heads to disperse them. Ford's residence was also trashed.

When the attackers finally left the embassy, Ford told the Marines to "get that God damned flag off my roof." He folded it and brought it, in the Cadillac the embassy used for ceremonial occasions, to the Syrian foreign ministry. He handed it to Faisal Mekdad, the deputy foreign minister.

"Mr. Minister, I have treated your flag with more respect than you treated mine. But I want mine returned," he told him.

"Robert, we are so sorry," Mekdad said. "What can I say? The people are out of control."

But though the government continued to insist that the attack was the work of ordinary citizens, they returned the American flag the next day. When Ford sent a bill for the damage, they paid it without complaint.

After the attack, Bill Burns, the deputy secretary of state, called Ford with words of support on a line he knew the Syrians were monitoring. "Well done," he told him. "I want you to know we're all behind you back here." He asked Ford if there was anything he could do to help, and Ford asked him to call the foreign minister, Walid al-Moallem, to demand an end to the harassment.

Ford's stock was rising in Washington. The administration's decision to send him to Syria, controversial when it was made, was now earning praise from both parties. Officials in Washington were looking to him to explain the protest movement, guide their dealings with it, and help shape their statements to the press. Ford also convinced Washington to make him the sole contact point for the Syrian opposition. Otherwise, he argued, expatriates with little popular backing in Syria could be lobbying officials across the government for Washington's support, as happened with Iraqi expatriates before the Iraq war.

On August 1, during a trip to Washington, Ford was summoned to the White House. He expected to confer only with lower-level officials. But Tom Donilon, the national security adviser, escorted him to the Oval Office to meet President Obama. Obama praised his efforts and asked his thoughts about what was next.

Ford's mother, in Colorado, saw a TV news clip of the meeting that night and called him to complain. She noticed there were no shirt cuffs poking out of his green summer suit. "Did you meet the president in a short-sleeved shirt?" she scolded. "I didn't raise my son to meet the president of the United States in a short-sleeved shirt." Ford protested that he hadn't been expecting to meet the president and, besides, it was a suffocating 95 degrees in Washington. Mom wasn't satisfied.

As the regime's crackdown continued, Obama came under growing political pressure to call on Assad to surrender power. Congressional hawks, human rights groups, newspaper editorialists, and even, in internal debates, some State Department officials were demanding it.

Ford had his doubts, worrying that such a pronouncement wouldn't change Assad's behavior and would make the United States look weak if Assad stayed and continued to pile up bodies. "They're going to keep shooting," Ford told his boss, Assistant Secretary Feltman.

Later in August the White House called to tell Ford that Obama was close to calling for Assad's departure. But they wanted to know if that would expose the embassy to danger.

"I understand you have political problems back there," Ford told them. "If you do it, we'll be OK here." When Obama made his declaration, on August 18, the Syrians ignored it. Critics said that by making the demand without the means to enforce it, Obama had made an amateurish mistake. Ford came to regret that he hadn't tried to steer the White House away from the statement.

Washington told him to use his own judgment on how much he wanted to challenge the Assad regime. Feltman called to tell him that it was his choice whether he wanted to continue denouncing the regime in the manner of Mark Palmer, a former ambassador to Hungary. Palmer was celebrated for his public criticism of the Hungarian government's crackdown on dissidents in the late 1980s. "If you decide to do a Mark Palmer, you'll have backing here," Feltman told him.

Ford decided to keep on challenging the regime. Later in August he defied the government's ban on his travel to visit the farming town of Jasim, which was then threatened with a bloody crackdown. Jasim, forty-five miles south of Damascus, had already seen bloody clashes. The mayor and town council had issued an appeal, promising that upcoming demonstrations would be peaceful and asking the central government not to intervene. Ford got in touch with city officials and they invited him to visit, hoping his presence would deter an attack.

But on August 23, when he and his defense attaché, Robert Friedenberg, drove from Damascus, they discovered there was little they could do to help. The city of 30,000 was overflowing with soldiers and heavy military equipment. They drove through the streets in their small Ford SUV under the barrels of Soviet-made tanks. There were no demonstrators, nor many other civilians, on the streets. Friedenberg went into a drugstore to ask what was going on. "We knew you were coming," the druggist whispered. "But there are no demonstrations. People are scared."

On the drive back to Damascus, Ford called the foreign ministry to acknowledge that he had made the trip without permission. Faisal Mekdad, the deputy foreign minister, complained bitterly but did nothing in retaliation.

Along with his travel, Ford had been lodging protests with the foreign ministry and getting on their nerves. In the first days of the uprising, Ford went to the office of Mekdad, one of the regime's most disagreeable officials, to complain about the crackdown in Dara'a. "We are getting reports that security forces are firing on and killing protesters," Ford told Mekdad. "We are very concerned."

"No, there are just some terrorists there," Mekdad told him. "This will all go away."

"We have not heard of any terrorism," Ford told him. "We have only heard of protests."

Mekdad, who happened to be from Dara'a, quickly lost his temper. "They're insulting my family name in the streets," he complained in Arabic.

To further irritate Mekdad, Ford asked his deputy, Mounir Ibrahim, whether he had understood Mekdad's Arabic correctly.

"Mr. Foreign Minister, insulting you or the president is by no means the definition of terrorism," Ford told him. "You should pick up the *New York Times* and see what people say about our president every day. We do not shoot the people who do this."

The government was also displeased to discover that Ford planned to attend a September 11 memorial service for Ghiyath Matar, a twenty-six-year-old tailor who had become a celebrated figure in the protests advocating a nonviolent approach. During protests, Matar had given Syrian troops water bottles and poked flowers in their gun barrels, earning him the nickname "Little Gandhi." But Matar's work had caused the first defections from the army, and the government saw him as a threat. The police arrested and tortured him for four days in early September, then returned his dead body, covered with burns and bullet holes, to his family.

Ford got in touch with Matar's family through Syrian contacts and asked if they would like him and other diplomats to come to the memorial service. Although he cautioned them that their presence might provoke a reaction from the government, the family wanted them to come. Ford showed up with seven other ambassadors, including the French, British, German, and Japanese. Their appearance, sitting in the front row under a canopy of Lebanese cedars, was filmed and the images were quickly uploaded to the Web. Soon Arab satellite stations and world news media were carrying the footage. As the service continued, some in the crowd began calling for the overthrow of the government. The diplomats, not wanting to be accused of endorsing a revolution, took that as their cue to leave. Within a few minutes the army and secret police burst in, halting the service, trashing the funeral tent, and arresting dozens, including members of Matar's family. Some were never seen again. The secret police spray-painted on the side of the family's house: "The Matar family is an agent of the American ambassador."

Ford had another brush with danger a few days later. He arranged to go see Hassan Abdul Azim, the head of the Democratic Arab Socialist Union, an Arab socialist party. Azim's party was one of the few officially recognized by the government, and it had reasonably good relations with top officials. In the previous week, diplomats from the United Kingdom and other countries had met with Azim. But tensions with Washington were especially high, because ten days earlier Obama had called on Assad to step down. The government decided to make a point when Ford came calling.

When Ford and aides arrived on foot near Azim's office, they were spotted and pursued by a group of about seventy-five men: Syrian intelligence posing as pro-government demonstrators. When they spotted the Americans, they chased them into Azim's building, pelting Ford with eggs and tomatoes. Ford and his group barely made into Azim's office, where they slammed the door and wedged a desk next to it to keep it closed. Ford and Azim went ahead with their discussion and sweet tea. But outside, the men continued banging on the door, chanting anti-American slogans, and effectively holding the diplomats captive. "Down with the ambassador!" they cried. "Down with the Americans!"

Ford's security aide called for reinforcements to try to get them out. When two armored cars arrived, the crowd turned on them, bashing the cars with crowbars and nearly injuring one of the staff. Ford decided he wasn't going to be getting out without a beating. But after several hours the crowd ebbed and Syrian police finally appeared and cleared a way for them to make it back to the embassy. Secretary of State Clinton, in Washington, denounced the attack as a violation of diplomatic rules and "clearly part of an ongoing campaign of intimidation."

Ford was also jousting with the regime on social media. The regime's control over local TV and newspapers allowed it to largely prevent the embassy from getting its point of view in the Syrian press. But Ford could make the administration's arguments and describe what they were learning of the protest movement on the embassy's Facebook page. He discovered that if he wrote in Arabic, he wouldn't even have to clear his statements with Washington. The Facebook site began to get likes from the opposition, but also denunciations—and death threats—from the regime and its supporters. Syrian protesters who were angry Washington wasn't doing more also weighed in. The site became a free-for-all—and a bracing departure from the usual bland State Department pronouncements. The Arab satellite TV stations followed it closely, and when Ford made news, it was quickly reported.

"Mujtaba Xr warns me that I will face being killed if I continue my criticism of the repression in Syria," Ford wrote on the Facebook site in October. "I take his post to be a perfectly good example of the kind of intolerance that has provoked such discontent in Syria." The embassy used the site to rebut stories, many wildly inaccurate, about what Ford and the embassy were doing. One false tale had it that Ford's motorcade had killed a young Syrian boy as it raced back to the embassy from Azim's office.

Ford went a step further and began posting satellite photos from U.S. intelligence to challenge Syria's claims about its military operations. During a campaign against rebels in the city of Homs, the opposition and aid groups began complaining that the government was bombarding civilians in the city. The government insisted it was only rockets from the rebels. Ford got permission from his superiors to post satellite photos of the government artillery emplacements. "Oh, that made the news," he said. He posted other photos to show that the regime was cheating on U.N.-sponsored ceasefires by moving armored vehicles short distances rather than withdrawing them from the battlefield. "The regime and the Syrian people should know they cannot hide the truth," he wrote. "We are watching." The regime's defenders challenged the pictures and gave Ford such names as "the lunatic barbarian criminal ambassador."

By the end of October, State Department officials decided it was too risky for Ford to remain in Damascus and recalled him temporarily to Washington. The state media was blaring accusations against him, including reports in the *Al-Thawra* newspaper that he was leading the uprising and had organized death squads during his posting in Iraq. "The kinds of falsehoods that are being spread about Ambassador Ford could lead to violence against him," said Victoria Nuland, the chief State Department spokeswoman. Ford returned to Syria in early December, after the government promised it would not harass him. But he discovered on his return that the embassy's situation was now even more perilous. It faced danger not only from a hostile government but also from the fighting that was raging ever closer. The conflict was changing from a peaceful popular uprising to a multi-sided international conflict, the deadliest war of the new century.

In an ominous sign, the Al-Nusra Front, an Al Qaeda–linked jihadist group, blew up the Syrian intelligence headquarters on December 23 with a pair of car bombs, the first use of suicide bombings in the war. The bombings, which killed forty-four, followed a pattern used in Iraq: one vehicle blew a hole near the entranceway, then a second followed, penetrating deeper with the second blast. U.S. intelligence believed the bombings were the work of two women sent from Iraq. But it raised worries that the U.S. embassy could become a target for the kind of truck bomb that had destroyed the U.S. embassy in Beirut in 1983. Embassies were required to have a one-hundred-foot setback from the street, high perimeter walls, and crash barriers in front. The Damascus embassy didn't have any of that. It was also constructed without reinforced steel, making it especially vulnerable to a bombing.

The Syrian government wanted to prevent the embassy from closing, to avoid creating the impression that the regime was under siege and isolated. The regime had been arguing publicly that Ford's continued presence in Damascus showed Washington wasn't serious in its declarations that Assad had to step down. They sent security specialists and military officers to the embassy with tape measures to explore ways to improve protections.

Dhu al-Himma Shalish, the head of presidential security and an Assad cousin, invited Ford to his home in the northeastern suburb of Harasta to discuss the issue over Johnnie Walker Blue Label Scotch. Amid the continuing war of words between the governments, cocktail hour at Shalish's place was a slightly surreal interlude. But the trip turned out to be a reminder of the war's growing dangers, even to top regime officials. Ford noticed that only a few blocks away fighting was raging and curtains of flame were slowly advancing. Shalish, too, would soon have to abandon his home, Ford knew.

In the end, Washington decided the embassy was too vulnerable to terrorist attack. "We were on borrowed time," Ford said. Ford and his team quietly decamped in early February to State Department headquarters. He was now an ambassador without an embassy but still envoy to the Syrian opposition and the administration's chief point man on the war.

Before he left Damascus, he had the unhappy duty of meeting one final time with the embassy's dozens of Syrian employees, some of whom had been working for U.S. agencies for decades. When they gathered at a room in the embassy, a Syrian employee named Jabr, who had been helping to promote sales of U.S. farm products for a quarter century, got up. "What's going to become of us?" he asked. Ford could offer no reassurances. The State Department would continue to send them checks for their salaries for some time, he said. But he told them that, based on what he knew, their country was descending into a full-blown civil war. If they could get out of the country, he said, they should. Many wanted to move to the United States, of course. He had to tell them that was not possible. "The message was *sauve qui peut*," he said. "It was not a happy time."

Ford returned to Washington, still upset over the departure, and was surprised to receive a hero's welcome. The Republicans who had opposed his nomination now praised him, as did Democrats and news outlets ranging from the conservative *Weekly Standard* to the *New York Times*. Ford was "an exemplary and courageous diplomat," the *Times* editorialized. After blocking his nomination for twenty months, on October 3 the Senate confirmed him unanimously as ambassador. "Wow!" Cheryl Mills, Secretary of State Clinton's chief of staff, emailed her boss.[3]

Ford's defiance had been a moment of moral clarity in a war with few of them. But now, with 7,500 dead, the opposition was turning to arms, and the Obama administration was under pressure to decide whether to join the fight. Ford's job was about to get a lot tougher. His posting in Damascus, where he had risked his life, turned out to be the easy part.

# CHAPTER 12

# Envoy to the Rebels

On February 15, 2011, two months after the beginning of the Arab Spring, Libyan police began firing on unarmed demonstrators outside a dilapidated police station in the eastern city of Benghazi. Police slaughtered dozens in follow-on demonstrations over the next few days, but the protests against the regime grew and spread across the country. When the country's dictator, Muammar el-Qaddafi, threatened to kill thousands more "like rats," the Obama administration faced a decision on whether to send the U.S. military to yet another troubled country in the Middle East.

The administration already had its hands full of wars and revolutions, and top officials were deeply split. But facing warnings of mass slaughter, combined with pressure from the Europeans and Arabs, President Obama agreed in March to join an air campaign led by NATO, the Western military alliance, to protect the rebels.

A first priority was to find a diplomat willing to plunge into the war zone to serve as a link to the little-known rebels. The choice of almost every top State Department official was Chris Stevens, who had been the number two at the embassy just two years before. He knew more about Libya than anybody, Secretary of State Hillary Rodham Clinton told lawmakers later, and was "one of our most accomplished diplomats." This was not a usual diplomatic gig: the State Department didn't usually send envoys to rebel groups, and it didn't parachute diplomats into the front lines of wars. But Washington was handicapped by a lack of good information, even from the intelligence agencies. And Stevens was willing to go. He accepted the job as soon as it was offered by Jeffrey Feltman, the top State Department official for the Middle East. Later, Feltman learned that Stevens was in the middle of buying and restoring a house in the Washington suburb of Chevy Chase, Maryland, a task that would be far tougher from a distance of 5,200 miles.

The Arab Spring revolutions in Egypt and Tunisia had made many in the West exultant that the stagnant Middle East was entering an age of renewal. But Stevens understood that the rebellion was likely to mean years of upheaval. Ousting the regime and creating a new state meant the trouble was only beginning.

A week after the clashes began, Stevens wrote friends and family that because Qaddafi had banned all political activity, "it is hard to see who or what might come after him." Since Qaddafi had snuffed all independent national institutions, the next leaders would have to create an entirely new nation. Whoever succeeds Qaddafi, Stevens wrote, "will have to start building these national institutions from scratch." Even beginning the new order would not be easy, since Qaddafi would never surrender his position peacefully, he predicted. The leader and his sons were "thuggish, violent and obsessed with holding onto power."

One of his first tasks was to help Clinton decide whether the rebels were worthy of U.S. military support. At a late-night meeting in Clinton's suite at the Westin Paris–Vendôme hotel on March 14, Stevens introduced her to the rebels' senior emissary, Mahmoud Jibril. Jibril, a polished political scientist who had been a Qaddafi aide and an American academic, made a winning argument. "He reminded her of Rwanda and the Balkans, where the world— translation: her husband—had failed to stop mass killings," journalist Mark Landler wrote in *Alter Egos: Hillary Clinton, Barack Obama, and the Twilight Struggle over American Power*.[1] Jibril's goals meshed neatly with the Americans': elections and a quick transition to a democratic, inclusive state.

Stevens sneaked into the country April 5 aboard a ship. He had a closet-size cabin on a Greek cargo vessel, the *Aegean Pearl*, with a toilet that was backed up and reeking. Stevens was carrying 60,000 euros and was accompanied by a junior foreign service officer, two U.S. disaster relief specialists, and eight diplomatic security agents.

Security was a worry from the beginning. Before leaving for Libya, Stevens flew to Stuttgart, Germany, to discuss with General Carter F. Ham, number two at the U.S. military command for Africa, how he might get in and how they might extract him if the danger got too great. U.S. officials first considered having Stevens bunk on a U.S. ship off the coast and sending him to Benghazi on day trips with military protection. But a U.S. military role was abandoned when Admiral Michael Mullen, chairman of the joint chiefs of staff, decided it would violate Obama's directive that there should be no American "boots on the ground"—even in civilian clothes—in the Libya operations.[2]

Stevens arrived in Benghazi with no specific instructions. "There was no protocol for how to move forward," Clinton recalled in her memoir. "No past precedent to follow. No list of important figures to look out for. Chris had to work from scratch . . . to carve out his own set of rules for working with the opposition." Clinton saw that Stevens understood the importance of diplomacy on the front lines. "After years of experience in the field, he understood that the difficult and dangerous places are where America's interests are most at stake, and where it's most important that we be represented with skilled and subtle diplomacy."[3]

Benghazi, an ancient trading and cultural capital of 1 million, was in chaos. The police and army had melted away in the fighting. Trash was piling up and utilities were breaking down. Militias, many little more than groups of untrained neighborhood men, were trying to fill the security void. But the city was also menaced by jihadist thugs and Qaddafi sleeper cells. Stevens and his team took rooms in the Tibesti Hotel, a faded fifteen-story waterfront tower then jammed with diplomats, journalists, and spies. He was amused to learn that his suite, with its garish gold-painted furniture and four-poster bed, had often been used by Abdullah al-Senussi, Qaddafi's intelligence chief and brother-in-law.[4]

Security threats began immediately. Five days after he arrived, Stevens almost had to pack up and leave. Qaddafi's army had seized Ajdabiyah, a city in the desert one hundred miles south of Benghazi. Washington feared the army might cut off power and water to Benghazi and begin a slaughter. Those fears proved unfounded. A few weeks later Stevens was awakened and told he should head to the hotel's basement because of fears that Qaddafi was preparing to launch a Scud missile at Benghazi. On another evening Stevens was dining at the hotel with the Swedish consul when they were startled by a crash. A gunman had fired through the window into the restaurant, sending diners fleeing. On June 1 a car bomb went off in the Tibesti parking lot, shaking the hotel to its foundation. That did it: the U.S. team decided the Tibesti was too big a target. They decamped and moved several times, finally settling in a thirteen-acre walled compound in the Venezia neighborhood south of downtown.

One Saturday afternoon shortly after he arrived in Benghazi, Stevens took part in a conference call with State Department officials. Joan A. Polaschik, who was the embassy's number two and had fled the U.S. embassy in Tripoli for Washington, asked him, "Are you sure you should stay?" She would have felt better if he had left. But "Chris had, I think, a different tolerance for risk than I did," she told Congress later. "Chris felt it was important to stay and felt that conditions were such that they should."[5]

As in his first posting, Stevens kept trying to make friends. He visited Libyans in their homes and shared meals sitting on the floor, Arab-style. Two weeks before Stevens arrived, a U.S. F-15E fighter jet had crashed a few miles southeast of Benghazi. The pilot was recovered by NATO forces, and then his partner, the weapons officer, was picked up by a friendly Libya militia with the help of Stevens's aide, Habib. But in trying to protect the airmen, a NATO warplane mistakenly strafed the militia and a young Libyan had lost a leg. The Americans offered compensation, which the young man's family had turned down. But Stevens wanted to do more. He visited the man's home, in a tiny town southeast of Benghazi, to express his regret and ask if there was more the Americans could do. The man was surprised but pleased to see the American envoy at his home.

Even after the bombing of the Tibesti, Stevens was venturing on foot into the streets, protected by only a couple of security agents. He visited Derna, an oceanside city east of Benghazi that had been one of Libya's most prosperous. Later it became a hotbed of jihadist groups, who closed beauty parlors and radio stations and insisted on gender segregation at the local university.[6] Stevens was undeterred. Meeting with a group in the city, he recalled it had long been known for a famous ocean diving club. "We should open it again!" he told the residents.

Through his contacts, Stevens was gathering a stream of information for Washington on personalities, politics, and military developments. "We didn't have boots on the ground, but we had Chris Stevens," said retired general David Petraeus, who became CIA director in September 2011.

For the Western campaign to succeed, the rebel group had to be competent enough to field a military force and provide rudimentary government services. So Stevens was inevitably drawn into helping unite the splintered Transitional National Council, make it credible enough that it would win support from Arab neighbors and world powers. When he entered the country, the rebels "didn't have money to provide food and medicine for emergency relief, or even to generate enough electricity to keep the lights on," Stevens told American journalists in August.[7] He helped arrange emergency aid, as well as nonlethal military equipment, such as boots, for rebel troops. At times he went to Benghazi's harbor in shirtsleeves to help unload the aid shipments.

Stevens tried to overcome differences between the political groups, large and small, that were springing up and wanted a say. "He was trying to find common ground within a lot of factions," Peter Sullivan, his brother-in-law, testified in an October 2017 federal court hearing. The opposition consisted of "about 156 of them, with an average of seven people each," he said.

Some of Stevens's contacts were like Jibril: Western-educated, English-speaking, and relatively cosmopolitan. They included doctors, lawyers, businesspeople and government officials. Others were rough-hewn former military men, merchants, and farmers. Stevens told colleagues of discussing with a rebel commander what the rebels needed to say to Western leaders to get their support. The Libyan was eager but didn't quite get it. "We will tell them we are democratic," the commander enthused. "We will tell them we will run Libya with a firm hand, like a king!"

Stevens lobbied Washington to recognize the rebels' Transitional National Council, rather than Qaddafi's regime, as the legitimate government. Recognition would give the group new credibility among Libyans and would also help convince other governments to recognize it and strengthen the rebels' claims to the $30 billion in Libyan government funds that were frozen in foreign banks. But first Clinton asked Stevens and U.S. Ambassador to Libya Gene Cretz to make sure the organization, which included Islamist groups, was worthy of American recognition. "She wanted us to make sure this really was a national uprising and not an Islamist takeover," said Cretz.

Stevens and Cretz gave her that assurance. Most Libyans supported the group, they said, and while Islamists were present, they weren't dominant. Clinton came to agree, and on July 15, after a series of high-level meetings in Washington, the administration announced it was granting diplomatic recognition.

Even so, there were questions about the rebel leadership. Two weeks after Washington gave its blessing to the council, rebel fighters assassinated the group's military chief, the former Qaddafi aide Abdul Fatah Younis, and two of his commanders. Younis's body was found by a roadside, badly burned, possibly in retaliation for a crackdown on Islamists he had carried out while working for Qaddafi. Some rebel leaders had begun to lose faith in Younis. But outsiders saw him as one of the group's most credible leaders, and the killing was a blow to international confidence in the revolution. Mustafa Abdul Jalil, the Transitional National Council chairman, launched an investigation "even though everyone knew who the culprits were," Stevens emailed friends in August. The rebels had no military chief for the remainder of the war. "Rebel leadership is on shaky ground," Stevens wrote.

As the summer continued, the rebels' progress on the battlefield ground into a stalemate. In Washington, criticism of the U.S. intervention was increasing.

Stevens was candid with his superiors about the leadership's failings. In late August, Stevens's boss, Jeff Feltman, and other U.S. officials came to Benghazi for a round of meetings with the rebel leaders, nongovernment groups, and foreign diplomats. Stevens briefed the group about the opposition's strong points but also about shortcomings that were increasingly apparent. Feltman agreed with Stevens's analysis and sent a long memo to Clinton laying out the troubling signs in the rebel council. The rebel leaders, he wrote, were largely passive, observing rather than directing the movements of the rebel troops that were fighting Qaddafi in the west. Mahmoud Jibril, the interim prime minister, made only cameo appearances in Benghazi and spent most of his time living in safety in Qatar. While Washington had committees trying to figure out how to end the military stalemate, the rebel leaders in Benghazi didn't seem to be giving it much thought, Feltman told Clinton. Their comments to the Americans on the situation were "passive analysis, rather than aggressive forward thinking," he wrote. Feltman found that the rebels had no ideas on how to rein in the proliferating militias, which became the country's foremost security problem. Some rebel leaders talked candidly about the need to get the growing bands of armed men under government control, but others "tried to avert their eyes to the troubles the militias could pose on the Day After," he wrote. "On reining in the militias, we heard no good answers." Feltman, Stevens, and the U.S. team cautioned the rebels that more feuding would jeopardize the rebels' support from world powers.[8]

During Feltman's visit, the U.S. delegation and Stevens had a meeting with Ali Tarhouni, the Transitional National Council's new deputy prime minister and a former American economics professor, that unearthed one encouraging piece of news. During one of Stevens's patient pauses, Tarhouni began to talk about the rebels' long-anticipated plans to finally take the capital, Tripoli. When would the operation begin? Feltman asked. Tarhouni looked at his watch. "In about an hour," he said. When Stevens and Feltman left, they turned on the news and found that Tarhouni was not kidding. "Sure enough, the Tripolitanians had risen up again!" Stevens wrote friends.

The next day Tripoli fell in a twelve-hour battle that killed 1,300. Qaddafi's sons Seif and Mohammed were captured in the battle, and the TNC leadership made sure they were brought in alive. "The TNC, including [chairman] Abd al-Jalil himself, intervened with the militias surrounding Mohammed's house to make sure they didn't harm him," Stevens cabled Washington on August 22. "They understood it would be harmful to the revolution and the TNC if he were killed." Stevens was relieved to hear that; he'd been cautioning the rebel leadership about it for weeks.

A few days later Clinton called Stevens for an update. With the rebels about to take power, she decided it was time to nudge Jalil to run his government like a responsible democratic leader. "She called the rebel president as I silently listened," Stevens emailed friends. "She encouraged him to be strong, do the right things, say the right things, so he could lead the country into the next, hopefully post-Qaddafi era."

Unfortunately, the rebel forces that captured Qaddafi on October 20 hadn't heard that call for restraint. When they found him hiding in a drainage pipe in the central city of Sirte, they beat and stabbed him, sodomized him with a stick, and shot him. "Why are you doing this, my sons?" he pleaded. The NATO campaign officially ended eleven days later.

The war's end brought a quick shift in American priorities. Administration officials were preoccupied with a revolution in Egypt and a war in Afghanistan, among other challenges, and viewed Libya as a peripheral player. They wanted the Europeans, who had pushed for the NATO campaign and had historical ties to the country, to take the lead. "For the United States, Libya must not be a state-building exercise," cautioned a September memo written by Clinton foreign policy adviser Jake Sullivan and other top officials. "Post-conflict stabilization in Libya, while clearly a worthy undertaking at the right level of investment, cannot be counted on as one of our highest priorities."[9]

Privately, Stevens and the other State Department Middle East hands would have preferred a greater American effort. They saw the country's inexperienced leadership starting a rebuilding with no central government, military, or other national institutions and threatened by dozens of heavily armed militias. They thought the United States could make a difference in the only Arab Spring country it had intervened to help. Stevens "played an important role in making the argument that the United States needed to have a very robust presence," said Gene Cretz.

Stevens's chief worry was that the administration wasn't paying enough attention to what was going on in Benghazi and in the eastern region around it. The city had been the cradle of the revolution and remained, in his view, the key to stabilizing the country. With the rebel leadership moving west to Tripoli to run the government, there was a risk that the ancient east-west tensions could flare again and split the new state. Some in Benghazi were already pushing for a loose federal system that would give their region greater power; a few were advocating violence to achieve it. U.S. officials also needed to deal with the growing threat of Islamist militias that were taking root in the east, Stevens believed. There had been increasing attacks from Islamists on other factions and on Western and international groups and officials. He told Ethan Chorin, a former State Department official in Libya, "he was concerned that we were at a turning point and things could go badly quickly," Chorin said.[10]

Stevens returned to Washington from Benghazi in November 2011. State Department officials had already asked him to take over as ambassador when Gene Cretz's tour ended in April. He needed to be in Washington for the next six months while Congress was considering his ambassadorial nomination. Stevens was excited about his appointment but worried while he was in Washington that he should be at work in Libya at a crucial time. His friend Roya Haka-kian invited Stevens over and found him looking gaunt and out of sorts, wishing he were on the job. "He had been separated from his purpose, which was back in Libya," she wrote later.[11]

Stevens had been staying in touch with his Libyan contacts and trying to keep Washington abreast of developments. In early April, Stevens was asked about one of the dozens of emails that were being sent to Clinton by Sidney Blumenthal, a longtime Clinton political aide and confidant. Blumenthal was reporting jitters in Tripoli that the Muslim Brotherhood, an old-line Islamist group, was gaining strength and might become a dominant factor in upcoming elections in July. The report was "very interesting," Stevens offered diplomatically. But his own contacts, he said, believed the Brotherhood was poorly organized and seen by most Libyans as an unwelcome interloper from Egypt.

At his Senate confirmation hearing in March 2012, Stevens sounded like a man who would have a preferred a more ambitious program than the one his administration was actually planning. Overcoming the damage done by Qaddafi's forty-year rule would take "some time and much effort," he said. "Libya's new leaders must build democratic institutions from scratch, consolidate control over militias, ensure that all Libyans are represented and respected in the new government, and dispose of the country's oil wealth fairly and transparently," he said. "It is clearly in the United States' interest to see Libya succeed as a stable and prosperous democracy." That outcome "would enhance our security and economic well-being."

Under questioning, Stevens told lawmakers the biggest threat to the country was from the 200,000 armed young men in hundreds of militias who were now wandering the country and battling each other. The new government hoped to reintegrate them into society, Stevens said, and remembered how the purging of Saddam Hussein's military after the U.S. invasion of Iraq had helped ignite a bloody civil war. The new government had several plans for dealing with the militias, but none that seemed likely to resolve the issue, he acknowledged. "I have to say it's not as organized as one might like it to be," he said. Asked about the U.S. role, Stevens said the United Nations was now leading the international effort, and the U.S. contribution would be largely in providing advice.

Stevens was sworn in as ambassador by Clinton on May 14. The secretary and her top officials were confident they were sending the best person for the job, and the mood at the Franklin Room was celebratory. Stevens had a "magic touch," Clinton said, and a "California sense of calm."

Before Stevens left, his family had a fiftieth birthday party for him in his former home of Piedmont, California. His mother asked, half teasingly, "And why do you have to go over there again?" And Stevens replied, also half joking, that it would serve Americans' interests and security if Libya were stable and prosperous, Stevens's friend Austin Tichenor recalled. When he talked to his former aide Bubaker Habib about his return, he made clear that however limited Washington's plans, he had a personal commitment to the recovery of Libya. "I had a role in getting rid of Qaddafi, and now my mission is to rebuild the country," he told Habib.

Before he arrived in Libya in May 2012, Stevens posted a video on his embassy's website to introduce himself. The three-minute clip told how a skinny Northern California kid in a backward baseball cap had been enchanted by the Middle East and in two assignments in Libya had come to see it as a second home. To a soundtrack of purring Arab strings, the video showed Stevens on a dusty roadside with smiling Libyans, swapping life stories and jokes. It followed him strolling around the Lincoln Memorial in Washington to explain how Libya and America, enemies for decades, were now alike. America had in its past to endure a bloody civil war to emerge as a modern state, he said, and the new post-revolutionary Libya, with American help, could do the same. "See you soon," he said.

# CHAPTER 13

# The Long Goodbye

Almost a decade after it started, the war in Afghanistan was still raging across much of the countryside in early 2011. And in the capital of Kabul, behind the razor wire and blast barriers that protected Afghan officials and the Americans who had come to help them, the fighting was also intense. Afghan president Hamid Karzai was barely speaking to the U.S. ambassador, Karl Eikenberry. U.S. military commanders were at odds with the civilian leadership of the American mission. And in Washington, the State Department and Pentagon wrestled with White House aides over the conduct of what was soon to become America's longest war.

President Obama, searching for a way to end the feuding, decided it was time to bring back Ryan Crocker. The five-time ambassador had closed a thirty-seven-year foreign service career in early 2009 and now presided as dean in the wood-paneled precincts of the Bush School of Government and Public Service at Texas A&M University. He had begun to make money as a foreign affairs consultant. When Vice President Joe Biden called to ask him to return to the crossfire as U.S. ambassador to Afghanistan, he resisted. But then he agreed.

Soon Crocker was in the Oval Office listening to Obama issue marching orders for himself and Marine General John R. Allen, who was taking over as commander of U.S. and allied forces in Afghanistan. Obama wanted to draw down the combined NATO force from 150,000 to 15,000 and turn leadership of the military

effort to the Afghans. He wanted to negotiate a long-term U.S. relationship with the Afghan government. And as a first step on the
new path he needed to end the internal frictions, especially those
with Karzai. "You know him," Obama told Crocker. "Get us to a
better place."

It was a return engagement for Crocker. He had led the U.S.
embassy in Afghanistan from January to April 2002, in the first
months after the five-week U.S. military campaign had toppled
the country's Taliban government. When he left, he was worried
that the shrinking Western support for the fragile new government
would allow a jihadist resurgence. He was right. By 2008 the threat
from the insurgents had grown so that some officials in the departing Bush administration feared the long effort to protect the government was near catastrophic failure.[1] To try to save it, Barack
Obama ordered in an additional 33,000 U.S. troops at the end of his
first year as president. But eighteen months later, despite 150,000
Western troops and U.S. spending of $150 billion a year, victory
was not in sight. The president was approaching his second presidential run and wanted to tell voters he had an exit plan that would
cut their costs in blood and treasure while preventing a return of the
Taliban and Al Qaeda.

As Obama knew, Crocker and Karzai had a bond from the past.
In the first days of Karzai's leadership in 2002, the two had met
almost daily to explore how they might bind a country that had
always been a collection of unruly fiefdoms and thousands of sub-
tribes. In those early days Karzai had been ebullient, thrilled at his
new power, and grateful at whatever help he received from Washington.

But in ten years, the American relationship with Karzai had
soured. The thirteen allied commanders and five U.S. ambassadors who had trooped through his office over the past decade had
come to see his government as weak, incompetent, and corrupt—a
source of the country's problems rather than their solution. Many
maneuvered to work around him and a few conspired to get rid of
him. Richard Holbrooke, the veteran diplomat who was regional

envoy for the first two years of the Obama administration, made little effort to conceal his distaste for Karzai. He and Eikenberry had encouraged other Afghans to run for president in the August 2009 presidential election in hopes of defeating Karzai. Robert M. Gates, the defense secretary from 2006 to 2011, later lamented how "our clumsy and failed putsch" had done lasting damage to the relationship with Karzai.[2]

By the time the new ambassador arrived, "he was a different Hamid Karzai than the one I had worked with a decade earlier," Crocker said. "Deeply suspicious, deeply embittered toward us."

Karzai's long tenure had also given him political skills that didn't make life easier for the Americans. He had learned that challenging the Americans, who were increasingly unpopular, could strengthen his own political support. He knew that by creating a crisis he could keep the Americans off balance and force them to listen to him. "He used erratic behavior as a technique," said former ambassador Marc Grossman, who succeeded Holbrooke as special envoy to Afghanistan and Pakistan.

On July 24, Crocker arrived at the embassy complex, a jumble of dirty-yellow office buildings and residential trailers that now had a $4 billion budget and a larger staff than any U.S. diplomatic facility in the world. He was sworn in as ambassador and made a promise to Afghans. Americans were weary of the war, he acknowledged to his audience, and wanted the Afghans to take a lead role in the fight. But America would not pull out abruptly as it did in the early 1990s, he said, because that had led to a devastating Afghan civil war and attracted to the country the Al Qaeda extremists who had planned the 9/11 attacks. "Frankly, we left the wrong way in the early 1990s, and we all know the history of those decisions: the civil war, the rise of the Taliban, sanctuary for Al Qaeda, and 9/11," Crocker said. "There will be no rush for the exits." Privately, he hoped Washington wouldn't make a liar of him.

After the swearing in, Crocker went with Allen to the presidential palace to formally present his diplomatic credentials to Karzai. Karzai greeted Crocker like an old friend, gripping his arm, his dark eyes twinkling. Crocker told how, in his first meeting with Karzai in 2002, they had met in the same small office, at a time when the palace's heating was broken and the windows had been shot out. Now he and Allen, he said, were going to build a partnership of equals with the Afghan leadership and would consult with the palace on all issues. It was what Karzai wanted to hear, and he welcomed the new team warmly. A new era of cordial relations, it seemed, had begun.

Or maybe not. Soon after Allen returned to his office, an aide rushed in with a copy of the press release that the presidential palace had put out about the meeting. "Have you seen this, sir?" the aide asked. The palace's statement was a stunner: it made it appear that Karzai had delivered an ultimatum to the general, demanding that the American halt all military operations that could harm Afghan civilians, including aircraft flights and night raids through Afghan homes. The impression was that Karzai had "imposed himself on the heathens that had come to see him," Allen said. "It was a lesson for me. There's the reality of the meeting, then there's the intended perception."

Karzai had gotten into the habit of holding friendly meetings with American officials, then blasting them minutes later in scalding public statements aimed at strengthening his support among Afghans. Karzai did it repeatedly to Allen—and also to U.S. defense secretary Leon Panetta and to President Barack Obama himself. The Americans ground their teeth but put up with it because they needed Karzai. "Never in history has any superpower spent so much money, sent so many troops to a country and had so little influence over what its president says and does," a European diplomat told the *New York Times*.[3]

Karzai didn't scorch Crocker. The two agreed in an early meeting they wouldn't publicly criticize each other and they largely stuck by it. Much as he had done with Prime Minister Nouri al-Maliki in Iraq, Crocker spent long hours listening to the Afghan president, showing the deference Karzai craved, and consulting him on decisions in a way Crocker's predecessors had not. Crocker understood the whipsawing political pressures on Karzai and knew he had been invited by the Taliban to choose the lamppost that they would one day hang him from. Crocker continued defending Karzai long after he left Afghanistan. While Karzai was emotional, scheming, and erratic, he was also, in Crocker's view, patriotic and resourceful in binding a country always on the verge of an explosion. "He's got the world's hardest job, and he's had it for more than a decade," Crocker said.

Crocker formed a partnership with General Allen, a thirty-five-year Marine veteran with a commanding voice and a classic high-and-tight Corps haircut. As he had done with General David Petraeus at the start of their Iraq posting, Crocker commiserated with Allen about the impossible challenges they faced. There simply might not be time, they agreed, to accomplish the mission they had been given. Allen had forty-four months to cut the troop level from 150,000 to around 15,000 and pare the number of bases from 830 to about 12. As he did that, he had to turn the lead role over to Afghanistan's 30,000 troops. "I had to keep all that from looking like a stampede," Allen said. "And I had to do it all while in contact with the enemy. We had our work cut out for us."

As Allen planned the military downsizing, Crocker had to scale back the mammoth U.S. effort to rebuild the country. The United States had spent $90 billion since 2002 to improve public services and infrastructure in hopes of winning the loyalty of average Afghans for the Kabul government. As regional envoy, Richard Holbrooke had pushed in the first days of the Obama administration for a "civilian surge" that would supercharge the aid program. By the time Crocker arrived, the embassy had 1,245 civilian specialists from eighteen federal agencies and around 1,000 contract employees—the largest American civilian force ever fielded for a nation-building effort. But Crocker and the U.S. team decided they had overshot the mark. The problem was not too little civilian help but too much.

These civilian teams, working with the military and Afghans, had built schools, health clinics, and irrigation projects, and sought to lay the groundwork for independent courts and honest public agencies. But it proved harder than expected to create a Western-style national system of public services. In some areas they made progress; in others it was held back by incompetence, corruption, or simple lack of public interest. Afghanistan, unlike Iraq, had never had such government services, and creating such a system was a radical social overhaul that would take decades. "We did a lot of really good stuff," said former ambassador James Cunningham, who after a year as number two succeeded Crocker as ambassador. "But the notion that we were going to use that to build up something that looked like a modern government—that's a long-term proposition. Much longer than we had time for."

In the meantime the rebuilding effort had become a parallel system of government. Afghans went to them when they wanted something, but it didn't build loyalty for the government in Kabul, because the locals saw the apparatus as another appendage of the American occupation. That enraged Karzai, who saw the system as another American effort to usurp his government's authority. "I turn on the TV and I see Americans doing things Afghans are supposed to do," he complained.

Many of the civilian specialists had never really made it into the villages and hamlets where most Afghans lived. Of the 1,245, some 700 were congregated in Kabul, where they seemed to fill their time holding meetings with each other. The size of this civilian force had another drawback: it meant there were lots of people whose safety the chain of command had to worry about. All this convinced the senior State Department officials on the scene that as the military force shrank, so, too, should the civilian host.

"One of our first jobs was to tell Secretary of State Clinton that we weren't putting any more people there," said former ambassador Marc Grossman, who succeeded Holbrooke in early 2011. "This idea that the counterinsurgency strategy would only work with more people—we were not buyers of that argument."

The embassy began a race to finish construction of the $1 billion worth of reconstruction projects that were on the books in early

2011. They needed to be finished, if possible, while there were still enough U.S. troops to ensure the builders' safety. But Crocker at times found it frustrating trying to speed up balky American agencies that had their own habits and priorities. At one morning staff meeting, Crocker fumed about the slow completion of an institute that was being built at the American University of Afghanistan to promote entrepreneurship. "The building is built—why are they telling me it's going to take two more years?" he demanded of his staff. "Just get it going. Do it."

Crocker overhauled the way the embassy worked. Eikenberry, Crocker's predecessor, was a punctilious former three-star general who had kept tight control over the embassy's information flow. He had embassy staffers filing regular reports and attending regular meetings to keep him informed of all they did. Eikenberry sometimes returned the reports with corrections. But many on the staff complained that their reporting duties prevented them from doing much else. Crocker junked much of the system. "What are these meetings?" he asked. "They're going away."

Crocker became convinced that the key to building a new Afghanistan was the younger generation, including the women, which was eager to connect with the outside world. Many of the country's young women had been left out of the education system for sixteen years of civil war and Taliban rule, and badly lagged behind the men. Crocker increased scholarship and remedial education programs for Afghan women and did what he could to encourage private groups that supported them.

One day he met with a group of eager students at the American University in Afghanistan who were trying to form a women's basketball team. When they told him their biggest problem was the lack of teams to practice with, he promised them that the embassy women's basketball team would play with them. When he returned to the embassy, he told the staff of his promise. Which embassy team was that? women on the staff asked. "The one we're going to form," he said. So women from the embassy and U.S. military units formed a team and scrimmaged with the Afghan women. They took up a collection to support the Afghans, including for purchase of the sports version of the hijab, the traditional women's head covering that relied on Velcro strips to keep them in place.

Crocker was impatient with the staff who complained about the hardships of life in Kabul. Even though the State Department had poured money into the embassy complex to make it more livable, the staff still had to put up with long hours of work, institutional food, separation from their families, and tight restrictions on their movements. For security reasons they were largely confined to the complex, sometimes called "the Kabubble." The embassy's bar was called "the Duck and Cover." All this came with the territory, in Crocker's view. "Where the fuck do they think we are, Brussels?" he told aides.

In September 2011, insurgents sent a scare through the embassy and NATO headquarters by raining down rocket-propelled grenades and small-arms fire from a half-built fourteen-story building nearby. The attack, an attempt by the jihadists to show Westerners were vulnerable even in fortress Kabul, lasted nineteen hours, killing sixteen. None of the casualties were embassy staff, but many on the staff were forced to stay in bunkers for half a day, and some were shaken by the experience.

Eileen O'Connor, the embassy's communications director, suggested to Crocker that he hold a staff meeting to talk over what had happened, reassure them, and thank them for their efforts. Crocker was skeptical.

"Is this Brussels? We've been under attack before," Crocker told O'Connor. When she pressed him again, he grumbled. "I don't do touchy-feely very well," he said.

"Well, try," she said.

He gave in, held the meeting, and told the staff he was proud of their efforts. He was sincere, and the staff was appreciative. He had done touchy-feely pretty well, O'Connor decided. The next time the embassy was attacked, he volunteered to hold a similar staff session.

After long years in war zones, Crocker had refined his approach to personal security. During his last posting in Iraq, he had usually traveled in thundering block-long motorcades that included up-armored Chevy Suburbans, military vehicles mounted with M60 machine guns, and a screen of Humvees. Everyone for blocks around knew the American VIPs were on the road, and it made them a large target. By the time he reached his sixth ambassa-dorship, he had decided he was safer traveling less conspicuously and leaving part of the security team at the embassy. He would go out with just a couple of Toyota SUVs that had no telltale fancy antennas and were muddied up enough to blend in with the grimy parade of Kabul traffic. "We looked just like everybody else out there," he said.[4] Sometimes, for security reasons, Crocker didn't give Afghan officials advance notice he was coming for a visit. If they didn't know he was coming, Crocker reasoned, neither would the jihadists.

From time to time Crocker slipped away from the embassy to take part in secret peace talks that had begun months before between the Afghan government and Taliban-allied groups. The Taliban's official position was that it wouldn't negotiate while there were foreign troops in the country. In fact, there were continu-ing contacts between the Afghan government and various jihadist groups, including the Quetta Shura, the Pakistan-based govern-ing council of the Taliban, and Hezb-i-Islami, a group founded by the brutal former prime minister Gulbuddin Hekmatyar. The talks made no headway, but both sides thought it was worthwhile to hear what the other side was saying. The jihadists sneaked across the Pakistani border and were guaranteed security once they reached Kabul. The meetings had to be top secret because of the risks to the Taliban from the Pakistanis. Islamabad feared a deal that would shortchange their interests and let it be known that if they caught a Taliban emissary en route to Kabul they would throw him in jail to rot. Obaidullah Akhund, a former Taliban defense minister, had been captured and jailed in those circumstances in 2010, and had died in prison. "If we get caught doing this, we're going to wind up like Obaidullah," the Taliban envoys told Crocker.[5]

Even when the meetings went nowhere, Crocker had to acknowledge he enjoyed contact with the wild-haired jihadis from across
the Sulaiman Mountains. "I like meeting the bad guys—it's kind
of fun," he said.[6]

His second Afghan tour was punishing for Crocker, even by the
standards of his past missions. His wife, Christine, did not accom-
pany him on the assignment, for the first time ever. His movement
disorder, worsened by stress, hampered his work. The doctors continued trying different drugs on the mysterious ailment but never
found the right one. He had to give up his running routine, his
favorite way of relieving stress. As the tour continued, his fatigue
increased. Some days he looked shaky, colleagues noticed.

Crocker was unhappy that, back home in America, the critics of the Afghan mission seemed to be winning the public debate
and undervaluing, in his view, the gains that had been made by the
American effort. Congressional analyses and intelligence agency
assessments painted a gloomy picture of the mission's prospects.
News stories about the war emphasized U.S. troop deaths, Afghan
civilian casualties, corruption, wasted U.S. tax dollars, and other
complications, large and small.

In August 2011 the embassy had to sort out what to do with the
dozens of feral cats that haunted the embassy complex. The animals
had bitten and scratched staff members, raising fears of rabies and
prompting the embassy staff to hold meetings to consider whether it
was time to thin the herd. When the subject caught the attention of
the press, the world's cat lovers were horrified. "Veteran diplomat
Ryan C. Crocker can handle Islamist insurgencies, hostile heads of
state and management of some of the world's largest embassies,"
the *Washington Post* wrote. "But what's he going to do about the
cats?"[7] More than two hundred readers wrote to the *Post*, most in
outrage. Crocker was not amused. "If anyone says the word 'cat' to
me, I'm going to kill them," he told the staff when he showed up at
his office that morning.

Crocker's posting as ambassador was, in fact, the second time
the Obama administration had made a run at hiring him. In the

spring of 2010, Secretary of State Clinton, angry at what she considered Eikenberry's insubordination, had proposed bringing in
Crocker to replace him. General Petraeus, then the CIA director,
had approached Crocker to sound him out. Crocker had seemed
open to the job but stipulated that he would not work for Holbrooke, who was special envoy until his death in December 2010.
Crocker knew of Holbrooke's battles with Karzai and Pakistani
officials and believed Holbrooke was only complicating U.S. relations with the region. "The only thing that the Afghans and Pakistanis agreed on was that they didn't like Holbrooke," Crocker
said later. But in 2010, officials on the White House national security staff were still firmly behind Eikenberry, and vetoed Clinton's
suggestion.[8]

When Crocker was finally hired a year later, he had a special
status. It was understood that, at this point in his career, Washington needed him more than he needed them. He had an easy relationship with Clinton that was much like the one he had had with
Secretary of State Condoleezza Rice when he was ambassador to
Iraq. When a problem arose, Clinton called him and asked to be
filled in. "It was, 'Tell us what's going on there—what should we
do about it?'" he said. "Not to give you ultimatums or orders."

When lower-level officials in Washington wanted Crocker to
stay up until 2:00 a.m. Kabul time for a videoconference meeting
on a topic he thought had secondary importance, he could refuse.
"You can hold that meeting, but you'll be looking at a bunch of
empty chairs," he told them. Crocker had worked with many of the
players in Washington and could call them directly to try to solve
problems.

On some issues he got his way. On others, he didn't win but
kept trying. In the internal discussions, Crocker and others on the
U.S. team in Afghanistan regularly made the case that Washington
should not pull out too abruptly from Afghanistan. Although President Obama had set 2014 as the target date for shifting U.S. forces
into a supporting role, the manner of the U.S. exit was unresolved,
with different factions arguing for a faster or slower unwinding.

The top embassy officials believed the U.S. mission would need to continue for years to strengthen the Kabul government enough to stand on its own.

"We were all fighting with Washington about that; the conversations were constant," said one diplomat.

A top priority was working out a pair of written agreements that would define a new relationship with the Afghans as U.S. combat forces drew down. One, a "strategic partnership agreement," defined in broad terms how the countries would support each other. The second, the "bilateral security agreement," would fill out the specifics of troop levels and continuing military ties. The agreements seemed like a manageable undertaking, since both sides wanted them. They would give Karzai a pledge of continued American support; they would signal that the United States was winding down its military commitment, although there would be a continuing effort to train the Afghan military, fight terrorism, and strengthen the Afghan state. Even so, in Crocker's ten months, the first of the two, the partnership agreement, constantly teetered near collapse as crises buffeted the relationship. Just as with the agreements Crocker negotiated with the Iraqis in 2008, these deals touched on the most sensitive issues of sovereignty and national pride. "We never knew where this was going to come out," said James Cunningham, the embassy's number two, who handled the nuts and bolts of the negotiations.

The Afghan officials negotiating the agreements, led by defense minister Abdul Rahim Wardak, were generally easy for the Americans to deal with. But all the real decisions were made at the presidential palace by Karzai. He would review all the important language. When he was upset, either about the negotiations or other events, he would demand concessions. Often he made demands the Americans would never accept. He would sometimes demand an ironclad mutual defense agreement that would obligate Washington to protect Kabul from any threat. Or he would ask for high-tech weapons, like top-of-the-line F-22 fighter aircraft, that his country could not afford to buy or maintain. Sometimes he balked at provisions because he thought their language implied that Afghanistan was a lesser partner.

Several times Crocker rose from the negotiating table and announced that the talks couldn't continue. "We have nothing more to talk about," he said. "You guys aren't serious. Call me if you come to your senses." And ordinarily the Afghan team would rush to the palace to try to convince Karzai that his latest demands had to be dropped.

Two chronic sources of conflict were the conduct of nighttime counterterror raids and the handling of Afghan prisoners. U.S. officials believed nighttime raids were an essential way to root out the most threatening jihadists, and conducted 2,200 of them in 2011. But Karzai was enraged by cases where civilians were killed or injured in operations and by what he saw as the routine humiliation of ordinary Afghans by the invasion of their homes. Similarly, U.S. military officials believed their detention of militants was essential. They needed access to the militants for interrogations and worried that if the Afghans were in charge, the militants might be freed or, following Afghan custom, tortured. The Afghans believed that, as a sovereign government, they should handle prisoners of their own country.

As the negotiations continued, relations between the governments were regularly disrupted by crises over U.S. military operations. Allen called these "meteor strikes." Sometimes they arose over military blunders, such as when Western troops fired on supposed Taliban fighters who turned out to be civilians—sometimes women gathering firewood. There were intermittent crises over the tragic road accidents that occurred when Afghan villagers were run down by military vehicles. U.S. infantry often patrolled with fourteen-ton "mine-resistant ambush-protected" vehicles, or MRAPs. The hulking vehicles were heavily armored to protect troops from roadside bombs, but their weight meant they were sometimes unable to stop fast enough to avoid hitting the pedestrians or civilian vehicles that darted in front of them. The casualties were often children.

Sometimes the top U.S. officials would show up at the palace with a long agenda of business to conduct and find that Karzai wanted to vent about a mishap. It might last an hour. "Karzai would growl at me and Ryan would put his hand on my arm and say, 'Now be calm, it's going to be OK. He's got some things to say—let him say them,'" Allen said.

Between the fall of 2011 and the following spring, there was a series of incidents that threatened lasting damage. In January 2012 there was an outcry over a YouTube video in which U.S. Marines in Helmand were seen urinating on the dead body of a Taliban fighter and posing with mutilated Taliban body parts. "What's wrong with your troops?" Karzai demanded of Crocker and Allen. "Why would they do this? No one touches a dead Muslim but a live Muslim."

The same month brought an alarming attack by an Afghan soldier on French troops who were trying to train his unit. Attacks by Afghan troops on U.S. and European trainers had been occurring intermittently for years. Now they were accelerating, in part because militants believed such casualties would build domestic pressure in Europe and the United States for troop withdrawal. Eighty-two military advisers were killed in fifty-two such attacks between the beginning of 2010 and mid-July 2012.[9]

In the January 2012 attack, an Afghan soldier in the eastern Kapisa Province turned an automatic rifle on French military trainers, killing four and injuring seventeen. The attacker believed he had been instructed in a dream to attack the Westerners over the video showing troops urinating on dead insurgents. The French accelerated the withdrawal of their 4,000 troops from Afghanistan, and it looked like other countries in the NATO alliance might also exit. The entire Western strategy revolved around training Afghan forces to manage the war, and if the advisers left, the strategy would collapse.

Marc Grossman, the special envoy, feared the attacks could be the beginning of the end in Afghanistan, shifting public support as the Tet offensive had done in 1968 during the Vietnam War. *If we have fifty of these things in the next two months, we'll be out of here*, he thought.

Karzai did not calm the uproar over the killings but fed it. The killings, he declared, were an understandable response to American abuses of Afghans. "You've been worse occupiers than the Soviets, you've walked on our sanctity at home, why should you expect not to be killed like this?" he told Allen and Crocker. "You're getting what you deserve." Allen put in a call to General Martin Dempsey, the chairman of the Joint Chiefs of Staff, and exploded. "Calm down, John, calm down," Dempsey told him. Allen and other U.S. officials visited NATO headquarters in Brussels to lobby the allies not to depart Afghanistan, and the threat diminished.

Another crisis erupted on February 22, when young Army soldiers at the prison at Bagram Air Base mistakenly threw five hundred copies of the Koran into a burn pit for destruction.[10] The staff at the detention center were taking away religious texts that prisoners had been using to send secret messages to each other. The plan had been to destroy the religious papers under the supervision of imams. Somewhere along the way, however, those plans were lost. When Afghan staff saw what was happening, they were horrified, and waded into the pit to try to save the holy books. Several were seriously burned.

Allen realized that this incident, too, posed a serious threat to the mission. One year before, a mob had attacked the United Nations mission in the north central city of Mazar-e-Sharif, killing seven, including three European diplomats, over the burning of a Koran by an anti-Muslim American preacher in Florida. The incident had drawn little attention in Afghanistan until Karzai had denounced it as a "disrespectful and abhorrent act." After that mob attack, Karzai said Americans should expect such reactions, words that seemed to excuse the violence.

This time Allen and Crocker understood they needed to try to get ahead of the fallout. They went immediately to the presidential palace to express their regrets to Karzai and to try to convince him to put out a statement asking Afghans to remain calm. Much as he had done in Iraq to forestall Sunni-Shia violence, Crocker helped fashion the statement. It was crafted so that Karzai was urging an end to violence, even while not excusing what Afghans would consider the latest American outrage. Karzai did what the Americans asked because he realized the public reaction could be so violent that he himself might be driven from office. Allen rushed out a videotaped message in which he apologized for the incident. "I assure you—I promise you—this was not intentional in any way," Allen said. Crocker reached out to other Afghan leaders to express remorse and try to absorb some of their anger.

Even so, a mob soon gathered outside Bagram's gates and began lobbing stones and gasoline bombs. In the first five days after the burnings, thirty people were killed, including four Americans, and more than two hundred were injured. Among the dead were two U.S. military advisers who were shot in the backs of their heads as they sat at their desks in police headquarters in Kabul. U.S. troops were ordered for two weeks to stay out of public view because the sight of them "would be just gasoline on the fire," Crocker said later.[11]

As the brutal week ended, with American nerves frayed, Karzai met with Crocker and Allen at the palace. Although Karzai had tried to calm the Afghan public, he wasn't willing to let the episode pass, lacing again into the American team. He again told the Americans that their troops were worse than the former Soviet occupiers, because the Russians hadn't burned Korans. "I wouldn't blame a lot of Afghan soldiers for wanting to kill American soldiers," Karzai said. Crocker had to restrain Allen from storming out of the palace.[12]

On March 11, as negotiators closed in on a final deal, a crisis erupted when U.S. Army staff sergeant Robert Bales went on a nighttime killing spree in Kandahar Province, murdering sixteen villagers, including nine children. Karzai exploded, demanding that by the following year U.S. troops be entirely confined to major bases and that plans for U.S. withdrawal be accelerated. His pronouncement threatened to wreck the carefully developed plan for a gradual NATO withdrawal. Crocker and Allen hurried to try to calm him down. Four days later, before going to bed, President Obama called Karzai to talk about their plans and had what he thought was a pleasant twenty-minute conversation. But later that day, after a meeting with relatives of the dead Afghans, Karzai became enraged once more and declared again that U.S. troops were to be confined to bases in 2013. U.S. officials decided they had no choice but to try to play down the dispute and hope they could soon get Karzai back on track. "Sometimes the rhetoric gets a little bit heated," Crocker told a television interviewer.[13] Karzai was coaxed, in time, to return to the agreed-upon plan.

Another point of friction was the secret peace overtures the Obama administration had been making to the Taliban for the past two years. With the earlier Kabul-Taliban talks yielding nothing, U.S. officials wanted to see if they could lay the groundwork for more productive negotiations. They also hoped that, as part of the discussions, they might win the release of Bowe Bergdahl, an Army infantryman who had deserted in 2009 and been captured by the Taliban. Karzai was deeply uneasy about the conversations, fearing Washington might make a deal with his enemies that would imperil his position and his government's.

In December 2011, during an international conference on Afghanistan in Bonn, Germany, Grossman and Crocker sat down with Karzai for a discussion of the talks. Grossman was about to head to Qatar for a meeting with Taliban envoys. But when Grossman gave his presentation, Karzai erupted, launching into a denunciation of the peace effort that lasted for more than an hour. At one point Karzai accused Grossman of killing Burhanuddin Rabbani, former head of the country's high peace council, who had been assassinated three months earlier by a militant who had wrapped a bomb in his turban.

"Marc, you killed Professor Rabbani so you could have these negotiations all to yourself!" Karzai told him. Grossman and Crocker were stunned. "We couldn't believe this was happening," Grossman said.

The following day, Karzai, Crocker, and Grossman had lunch with Secretary of State Clinton. Karzai boiled over again. "Why

have you not kept me informed of these talks?" he demanded. He had, in fact, been kept up to date, and a few months earlier had even urged the Americans to accelerate the conversations. Karzai accused the officials of trying to exclude the Afghans and insisted that his team had to be part of any future conversations. Grossman realized he had no choice but to cancel his imminent meeting with the Taliban. Taliban officials were outraged at the cancellation, viewing it as proof of American bad faith. The Bonn sessions "turned into a disaster for our peace efforts," Clinton wrote later.[14]

The following month, in January 2012, Grossman decided to try once more to get Karzai on board with the Taliban contacts. When he and Crocker showed up at the presidential palace, Karzai again erupted repeatedly. Each time, Crocker asked Grossman to put up with it. "Be patient," he whispered. "This is going to be OK." Sure enough, the next day they returned to the palace and found Karzai in a completely different mood. He was fine with the meeting with the Taliban. Grossman flew to Qatar, but the Taliban, still angry over January's snub, shut down the talks.

The negotiations on the partnership deal, meanwhile, gained ground slowly. The two sides finally worked out compromises that seemed to resolve their battles over American night raids and control of Taliban prisoners. In March the two sides signed a compromise deal that promised to give the Afghan government control of all 3,200 prisoners over the next six months while providing U.S. forces a veto over which militants could be released. In April they worked out a compromise on the night raids as well. This deal put the Afghans officially in charge of the night operations but allowed the U.S. officials to seek Afghan permission for raids and gave them an important continuing role in carrying them out. U.S. officials were confident they would continue to have a chance to interrogate the prisoners when they felt it was crucial. Washington would continue paying billions to cover Afghan military expenses, and that gave the Pentagon powerful leverage.

With the issues seemingly settled, the negotiating team reached agreement on the strategic partnership agreement in April. The deal was still controversial among some Afghans, who feared it meant an indefinite American presence. Iran, also alarmed at that prospect, spread money among Afghan peace council members to buy votes against it. The council members, showing customary Afghan independence, took their money—and voted for the deal.

President Obama flew to Kabul on May 1 to sign the agreement. Arriving in the middle of the night for security reasons, Obama brought differing and somewhat contradictory messages for the several audiences he wanted to reach. In his remarks he promised Americans at home that he was winding down the war. He told Afghans that America was still committed to helping them, and tried to convince the Taliban that Washington would not allow them to retake control of the country.

The partnership deal committed the United States to supporting the Afghan government for a decade after its combat troops departed at the end of 2014, in addition to helping build its institutions and education system. Washington didn't make specific financial commitments, which led some observers to describe it as a largely symbolic event. Crocker and Allen saw it differently, as an important commitment that had reached a successful conclusion despite constant threats.

The agreement was in peril up to the moment it was signed. Karzai had invited hundreds of Afghan officials from all over the country to attend the ceremony. But in the early hours of the morning, the U.S. Secret Service added a requirement than anyone who wanted to attend had to agree to have his turban searched. This was necessary, in the Secret Service's view, because the Taliban had begun planting bombs in turbans. From the Afghan perspective, routine security pat-downs were offensive and turban searches were a humiliation. Karzai was outraged and threatened to avoid the ceremony altogether. He wasn't willing to ask the visiting tribal leaders, a key part of his political coalition, to submit to a search. It fell to Crocker and Allen to find a solution. In the minutes before the signing, they worked out an arrangement in which dozens of the Afghan VIPs wouldn't need to come through security checks but would watch the events on television from Karzai's residence, two hundred meters from the signing. "Those are the kinds of things that never make it into the history books," said Allen. "But they happen. It was a difficult moment."

Three weeks after Obama's visit, the State Department announced that Crocker would leave his post one year ahead of the original plan. Crocker's illness, exacerbated by stress, was getting worse. Crocker had done what Obama had most wanted, restoring the conversation with the palace and completing the partnership deal. In July, after a final NATO meeting in Chicago where other alliance members promised to continue to pitch in to support Afghanistan, Crocker ended his last tour. He said goodbye and thanked his aides. It wasn't his habit to be effusive in such moments. He caught up with his deputy, James Cunningham, in a hallway. "This deal wouldn't have happened without you," Crocker told him. It was a succinct and unemotional conclusion to a year of tempest. "But this was high praise and I appreciated it," said Cunningham.

As in Iraq, a large part of Crocker's contribution had been in keeping the strained relationships functioning. "Ryan had come as close as anyone to having working, sensitive, positive relations with Karzai," said Grossman. Even then, the harmony was often short-lived.

In the months after Crocker left, the two sides resumed work on the bilateral security agreement, spelling out the details of the continuing military relationship. The battles over the night raids and prisoners resumed with new ferocity. Allen and Karzai had a series of ugly confrontations at the presidential palace. Although Karzai had signed an agreement on prisoners in the spring of 2012, he began to balk at its terms by the fall of the year, insisting that he have full control over who was to be freed. In one session Karzai demanded that Allen turn over all the Afghan prisoners by 4:30 that afternoon. "Mr. President, that isn't going to happen," Allen told him. "Not only isn't it going to happen, this meeting is over." When Allen shifted forward in his chair, Karzai and his aides looked alarmed. Their eyes widened. "For a brief moment, I think the Afghans were afraid the meeting was going to take a really bad turn," Allen recalled later. After he left the palace, Karzai issued a blistering press release that stopped just short of calling Allen a war criminal.

Yet through the fights and frustrations, Allen and Karzai needed to preserve a working relationship. They found a way. When Allen left Afghanistan in February 2013, they were on cordial personal terms, as Karzai and Crocker had been.

In the four years after Crocker left, Obama administration officials continued a long internal debate about how much of a continuing commitment they wanted to make to Afghanistan. The White House went back and forth on how large a force would remain and how long it would stay. The commitment ended up smaller and briefer than was expected when Crocker and his team arrived in 2011. And the U.S.-Afghan partnership deal was "undercut by the uncertainty . . . and the appearance that we were withdrawing rather than establishing a long-term relationship," said Cunningham.

As soon as he left the post, Crocker began making his case publicly that the administration could not afford an abrupt exit from Afghanistan. He told American audiences that the country's $1 trillion expenditure had given a new generation of young people a chance to make Afghanistan into a normal modern society. If the Americans exit too soon, "who would get it in the neck?" he asked. "All those people we've made promises to. Starting with the women."[15]

# CHAPTER 14

# Libya Loses a Friend

Chris Stevens returned to Libya as ambassador in late May 2012 and found a country intoxicated with its liberation. Cars roared along the Tripoli waterfront with tricolored Libyan flags whipping from their antennas. Spray-painted graffiti hailed the revolution and denounced the fallen dictator. Posters advertised the names of the new political groups that were organizing for elections. And Libyans were grateful to the Westerners who had helped deliver them. They honked and waved to Stevens when they spotted him crossing the street. Many had already met him, and those who hadn't knew he was a celebrity. "The whole atmosphere has changed for the better," Stevens emailed family and friends. "People smile more and are much more open with foreigners. American, French and British are enjoying unusual popularity. Let's hope it lasts."

At the same time Stevens saw the country faced sobering challenges. Support for the shaky rebel government was declining. The country had no army or police, no traffic control, and no trash pickup. The hundreds of rival *katiba*s, or militias, were refusing to give up their weapons and battling among themselves. The militias threw up checkpoints to control streets and challenged other armed groups and the remnants of the Libyan army. The European and Arab governments that helped engineer Muammar el-Qaddafi's downfall were turning their attention elsewhere.

With the war over, officials in Washington, too, were spending less time thinking about Libya and looking for a new, lower-cost approach. In the period before Stevens arrived, the small U.S. mission in Tripoli seemed adrift. Officials in Washington worried that the embassy team didn't have the expertise to collaborate with U.N. officials in helping Libyans build a normal state. To the U.S. team on the ground, it looked as though officials in Washington were indecisive about what they wanted from the embassy. It required six weeks of internal debate for Washington to figure out whether to add a defense attaché or if that would violate the president's prohibition on "boots on the ground" in Libya. Senior officials looked to Stevens to figure it out. Before the new ambassador left Washington, Deputy Secretary of State Bill Burns asked him to spend the next six months assessing the country's condition and preparing a proposal on what the administration should do in Libya.

With the embassy sacked during the insurgency, the U.S. diplomats were working from a converted house and living in a high-walled compound near the Tripoli airport that had formerly housed Norwegian oil workers. The compound had about fifteen buildings, each of which now housed a handful of Americans. Stevens moved into the elegant villa with pool, patios, and resplendent lawn that had been occupied by his predecessor, Gene Cretz.

Stevens threw himself into renewing old relationships and fattening up his Rolodex with the names of everyone who was important or might be. Even after his earlier two tours, he believed the U.S. team still lacked needed details about Libyan society and politics because of America's four-decade absence. He was up every morning at 6:00 a.m. to go jogging with his security detail. Then he would sit down at his breakfast table with political section chief David McFarland and divide up the contacts they needed to make that day. Phone communications were poor, so Stevens relied on a primitive Toshiba gadget that allowed him to text his contacts. The device required digital calisthenics, but Stevens had become an expert at banging out the letters.

In his first month as ambassador, Stevens and his team focused most closely on the upcoming July 7 parliamentary elections. The elections, the first democratic balloting since 1964, were an important step toward creation of a legitimate government. "The conventional wisdom was, if we get through this election, we'll have Libya on a path where it will be all right," said Lieutenant Colonel Brian Linvill, Stevens's defense attaché.

Stevens and his team offered help on almost all aspects of the election: advising on security, paying for printing of ballots, and counseling officials on steps to make sure the elections were free and fair. As the election approached, there were worries that the polling might be marred by violence or fraud or would simply be ignored by Libyans. There were fears that the Islamists, who seemed best organized, might emerge with the strongest hand in the new government.

But the elections exceeded expectations, with a 62 percent turnout and 94 percent of polling places opened as expected. The coalition led by the interim government's executive board chairman, Mahmoud Jibril, a relative moderate, took thirty-nine of the eighty parliamentary seats reserved for party-list candidates. The Justice and Construction Party, an Islamist group dominated by the Muslim Brotherhood, was a distant second with seven. The Al Watan Party of Abdelhakim Belhaj, who had been a jihadist in Afghanistan, won no seats, although it had tried to portray itself as moderate by putting an unveiled woman at the head of its ticket.

The election opened the way for the transitional government to hand power to a democratically chosen General National Congress. The election "has gone better than I think almost anybody in the international community or the international media expected," said Ian Martin, the Briton who then led the U.N. mission in Libya. President Obama congratulated the Libyans for "another milestone on their extraordinary transition to democracy."

But Stevens and his staff cabled Washington with some cautions. The results should not be read, they said, as a sweep for the liberals. The political leanings of the lawmakers without party affiliations, who held 120 of 200 seats, were still unclear. And Islamists still had enough leverage to hold up action in the parliament because of rules that required a two-thirds vote to pass legislation. In time it became clear that many of the unaffiliated members did, in fact, have Islamist leanings.

Stevens had a nuanced view of Libya's prospects. He had high confidence in the many friends he had made in the country and believed that with its oil riches Libya could become the greatest success story from the Arab Spring revolutions. Before returning to Libya, he had defended the country's prospects in a conversation with his friend Roya Hakakian. Hakakian told him she feared that the Libyan revolution, like the 1979 Iranian revolution she had lived through, was at risk of a takeover by radicals. The United States had only a narrow window, she told him, to prevent that from happening. "Chris' face was unusually flushed as he listened," she wrote later. "He was far more hopeful about the future. This was not the first time we had disagreed. Only this time I felt I had hurt him. Chris had fallen in love with Libya's revolution."[1]

But Stevens also recognized the country's weakness. The government and military were gossamer, the militias strong, and the national institutions that bind most countries nonexistent. In cables to Washington, he and the team would hedge. In the customary comment section, they would write that while the outlook was generally favorable, uncertainty remained, in part because of the troubling figures who were joining the government. Among Stevens's regular contacts were some tough customers, including some Islamists in the small coalition of Muslim Brotherhood–related parties who had been held as terrorism suspects at the U.S. military prison in Guantánamo Bay, Cuba. "He met with some pretty bad characters," a diplomat said. One of them, a former jihadist, became a deputy defense minister, an official the Americans had to meet with regularly.

Stevens tried to keep channels open with the militants, both to gather intelligence on who they were and to try to win cooperation. He ventured into militia barracks, usually former schoolhouses or police stations that now bustled with armed men in fatigues and round Afghan *pakul* hats. He stayed up one night until 3:00 a.m. with a commander who had waged jihad in Afghanistan, roaming between topics ranging from the radical Islamic theorist Sayyid Qutb to East German political philosophy. The long gab didn't change the jihadist's convictions but seemed to make a personal connection. The result was: "There's one more Islamist coming away thinking, 'Hey, it's OK to talk to the ambassador,'" a diplomat told Middle East scholar Frederic Wehrey. "This was exactly the sort of meetings Chris had."[2]

Stevens urged U.S. military officials to move cautiously in dealing with the Libyan armed forces. A young U.S. Army officer, Lieutenant Colonel Gregory Arndt, had been sent to Libya to oversee the arming and training of the national military. He had ambitious plans for improving the Libyans' capabilities. Stevens pointed out that the military was a hollow force and that there was much the Americans didn't know about the commanders. They might regret providing high-tech American weapons to Libyans who might not be trustworthy, he said.

Arndt came to recognize the wisdom of Stevens's advice. Libyan military officers approached him asking for some of the Pentagon's flashiest weaponry, including V-22 Osprey tilt-rotor aircraft and sophisticated antiaircraft missiles. But when Arndt talked to the officers, he realized few knew anything about weaponry or even the basics of the military craft. When he visited what had been described to him as an infantry battalion, he would find a handful of men sitting around on chairs holding rifles. "It wasn't until my third or fourth month there that I realized—there's nothing behind this curtain," Arndt said. "Ambassador Stevens understood that."

Washington assumed the Libyans had money from oil revenues to pay for the military they wanted. But when U.S. officials worked up estimates for the Libyans of the cost of the arms and services they requested, the Libyans wouldn't have the needed cash and the plan would die. Much of the new government's limited resources was going toward an expensive government commitment to pay salaries to the tens of thousands of militiamen.

The militias, meanwhile, were learning that when the new parliament issued orders to try to control them, the commanders could simply ignore them. "Power under Qaddafi was in the hands of one man," said Brian Linvill, then Stevens's defense attaché. "Power, post-Qaddafi, was in the hands of every man who carried a Kalashnikov."

The militia commanders constantly pressed the American officials for arms and training and other help. But the commanders' place in the real power structure "was completely opaque," Linvill said. "You'd meet a militia chief who said he was a brigade commander when in truth he commanded a hundred guys. You didn't know. It was all kind of rumor and hearsay."

Another of Stevens's assignments was helping in the roundup of Qaddafi's vast weapons inventory, which was scattered at bases and arms depots all over the country. Qaddafi had left behind a mountain of rifles and small-arms ammunition, shoulder-mounted antiaircraft missiles, chemical weapons ingredients, and the uranium concentrate called yellowcake used in the production of nuclear weapons. The highest U.S. priority was on getting hold of Soviet-built SA-7 shoulder-fired missiles, which officials worried could fall into the hands of terrorists and enable them to shoot down commercial aircraft. Stevens oversaw a force of contractors who roamed the country, negotiating with tribal and militia leaders to buy the missiles, then disabling them by smashing their infrared sensors with hammers.

Stevens thought Libya's nongovernment groups held the greatest promise, and he devoted time to working with charities, women's and youth groups, and private health and education organizations. The groups included many returned expatriates and some of his best friends. He was eager to increase scholarships for young Libyans and supported a public-private effort to build a new emergency medicine and training center at the Benghazi Medical Center.

Stevens built a circle of personal friends. He assembled a group that got together on weekends to barbecue, drink, and talk about nothing in particular. Liquor was officially banned in Libya, but his Libyan friends trusted Stevens to see that his parties wouldn't get them in trouble with authorities. It was a diverse group. One friend was the Libyan who had written the first draft of the Libyan constitution. Another was a man who had lived illegally in the United States for twenty years, running a liquor store in eastern Pennsylvania, and was deported after the 9/11 attacks. Stevens had no reason connected to work to cultivate him but happened to like him. Stevens came across a Libyan tennis pro who had trained some of the country's best players, and made him a regular hitting partner.

But even in his time off, Stevens began picking up worrying signs of the growing dangers he faced. One day the U.S. team discovered militants had posted on the Web a map of Stevens's regular running route through Tripoli. It was an alarming hint: either they were planning to attack or kidnap him or inviting others to do it. Stevens continued to run but varied his route.

While many Libyans remained grateful to Westerners, a dangerous minority were intent on driving them out. Diplomatic delegations, and international aid and nongovernment groups were increasingly a target, especially in the country's east. Many were gradually pulling out. Attackers fired rocket-propelled grenades at the Red Cross offices in Benghazi and hurled a homemade bomb at the United Nations envoy's motorcade. When militants fired a rocket-propelled grenade at the British ambassador's convoy and hit a parked vehicle, the British closed their Benghazi mission. The U.S. special mission in Benghazi was hit repeatedly. In April a Libyan on contract to guard the compound threw a homemade bomb over the mission's perimeter wall. In June, attackers blew a hole in the wall with another improvised bomb.

Some of the Islamists in Benghazi were demanding that the Americans all depart immediately. Ahmed Abu Khatallah, a former mechanic who led a small jihadist militia, raged about the U.S. compound that he mistakenly believed was a CIA station under diplomatic cover. "How can this be?" Abu Khatallah told a gathering at a Benghazi mosque in late 2011. "How can we allow spying among us?" A year later, he led the attack on the compound. In 2014 he was arrested by U.S. authorities, tried, and in 2018 sentenced to twenty-two years in a U.S. prison.

The U.S. team struggled to understand the militias of Benghazi. They were being paid and armed by the government to protect the public, including foreign governments' diplomatic missions. The city of Benghazi was supposedly protected by a coalition of militias cobbled into a single force. In reality it was run by a patchwork of local Islamist militias whose strength ebbed and flowed depending on the shifting alliances and loyalties of individual leaders.[3] Two militias might battle each other one day and work together the next. Many fighters belonged to multiple militias. And their attitudes about who and what they supported seemed constantly shifting.

On September 9, David McFarland, the political counselor at the embassy, met with Benghazi's most powerful militia leaders to try to get some answers. In a session at a Benghazi banquet hall, the Islamist commanders Wissam bin Ahmed of the Libya Shield 1 militia, and Muhammad al-Gharabi of the Rafa' al-Sahti Brigade and Libya Shield 2, laid out their strong but conflicted feelings about the Americans. They were grateful that U.S. forces had helped oust Qaddafi and loved American fast food and cars, they said. But they accused the Americans of supporting the former interim prime minister Mahmoud Jibril in upcoming elections for prime minister over the Muslim Brotherhood candidate they favored. If Jibril won, they warned, they would stop providing protection. They asked for more aid and wanted Washington to pressure American companies, including fast-food chains, to invest in the region. They couldn't clear up what various militias stood for. "They debated—hotly and without resolution—which brigades supported or opposed specific causes," McFarland wrote in a cable that went out under Stevens's name on September 11.[4]

McFarland got to his bottom line: "Is it safe for us in this city?" he asked. The answer was not clear.[5]

In July, Stevens received a visit from Bill Burns, the deputy secretary of state, who had been his boss for years in the Near Eastern Affairs bureau. Burns considered Stevens the most knowledgeable hand on Libya in any U.S. agency. After a day of meetings, the pair had a beer in Stevens's villa. Stevens was cautiously upbeat about the country and optimistic about his ability to make connections with the Libyans, while acknowledging the troubling security situation. Stevens told Burns he would be careful, for his own sake and that of the mission. But he said he knew "there was no such thing as zero risk in our profession," Burns wrote in his memoir. "That conversation has haunted me ever since."[6]

At least three times between June and September, Stevens asked Washington for more security for the U.S. facilities and staff. But the improvements were limited.[7] Lower-level security officials told him the department's security resources were stretched everywhere, and the Benghazi compound had low priority because of its temporary status.[8]

Stevens also turned down an offer of more help from the Pentagon because he feared a U.S. military contingent would increase risks rather than reduce them. The embassy in Tripoli had had a unit of sixteen special forces soldiers called a "site security team." But one night earlier that summer the special operators had tangled with some young Libyans living near the embassy. The U.S. team had gone out for an unexplained reason—possibly a jaunt to the beach, a trip that embassy officials would have frowned on. They were quickly stopped at a checkpoint in what the young Americans thought was an attempt to steal their vehicle. One of the U.S. troops fired at the Libyans, apparently hitting one of them.

Stevens had the shooter sent home to the United States. But he worried about the repercussions. The soldiers had no diplomatic immunity, and the Libyan government might try to have them arrested. Or members of the victim's clan might, following Libyan custom, try to retaliate against the Americans. Because the U.S. troops were under military command, Stevens didn't have authority to tell them what to do and most of the time didn't even know where they were. Stevens had pressed Washington to give him control over all armed personnel at the embassy but was rebuffed. The U.S. military command for Africa, called AFRICOM, insisted the unit should continue to report to them. The disagreement was part of a long-unresolved dispute over the competing authorities of ambassadors and military field commanders.

On August 16, Stevens sent out a cable detailing the increasing security threats in Benghazi. When General Carter Ham, AFRICOM's deputy commander, saw it, he called Stevens and offered to extend the security team's stay. Stevens turned him down.

Stevens saw Benghazi as a key to stabilizing Libya and remained determined to increase the U.S. presence there. He had taken it up with Clinton in his final conversation with her before leaving for Tripoli, and she said she shared his desire to make the Benghazi mission a permanent post. Stevens decided to visit Benghazi in September, with multiple goals in mind. He wanted to renew contacts with local leaders who were feeling neglected by the United States. He wanted to open a new public outreach office and library for Libyans, to be called the American Corner. And he hoped a visit would help him make the needed preparations for announcing during a planned visit by Clinton in October that the Benghazi mission would become a permanent consulate. He knew a visit entailed risks and was cautioned by the top U.S. diplomatic security agent in Tripoli. But he believed a visit was important.

"I haven't been up there since I first arrived and I have a lot of contacts," he told Beth Jones, who was then acting assistant secretary for the Middle East. "Fine," she said.

The night before he left, Stevens was feeling the strains of the job. He hadn't been sleeping well, he wrote in his diary. "The usual bundle of worries—family, bachelorhood, embassy and work-related issues. . . . Too many things going on, everybody wants to bend my ear. Need to pull above the fray."

Stevens had taken a vacation at the end of the summer—first to Stockholm, to take part in a friend's formal wedding, in white tie and tails. It was "a boisterous dinner for 100, with 13 toasts, some of which were clunkers. Dancing until 2 a.m.," he recorded in his diary. Next he traveled to Vienna, where he saw more friends, toured a museum that explored the country's Habsburg past, and enjoyed beer and Wiener schnitzel in the Naschmarkt, the city's biggest market. But his thoughts turned gloomy after he spent the rest of the afternoon in his hotel room reading the Swedish crime writer Henning Mankell's *The Troubled Man*. The hero was a brooding police detective who at age sixty was seeing his faculties deteriorate and his life unravel. "He's divorced, lives alone with his dog, and slowly descends into Alzheimer's," Stevens wrote in his diary. "I'm only eight years away from 60—I need to avoid such an ending!"

The accumulating dangers were weighing on him. "Security vacuum," he had written three days earlier. "Militias are power on the ground. Dicey conditions, including car bombs, attacks on consulate, British embassy, and our own people. Islamist 'hit list' in Benghazi. Me targeted on a pro-Q website (no more off-compound jogging.)"

Even so, he was looking forward to returning to Benghazi, a city he loved. The second city had "the smaller town feel and the moist air and green and spacious compound," he wrote. "Benghazi and friends tomorrow," he wrote on September 9, the day before he left Tripoli. "Something to look forward to."

His visit began like a homecoming. He flew into Benghazi with two security officers and was met at the airport by Habib, his fixer and friend from 2011. "Welcome back!" Habib told him. "It's great to be back home," Stevens replied as they embraced. Stevens had sent an email to Habib on September 8, asking him to set up his meetings at the U.S. compound in light of the security threats: "For security reasons, we'll need to be careful about limiting moves off-compound and scheduling as many meetings as possible in the villa."

But Habib told him it might be a mistake to make the newly elected Benghazi city council come to meet them in the compound—it would look to many Libyans like the council members were American puppets. So, with Stevens's approval, Habib arranged to have the meeting at a neutral location, the El Fadeel Hotel, on the waterfront. The meeting went off well, Stevens wrote afterward, although there was mild griping, as he expected, that the new government in Tripoli was not paying enough attention to Benghazi.

Later that night, after returning to the U.S. mission, Stevens had time for a toast with his diplomatic security team. Scott Wickland, one of the agents, testified later that Stevens had an unusual warm relationship with the men who protected him. Most ambassadors, he said, keep the security staff at a distance. Stevens "came right up and shook my hand and said, 'Thank you for what you're doing.' That's not exactly normal." One of the six agents broke out a bottle of premium whiskey. "Welcome back to Benghazi, we're really happy to have you here," they told him. They weren't supposed to be drinking on the job, but it was a special occasion, Wickland said.[9]

The following day, the anniversary of the September 11 attacks, Stevens held all his meetings at the compound. There were troubling signs. A Libyan in a police uniform was seen taking pictures of the compound from a construction site across the street. In the afternoon the Americans learned that a mob of 2,000 Egyptians had attacked the U.S. embassy in Cairo to protest a film, made by a U.S. immigrant who was an Egyptian Christian, that mocked the Prophet Muhammad. Stevens held meetings with a judge, a shipping company owner, and a political analyst before dining with the Turkish consul general. At 7:39 p.m. he escorted the Turkish diplomat out the front gate, where all was peaceful. He returned to his room. "Never ending security threats," he wrote in his diary that evening. It was his final entry.

The diplomatic mission was about three hundred yards long and one hundred yards across. It had four buildings, including a security command post, a dining hall, and Villa C, a yellow one-story structure with several bedrooms. Stevens and Sean Smith, a State Department IT specialist, were staying that night in Villa C. Since the property had been leased more than a year before, U.S. officials had spent $100,000 to make a variety of security improvements. They had raised the perimeter walls to nine feet high and topped them with an additional three feet of barbed wire and concertina wire. They added concrete Jersey barriers and steel drop bars at the gates to control traffic. There was a guard house manned by a friendly militia, the February 17 Brigade. The perimeter was also patrolled by Libyan employees of a Welsh security company, Blue Mountain Group. But the new measures, it turned out, were not nearly enough.

At 9:42 p.m. the Americans heard a deafening roar of explosions and automatic gunfire. About sixty men in knit face masks, some in military fatigues and others in Afghan clothing, burst through the gates. Carrying AK-47 assault rifles and rocket-propelled grenades, they scattered the Libyan guards and began charging across the grounds toward the buildings. Close behind followed pickup trucks mounted with machine guns and flying the black flag of jihad. "*Allahu Akbar!*" the attackers cried.

Stevens had retired to his bedroom for the night, and Smith, the IT specialist, was in his room playing an online sci-fi game. Wickland, hearing the commotion, rushed to put on shoes and herded the pair into the villa's safe room, a fortified space at the rear of the building that was stocked with food and protected with a heavy metal bars and reinforced windows. "This is the real deal," Wickland told them. He handed his cell phone to Stevens and told him to call anyone he knew who might help. Stevens had slipped on body armor and a helmet and began dialing. "We're under attack," he told Gregory Hicks, his deputy chief of mission back in Tripoli.

The attackers rampaged through the villa, overturning furniture and smashing computers and televisions. The three Americans crouched in the interior of the safe room, concealed in shadows where they couldn't be seen. Wickland trained his M4 rifle on the group, which he could view through the metal grille of the safe-room door. Stevens sat quietly, his eyes closed. Wickland offered Smith a shotgun but, noticing that Smith was rattled, took it back. The attackers began battering the lock on the safe-room door with the butts of their AK-47s. The locks held. But Wickland worried that they might next try to blow it up. "If they put the grenades on the locks, I'm going to start shooting," he told Stevens and Smith. "And when I die you need to pick up my gun and keep on fighting." His words were "pretty devastating news" for the two men, he said. "You could just see from their eyes that their hope had been destroyed." Wickland thought that if the Libyans succeeded in breaking in, he might be able to kill ten. But, *Well, there's 30 more,* he thought. "I was confident I was going to die."

Instead the attackers gave up on the locks, turned, and left the building. But soon a few returned with jerry cans of diesel fuel, which they sloshed over the overstuffed furniture and ignited. Soon flames and a toxic black smoke were pouring from the villa's windows. Wickland told Stevens and Smith he wanted them to crawl after him out of the safe haven, around a corner, to a bathroom about eight meters away. From there, he thought, they could escape through a window. He began to crawl, but when he had gone a few meters, he realized no one was following him. "To this day, I don't even know where they went," Wickland testified. "I had a hand on Chris Stevens, then he disappeared." He doubled back toward the safe room and couldn't find them. Wickland eventually made it out a bedroom window and onto a patio that was partially shielded by sandbags but taking attackers' fire. He went back into the flaming house repeatedly, choking on the smoke and fighting to remain conscious, to look for Stevens and Smith. He never found the two and eventually staggered up a ladder to seek cover on the roof.

Meanwhile, other diplomatic security agents who had been battling the attackers arrived at Villa C and began searching for the lost Americans. At about the same time a six-member quick-reaction security team from the CIA annex two kilometers away entered the grounds, joined by sixteen militiamen from the friendly February 17 Brigade. The diplomatic security agents eventually found Smith's body and, with help from the annex security team, removed it from the villa. By 11:00 p.m. the Libyan militiamen warned that the attackers couldn't be held off much longer. The five diplomatic security agents with Smith's body lifted it into an armored Land Cruiser and were first to leave the mission, at 11:16. They barreled through the front gate, taking heavy fire from the attackers, and headed toward the CIA annex. Traffic was heavy and they could move only slowly at

times while absorbing fire from assault rifles, grenades, and gelignite bombs. Soon the quick-reaction team also left the diplomatic mission headed for the annex.

When they arrived there, some took shelter on the roof and others took positions around the grounds. But soon the annex, which held thirty Americans, began to come under attack, too. At 5:00 a.m., a seven-person U.S. security team that had flown in from Tripoli arrived. But the battle only seemed to intensify. At 5:17 a.m. the attackers began lobbing 81-millimeter mortar rounds into the annex, killing CIA security contractors Tyrone Woods and Glen Doherty and badly wounding a diplomatic security agent. The U.S. team fled the annex at about 6:30 a.m. and headed to the airport, where they boarded a chartered plane and at about 7:30 a.m. lifted off for Tripoli.

At the American mission, a crowd had been gathering since shortly after the first moments of the attacks. Some wanted to tear down the diplomatic mission and some wanted to loot. Others, it turned out, were more sympathetic to the Americans. "Bring down the flag!" some chanted. The crowd broke through a window of Villa C and stumbled across Stevens's body, still next to the steel grille protecting the safe room. At about 1:00 a.m., a young Libyan's smartphone recorded images of the crowd dragging out the body of the diplomat, his feet bare, his face blackened with soot. Someone put a finger on his neck and felt a pulse. His eyes were moving. "He's living! He's living!" they shouted. "God is great!" Six Libyans, believed to be Good Samaritans, lifted Steven's body into a car and rushed him to the emergency room of the Benghazi Medical Center. They arrived at about 1:15 a.m.

The staff at Benghazi Medical Center tried to revive Stevens for ninety minutes with CPR but found no signs of life. They moved him to the hospital's morgue. After 4:00 a.m., a Libyan official confirmed Stevens's identity with officials in Tripoli. Soon a group of Libyan militiamen arrived, loaded his body onto a bread truck, and took it to the airport. There was a last-minute complication: some Libyan officials wanted the body held for autopsy. Instead, it was lifted onto a Libyan C-130 military transport plane with the remains of Smith, Doherty, and Woods. At about 10:00 a.m. they took off for Tripoli. The embassy staff in the capital, fearing they could be attacked, too, packed quickly and boarded the plane. They flew back to Washington with the bodies of their fellow Americans but no real explanation of what had happened.

Stevens's sister was distressed when Secretary of State Hillary Rodham Clinton called her at 5:30 a.m. the morning after her brother's death and promised to track down the killers. "She said that justice would be done," Anne Stevens Sullivan, a pediatric rheumatologist, wrote on a memorial web page. "This upset me. Chris was not focused on revenge. He wanted the Libyan people to have a free and democratic society. 'I hope this will not prevent us from continuing to support the Libyan people, from moving ahead,'" she told Clinton.

Two days after the attack, the C-17 cargo plane with the four victims' bodies reached Joint Base Andrews in suburban Maryland for one of the solemn memorial ceremonies that had become all too familiar over the past decade. "It was the longest plane flight I can remember, sitting in that cold, cavernous C-17 aircraft across from four flag draped coffins," Bill Burns, who accompanied the remains, wrote in his memoir.[10] With President Obama and Secretary of State Clinton looking on, and a military band playing "Nearer, My God, to Thee," Marine pallbearers carried four flag-draped metal caskets to black tables in the center of a vast hangar. Stevens was the sixth U.S. ambassador killed in action, and the first since Ambassador Adolph Dubs was killed in a shootout in Afghanistan in 1979. "They knew the danger, and they accepted it," Obama told the gathering of eight hundred. America, he declared, "will never retreat from the world."

Stevens was remembered in multiple memorial services, including one under the rotunda of San Francisco City Hall, and in an outpouring of postings on memorial websites. He left behind "a legion of best friends and broken hearts," wrote ambassador William V. Roebuck, a colleague who had been overseeing North Africa issues from Washington, in a poem of tribute. Another colleague later recalled going to a memorial service and meeting three mourning women who each believed they were Stevens's true love.

The attack stunned the tiny staff in the embassy in Tripoli. Despite the rising violence, the general view among the diplomats was that Libya was on a path for better things. "It was like a monster come out of the sea," one diplomat said. Colleagues had the sad duty of gathering up Stevens's things from his apartment to send home. They boxed up suits and workout clothes, tennis gear, a "Free Libya" mug, a bottle of Laphroaig Scotch, a biography of a minor president, and a pair of Dickens novels.

Among Libyans, the attacks brought an outpouring of grief and anger against the militias. Ten days after the attack, tens of thousands of Libyans marched in Benghazi to protest the militias and to remember Stevens. Hundreds stormed the compound of the Ansar al-Sharia militia, which had claimed responsibility for the attack. The demonstrators drove out the militiamen, ripped down the group's flags, and set a vehicle afire. Other marchers turned out only to share their sadness. "Libya lost a friend," signs read. Stevens's family received some 40,000 letters of condolence from Libyans and others in the Middle East.

In Washington, the deaths set off a partisan battle that raged for years. Republicans mobilized to try to prove that Clinton and the administration team had failed to provide proper security and sought to cover up their failures. Hearings started on October 20 and ground on through seven congressional investigations, thirty-two hearings, and eleven government reports. They dredged up little beyond what the State Department's internal investigation had unearthed in the first three months after the attack. The final report of the Benghazi committee found no specific fault with Clinton. But Kansas Republican representative Mike Pompeo, who became secretary of state under President Trump, joined Republican representative Jim Jordan of Ohio in adding an addendum that accused Clinton of failing to address the security shortcomings in the month before the attack. Benghazi became a new front in the Republican attack on Clinton's character. Stevens's family found it anguishing to see him, a dedicated nonpartisan, in the cross fire.

Stevens's skills and contribution in Libya were praised by both sides. But the State Department's internal investigation of the attack laid responsibility for the attack on him, along with diplomatic security officials in Washington and superiors in the Near Eastern Affairs bureau. "As the president's personal representative, the chief of mission bears direct and full responsibility for the security of [his or her] mission and for all the personnel for whom [he or she] is responsible," the accountability review board wrote. The panel's chairman was Thomas Pickering, a six-time ambassador who had been Stevens's boss in the 1990s and was the diplomat he most admired.

The conservative media painted the attack in lurid colors. Sean Hannity of Fox News, citing a news story that was later retracted, reported inaccurately that the mob had sodomized Stevens and dragged his body through the streets. Websites reported incorrectly that Stevens was about to convert to Islam; others said incorrectly that he was gay and condemned the administration for sending him to a region where his life would be in danger. There were reports that Stevens had organized the smuggling of arms from Libya to jihadists fighting to overthrow the government in Syria.

Elsewhere, Stevens was depicted as simply clueless. *13 Hours*, a 2016 film from the action-movie director Michael Bay, portrayed Stevens as a cosseted pretty boy who spouted diplomatic clichés but was oblivious to danger. The heroes of the film were the brawny security contractors who tried to save him. The film was a box office bust but won fans in some conservative circles. Candidate Donald Trump praised the film and screened it for free for supporters before the 2016 Iowa primary caucuses.

Among Stevens's peers in the diplomatic corps and other agencies, opinions were split on whether he had taken unwise risks. When other foreign delegations and aid groups pulled out of Benghazi, the American team should have gone, too, some argued. Some cited a maxim from the Foreign Service's pre-9/11 era: "When in doubt, pull them out." "The one person most to blame for Benghazi is the guy who got killed," said one former top U.S. official. The diplomats who worked most closely with him in Libya insisted Stevens heeded security officials but was ready to take some risk when it was important to the mission. "He took his personal security very, very seriously," said Greg Arndt, the former defense aide. "He had been put in a precarious situation."

Other foreign service veterans argued an occasional tragedy was the price of a noble but dangerous calling. "The reality is we do business in dangerous areas," said Ryan Crocker, who had known Stevens for decades. "We can manage risk, but we can't prevent it if we do our jobs."[11] The political fallout from the attack was a blow to the diplomatic corps, Crocker said, because it would make senior officials fearful of sending staff on risky missions that could get their superiors in trouble. His former colleagues noted the sad irony that Stevens, a leading example of expeditionary diplomacy, was now the reason diplomats could not get out and do the job.

Stevens's sister, Anne, said her brother was fully aware of the risks and was willing to take them because he thought the visit was important. But the trip, she concluded, was a mistake. "I don't think we'll ever know why he made the decision to take the risk of going to Benghazi, knowing there were multiple attacks. It was clearly a bad decision," she said.[12]

The Obama administration, in any case, wanted less risk-taking and less involvement with Libya.[13] After the Benghazi attacks, the embassy staff bulked up on security staff and cut back on contacts with Libyans. In the fall of 2012, the embassy had a complement of about one hundred, but among them only two permanent staff were assigned to deal directly with Libyans. The remainder were diplomatic security, intelligence, support staff, and FBI agents sent to track down the Americans' killers. The embassy also had the additional protection of a Marine counterterrorism team of fifty-one. Washington kept an intense focus on the mission's security: every time the diplomatic staff was increased or decreased, President Obama was personally notified. The embassy had the flavor of a forward operating base in Iraq or Afghanistan. The result was that Washington knew less, and helped less, as the country unraveled.

Former ambassador Laurence E. Pope II, a thirty-one-year foreign service veteran, ran the embassy for three months starting in October 2012. He had called Burns and volunteered to come out of retirement to handle the post temporarily. Pope concluded soon after arriving that the security rules meant little useful diplomacy was being done. Any meeting outside the gates required elaborate advance planning and reliance on a team of diplomatic-security agents to secure the travel route and destination. Washington seemed to prefer that he not venture beyond the gates at all, Pope said. Their aversion to risk "could hardly be overstated," he said. "And if all you're doing is protecting yourself, you might as well not be there."

Pope noticed that one of the swimming pools in the embassy compound had been drained and was now occupied by a large crate. When he asked what it contained, he was told it was the embassy's inventory of antitank missiles. "If they come at us with tanks, I'm inclined to surrender," Pope joked. Nobody laughed.

Deborah Jones, a veteran foreign service officer, took over as ambassador to Libya seven months after the Benghazi attack. The complement of Marines protecting the embassy had by then been increased again, from fifty-one to eighty-seven. Jones soon found herself devoting hours of her time to sitting with young American staff members to give them a chance to talk through their anguish over the attack. Even then some remained traumatized and wracked by survivor's guilt, she said. Jones sent a stream of messages on Twitter to 20,000 Libyan followers, because security rules meant that in most cases it was her only way to keep in touch. The Libyans were not pleased that America seemed to be turning its back on the country. Many of their Twitter replies were "vociferous," said Jones, putting it diplomatically. The embassy's enforced isolation added to the psychological strain on the staff, she said.[14] Officials in Washington said it became tougher to recruit staff for Libya than for anywhere in the greater Middle East, including Iraq, Pakistan, and Afghanistan.

In the Benghazi committee hearings and afterward, Clinton continued to stress that diplomats had to continue working on the front lines amid danger. Stevens "understood that the difficult and dangerous places were where America's interests were most at stake," she wrote in her 2014 memoir. Stevens believed that "when America is absent, especially from unstable environments, there are consequences. That's why I sent Chris Stevens to Libya in the first place; it's also why he wanted to be there."[15]

Even so, the consensus in Washington was changing. The growth in State Department spending in the final Obama years was not for more diplomats but for more diplomatic-security agents, security training, and equipment like surveillance cameras and fire-survival gear. Spending on diplomatic security leaped from $200 million in 1998 to $2.6 billion in 2012.[16]

Soon after Stevens's death, the Libyan government that had been launched in the 2012 elections became paralyzed by divisions. The Libya that a year earlier seemed to be embarking on a golden age now writhed in civil war. It became a haven for groups like the Islamic State; violence increased, as did the traffic in arms, drugs, and migrants heading across the Mediterranean. The country looked like a failed state, a threat not only to its long-suffering citizens but to all of North Africa and Europe as well.

Obama lamented in early 2016 that the failure by his team and U.S. allies to plan for the Libyan war's aftermath was the worst mistake of his presidency. To aides in private he pronounced Libya a "shit show." It further reduced his calculation of how much America could do to repair countries torn by war and civil upheaval. Libya's meltdown helped convince him it would be a mistake to get involved in the catastrophic civil war in Syria.

Bill Burns, the former deputy secretary of state, concluded that in the absence of a strong American presence after the war, neither the Libyans nor foreign powers played the role that was needed. "Without a strong post-intervention American hand, our neat 'long game' coalition stumbled—the incapacity and irresolution of most of the European players exposed, most of the Arabs reverting to self-interested form, and the rival Libyan factions unified only by their ardent opposition to any meaningful foreign support and engagement," he wrote.[17]

In his reluctance to get involved, Obama was not alone. Stevens's death helped convince many Americans "the place is just way too dark, and let's stay out of it," said Roya Hakakian, the writer who was Stevens's friend. The shift distressed her deeply, she said, and would have distressed Stevens as well.

Stevens's family and friends kept the faith. After his death, his family decided the best way to honor his memory was to expand the human contacts that were his passion. They set up a fund and an educational program called the Stevens Initiative that aimed to connect young people from the Middle East and United States. A main focus was international computer-linked classes that taught teens and connected peers in the Middle East and the United States. With support from corporate sponsors, the State Department, and Middle Eastern countries, the program in its first year, 2016, brought together 21,000 students from seventeen Middle Eastern countries and twenty-five U.S. states. The goal, said a family friend, was to "create more Chris Stevenses."[18]

CHAPTER 15

# Arab Spring and Fall

When Anne Patterson was chosen to be ambassador to Egypt, she thought the new job would be a lot quieter and more comfortable than her last. Egypt seemed stable after thirty years of Hosni Mubarak's autocratic rule. The embassy in Cairo had long been the crown jewel of U.S. diplomatic assignments in the Arab world, and the ambassador's post had always been one of most prestigious. Patterson thought she and her husband, David, a Middle East hand now retired from the Foreign Service, would have time to explore the Ptolemaic ruins and Nubian villages of the ancient Arab heartland. "We could see all the sights," she said.

Soon she realized she had that wrong. She was nominated for the post in October 2010 and returned from Islamabad to Washington to study Arabic and prepare for the job. When she turned on the television in late January 2011, she saw police with clubs and rifles chasing demonstrators in Cairo's Tahrir Square, 1,200 feet from the U.S. embassy. Egypt, long becalmed, was in upheaval. After eighteen days of protests, Mubarak was forced to resign.

His departure was not the end of the upheaval in Egypt but the beginning. Patterson, fresh from a conflagration in Islamabad, found herself in a new blaze.

U.S.-Egypt relations were a cornerstone of the U.S. security strategy in the Middle East. Washington relied on Egypt's military and civilian establishment to keep the peace with Israel, to help fight counter-terrorism, and to keep the sea-lanes open for the global oil trade and U.S. Navy ships. But as the Arab Spring reached Egypt, a struggle began between officials who wanted Washington to side with the protesters and change, and those who feared instability in the most populous Arab country could damage American security interests throughout the region. The reform advocates were mostly younger and lower ranking, including White House human rights adviser Samantha Power and national security deputy Ben Rhodes, while those most focused on stability were older and more senior, including Secretary of State Hillary Clinton and Defense Secretary Robert Gates. The administration wrestled for the next five years over this classic choice between reform and stability without fully resolving it.

Mubarak's fall had caught the administration by surprise, angering President Obama and shaking his faith in the national security team's understanding of Egypt. While some State Department and intelligence officials had warned of unrest, the majority view was that Egypt remained stable. A CIA analysis from late 2010 had predicted that the transition from Mubarak's rule to his successor, probably his son Gamal, would be smooth. They had it wrong. And after the revolution, Washington continued to be blindsided by developments in Egypt. "We were always sort of behind the curve," Patterson said. "Events moved more rapidly than we could respond to."

Officials in Washington were also second-guessing the team at the U.S. embassy in Cairo. Many in the administration thought U.S. diplomats on the ground had been too focused on getting along with the Mubarak regime and had paid too little attention to the young protesters on the street. White House officials prodded the embassy to reach out to others, including Egyptians they knew, and raised pointed questions whenever the U.S. team was surprised by some development. "It was basically intensive micromanagement at a very operational level," said a former top State Department official. "Basically, everyone in the White House who had been on a Nile cruise thought they were an expert on Egypt."

In addition, Patterson arrived at a moment when Egyptians were furious at Washington. Reform advocates were angry that Obama had not called for Mubarak's departure until a few days before he stepped down. The powerful Egyptian military and civilian establishment were outraged that Washington had abandoned America's longtime ally. The Islamist groups, who had the support of nearly 30 percent of Egyptians, had never been consulted. America had long had an image problem in Egypt, but never before had it been under attack by all sides at once.

Patterson began her work on the Egypt portfolio even before she took over as ambassador. In the first days after Mubarak's departure, the Obama administration wanted to quickly show it supported democratic change in Egypt. Secretary Clinton enlisted Patterson, a fellow Wellesley alum she had worked with in Pakistan, to oversee how the U.S. spent its aid. The assignment sounded sensible, but it made her arrival even more difficult.

The Obama administration had been wrangling with the transitional government over whether Washington could parcel out $65 million to U.S. and Egyptian pro-reform groups to accelerate the formation of political parties and jump-start democratic politics. Although the amount was a relative pittance, Egyptian officials were deeply suspicious of the nongovernmental organizations (NGOs). They saw them as part of a long effort, seen earlier in President George W. Bush's "freedom agenda," to reshape Egyptian government. They believed the revolution had been promoted by Washington. And they thought they were entitled to decide how aid should be spent.

Even before she arrived, Patterson was being bashed by Egyptian news outlets at the encouragement of the Egyptian military and intelligence. The Egyptians had a long tradition of denouncing U.S. ambassadors, partly to strengthen domestic support for the Egyptian leadership and partly to deflect U.S. pressure. Margaret Scobey, Patterson's predecessor, had ruffled feathers in Egypt by raising the country's poor human rights record during her 2008 nomination hearing. When Scobey arrived in March 2008, Egyptian press outlets complained it was an insult to have a woman sent as ambassador. Three months after Scobey arrived, one of her dogs was found poisoned in a garden, in what U.S. officials suspected was another part of the harassment campaign.

During her nomination hearing, Patterson had reaffirmed that the administration intended to hand over the aid money to the NGOs. The Egyptians noticed the comments and made known their displeasure. When it came time for her to formally introduce herself to the Egyptian government and present her diplomatic credentials, she was not received in a separate ceremony, as had been customary with U.S. ambassadors. She was ushered in in a cattle call of ten new ambassadors, sandwiched between envoys from Sudan and tiny San Marino.[1]

The state-owned press gave Patterson no quarter. *October* magazine described her in a cover story as "The Ambassador from Hell Who Lit a Fire in Tahrir Square." The illustration showed Patterson casting flaming dollar bills into a burning Tahrir Square. As ambassador to Colombia and Pakistan, the article said, Patterson had played a role that was "closely linked to conspiracies and stirring up unrest and discord."[2]

On Patterson's arrival, then, "she was caught between a suspicious White House and a suspicious Egyptian elite," said a former senior State Department official. "It was a no-win situation." Even so, she took charge of her new portfolio as she had done in Islamabad and Bogotá. She made herself the authoritative voice on Egypt in senior administration debates, took control of nonmilitary aid, and built ties to the U.S. defense and intelligence officials involved with Egypt. The CIA station chief would check with her before making a presentation to the White House. She was a master of bureaucratic procedure, knowing just when to submit position papers to the White House to give them maximum impact in internal debates. She could build a case for her views based on her long experience abroad in a way that was difficult for others to challenge. "She was a badass diplomat and I would definitely want her on my team," said a former State Department official who at times disagreed with her.

Though the generals were stoking criticism of the embassy

in the Egyptian press, in private meetings they got along reasonably well with Patterson. She was plain speaking and unemotional. Unlike some other U.S. officials, she knew how to explain what Washington wanted without seeming to lecture them on their moral failings. "These are, to put it bluntly, thuggish generals," said Prem Kumar, who worked closely with Patterson as a senior National Security Council staff member for the Middle East. "They're not going to agree with you. They don't care about democracy. If you come across as a preachy activist, they're going to dismiss you immediately." Although the Egyptian press was sexist in its attacks on her, Patterson never thought sexism was an issue in her dealings with Egyptian leaders.

In her first months in Egypt, Patterson's most important contact was Field Marshal Mohamed Hussein Tantawi, the leader of the Supreme Council of the Armed Forces (SCAF) and interim head of state. Tantawi was a courtly, tired seventy-five-year-old career officer who had been chosen by Mubarak for the top military post because he was thought to pose little threat. He had pledged as soon as he took the top job to return power to civilians. But soon it seemed that Tantawi and the generals weren't sure they wanted to surrender power over the government and the state-owned businesses that provided the military elite with a comfortable life. They wavered and hedged. Months passed, and the question of when the generals would step back remained as murky as when Patterson had arrived. "The process has been fraught with uncertainty from the beginning and decisions are made on a day-to-day basis," she told journalists in October, after a meeting with the generals and Defense Secretary Leon Panetta.

The delay and other grievances were setting off angry demonstrations and riots almost every week. The military handled the demonstrators ineptly and harshly, compounding the conflict. When members of the country's Coptic Christian minority turned out on October 9 to protest attacks on their churches, the military plowed into the crowd with twelve-ton armored personnel carriers, crushing thirteen protesters.

Patterson told Tantawi the military had to give up power if it wanted a stable Egypt. "This is not sustainable," she told him. Tantawi said he agreed, and the two began discussing the timing of elections.

Elections for a new parliament were scheduled to begin in late November. But as the date came closer, Patterson began to fear they might be postponed. Protests were again growing, and there were hints that the military might use the clashes to justify a delay in the elections. Patterson pressed the generals to stick with the schedule and asked the White House to have President Obama issue a statement calling for them to be held on schedule. In the end, the elections took place as planned.

Their results provided a clear signal of the struggle ahead. The Muslim Brotherhood, a long-outlawed Islamist group that was now the country's most well-organized faction, won 47 percent of seats. There had been signs for some time that the Muslim Brotherhood would do well. "You would see these huge trucks coming to the polls, and they would disgorge hundreds of women, dressed head to toe in black, and they would vote," said Patterson. The bigger surprise was that the Salafists, followers of a harsh Muslim fundamentalist ideology, had come in second, with about 25 percent of seats. Together, the Islamists had almost 75 percent of the seats.

Even so, the parliamentary election had gone off relatively smoothly. When Patterson and a congressional delegation that had come to Cairo to watch the election had a dinner afterward, they toasted its success. It appeared that the transition to a more democratic government was finally under way.

But the squabble over U.S. aid to the pro-reform groups was again intensifying, making it harder to transact other business between the governments. Patterson spent hours with the generals trying to convince them that the groups were focused on elementary political tasks. One of the courses they taught was on how to prepare a budget for a political party, she pointed out. Another was titled, Women, Are You Ready for Political Office? "Does that look like it really threatens you guys?" she asked the generals. "It was sort of grassrootsy stuff," she said later. "And totally harmless, frankly."

The generals were not placated. Importantly, it wasn't just the military that saw a conspiracy in the U.S. government's promotion of reform. "It was also—and this took me longer to realize than it should have—the Egyptian public," Patterson said. Egyptians "found it sort of offensive that with their 7,000-year-old civilization a bunch of Americans would parachute in and talk to them about how to order their political system."[3]

The fight over the groups was also politically sensitive in Washington, for a different reason. The revolution had strengthened support in the administration and both U.S. parties for efforts to advance political reform. The American pro-democracy groups had powerful political support. One of them, the National Democratic Institute, was chaired by former secretary of state Madeleine Albright, while another, the International Republican Institute, was chaired by Senator John McCain of Arizona.

The conflict erupted again on December 29 when police in riot gear raided and then shut down seventeen offices of ten American and Egyptian NGOs. Police seized files and computers and barred the departure from Egypt of a handful of American staff. One of them was Sam LaHood, the boyish-looking thirty-six-year-old Egypt director for the International Republican Institute and the son of transportation secretary Ray LaHood. Fearing arrest, he and six other Americans fled to the safety of the U.S. embassy. They arrived looking tired and bedraggled and slept on mattresses on the floor of an auditorium until Patterson found them accommodations in the ambassadorial residence. LaHood's presence made the fight over the groups, already a headline issue, a full-blown international incident.

At a moment when campaigning for a pivotal presidential election was beginning and violent protests raged, Obama administration officials found themselves spending their time trying to find a way to resolve the dispute and extricate LaHood. Obama, Clinton, CIA chief Leon Panetta, and others devoted hours to entreating and threatening the Egyptians. "This became a sort of touchstone for the relationship, in a way it shouldn't have been," Patterson said.

Over the next two months U.S. officials threatened to withhold the $1.3 billion in annual military aid that was at the core of the relationship and suggested they might also block badly needed billions in economic aid for Egypt from the World Bank and International Monetary Fund. None of it made a difference. Egypt defied its superpower ally, announcing on February 5 that it would put nineteen Americans, sixteen Egyptians, and six nationals of other countries on trial.

When the trial date came, the defendants were marched into a courtroom and locked in a metal-barred cage for the duration of the proceedings. No Americans, however, were among them. LaHood and five other defendants had been flown out of the country on an aging DC-3 on March 1, after the military agreed to free them in exchange for $4 million in bail. Back in Washington, LaHood rejoiced that after five weeks of embassy confinement he could now go on a long-delayed honeymoon. Patterson shared the credit for negotiating their release.

U.S. officials ended up subtracting the $4 million bail from the money Washington provided in aid that year, to the irritation of the generals. But there was no other penalty for the regime. The issue was a political winner for the official who had done most to promote it, Fayza Abul Naga, the foreign aid minister. She basked in the glory of her victory over America, and two years later, in a successor government, was promoted to national security adviser.

Human rights advocates and some U.S. lawmakers, such as Senator McCain, felt the administration should have pressed harder to win protections for the groups, rather than trying to smooth over the dispute. Officials of the American NGOs were unhappy that they were asked to mute their public criticism so that the standoff could be ended and U.S. officials could move on to the larger issue of the democratic transition. Harold Koh, the State Department's legal adviser, had told National Democratic Institute officials in a Cairo meeting also attended by Patterson that the goal was to reach a settlement with Egypt rather than to wring concessions from them. "Your job is just going to be to suck it up," Koh told the group. "Bigger things are at stake."

Les Campbell, the National Democratic Institute's top official for the Mideast, believed the stakes in the NGO fight were plenty large. The military government wanted to end all foreign support to try to ensure there would never again be an Arab Spring–style uprising in Egypt, he said. The campaign against the groups was a "planned, intentional, strategic attack," Campbell said, designed to "freeze, intimidate, disrupt, and destroy basically the entire democratic middle."

The young Egyptians who had pushed in the streets for Mubarak's ouster were heroes in America. Patterson, Clinton, and some other administration officials had an ambivalent view of them. While they had been urging the Egyptian government to give the activists more space, they viewed them as a tiny group with limited public support and often little interest in working through the political system.

In her first trip to Egypt since the revolution, Hillary Clinton met with the students and activists to explore their plans. She asked if they had thought through how they were going to try to influence the writing of a constitution and contest the upcoming election. "They looked at me blankly," she wrote in her memoir.[4] The young activists feared the new government was as corrupt as the old, and battled among themselves.

The next major political face-off came in June 2012, when the Islamists and the old guard challenged each other in the final run-off round of a presidential election. The Islamists' candidate was Mohamed Morsi, a little-known engineering professor from an impoverished Nile Delta village, who had served as a doctrinal enforcer for the Muslim Brotherhood. The establishment's candidate was Ahmed Shafik, a seventy-year-old former air force general and prime minister who said he wanted to restore a government like Mubarak's.

As the election approached, there were increasing hints that the military might be preparing to block a possible Islamist victory. Patterson appealed repeatedly to the generals not to take such a step. She reminded them that Egypt's first freely elected parliament had won them international goodwill and given them a means of deflecting political blame. But the generals would not be deterred. Just two days before the presidential election, a panel of judges dissolved the Islamist-dominated parliament and stripped the presidency of key powers. The moves were denounced by Islamists and liberals as a naked power grab by the generals.

In Washington there were growing fears that the military intended to prevent an election victory by Morsi, a move that could again set the country aflame. The administration called on the generals to accept the legitimate victor and threatened to withhold U.S. military aid.

To show American concern, Patterson and Representative David Dreier, a California Republican, toured Cairo polling places on the last day of voting. They were received politely at most stops, although in the poor Cairo neighborhood of Dar al-Salam a judge blurted out his suspicions of their motives. "America hates Arabs!" he said.[5]

When the ballots were counted, Morsi had 52 percent and Shafik 48 percent. There were some irregularities, and a number of ballots were nullified because voters had scrawled insults rather than checking a box. At the end of the tally, Morsi led by 800,000 votes, a margin too large to be entirely the result of fraud.

But would the generals acknowledge the Islamists' victory? The commission overseeing the election delayed announcement of the results for a week without explaining why. For those seven days, anxiety continued to grow. In Washington the National Security Council held meetings nearly around the clock as officials debated what to do if the generals declared the victory for Shafik. Ominously the Egyptian army positioned troops and tanks around Tahrir Square and other key intersections.

The electoral commission announced it would hold a press conference on Sunday afternoon to disclose the winner. What U.S.

officials were hearing from their best intelligence sources was not encouraging. When the chief of the electoral commission began a long speech to explain the outcome, Patterson was on a video tele-conference with senior U.S. officials at the White House, telling them the American effort to apply pressure had failed and that the generals had chosen Shafik. It was time, she said, to consider how the administration would respond if violence broke out. But an aide broke into the call to say that the commission president Farouk Sultan had finally announced the winner—and it was Morsi. Three days later the embassy's political counselor learned what had hap-pened: two members of the five-person electoral commission stood fast against the plan to throw the election. "They just refused to go along," Patterson said.

In Tahrir Square, 100,000 Morsi supporters exulted. "Down, down with military rule!" they chanted. Fireworks streaked across the night sky. The win was the greatest political accomplishment for Egypt's political Islamist movement in its seventy-five-year history. Obama administration officials said the outcome was for the best. But that didn't end their anxieties about what came next.

The Morsi victory again exposed divisions within the Obama administration. Many senior officials were suspicious of the Mus-lim Brotherhood, viewing them as, by definition, foes of plural-ism and democracy. Obama and others wanted to give the Muslim Brotherhood a chance to show what it could do. It was worth a try: maybe there was a chance for a moderate Islamist brand of lead-ership, akin to what seemed then to be developing in Turkey. If America could work with such a government, it could undercut the appeal of violent groups. And after all, the election had shown Islamists had huge popular support among Egyptians. This was democracy.

On the night of Morsi's election, Obama had called to congratu-late him and in a separate statement had reminded him of his prom-ises to uphold universal values and respect the rights of women and minorities, such as the long-persecuted Coptic Christians.

After the election Patterson lost no time meeting with Morsi in the presidential palace to try to pin him down on his promises. The administration wanted to know that he would respect commitments Egypt had made in the past, including on the peace treaty with Israel and the security relationship with the United States. Officials wanted to know that he would respect human rights. Morsi was polite but noncommittal. It was not reassuring.

The Egyptian press gave front-page play to all meetings between Patterson and Morsi, suggesting that the new president and the ambassador were in an unholy alliance to run the country. The suggestion was laughable to Patterson: she knew she was making no headway with Morsi. Morsi was "one leader I could never get through to," she said. She soon concluded that Morsi lacked the skills and temperament needed for the job. A short, stocky man with a close-cropped beard, Morsi was awkward in meetings, politically tone-deaf, and a poor public speaker. He was unable even to make the small talk that is the lubricant of politics. American officials tried to build a bond with him over his years living as an engineering student at the University of Southern California in Los Angeles. But he viewed such chitchat as frivolous, even improper. He did like to point out that his son had been born in California and therefore was entitled to run for office in America. "He could be president of the United States!" he told the Americans. The idea amused him.

Patterson continued to press him. "She was having to go and really bend his fingers back," said former ambassador Beth Jones, who was then acting assistant secretary of state for the Middle East. But it had little effect.

Patterson lobbied Clinton to make a July trip to Cairo, hoping the secretary would have more success coaxing Morsi in the right direction. Other U.S. officials disagreed about the visit, arguing Clinton should not honor him with such a meeting until Morsi had begun delivering on his promises. But Patterson persisted, and Clinton showed up on July 14, just two weeks after Morsi's inauguration. Morsi received her at the presidential palace, and when they allowed press photographers in to shoot pictures of them sitting

in a formal meeting room, they chatted amiably. The private conversation that followed, however, was not happy. Morsi was again
laconic and noncommittal. He appeared ready to break off security
cooperation with Israel, sharpening anxieties in Washington. "He's
an awful man," Clinton told aides after the meeting.

Clinton noticed how much had changed in Egypt since her last
visit, in the first days after the revolution. When she had walked
through Tahrir Square after Mubarak's fall, Egyptians were warm
and welcoming. This time crowds encircled her hotel to protest her
arrival, taunting the secretary with chants of "Monica! Monica!"—
referring to the White House intern who had an affair with her
husband. Protesters beaned Clinton's spokeswoman, Victoria
Nuland, with a tomato and threw shoes at Clinton's motorcade. One
agitated Copt confronted Clinton with an accusation, picked up
from right-wing media in the United States, that Clinton's personal
aide Huma Abedin was an agent of the Muslim Brotherhood. In
the Egyptian press, meanwhile, articles claimed that Clinton was in
town to toast the Islamist victory that Washington had engineered.

With Morsi's ascent, U.S. officials "faced our classic dilemma:
should we do business with a leader with whom we disagreed on so
many things in the name of advancing our core interests?" Clinton
wrote later. "We were back on the high wire, performing the bal-
ancing act without easy answers or good options."[6]

Patterson believed that, despite Washington's growing distaste
for Morsi, she needed to preserve a strong enough tie that U.S.
officials would know what the regime was doing and could try to
influence them when it mattered most. While she pressed Morsi
with demands, she also gave him slack at times because she understood that he was locked in a struggle with an old regime that was
plotting a comeback. The judges, prosecutors, police, and military
from the old regime were all trying to frustrate what Morsi and his
team were trying to do. For the first six months of Morsi's rule, she
prodded his team in private but said little or nothing in public about
the disagreements. Such bullhorn diplomacy would only reduce the
chances of concessions, in her view. When officials in Washington

wanted to criticize Morsi publicly, she sought to tone down their language. When Morsi hinted that he wanted to expand his powers or make other moves that the administration didn't like, she would not speak publicly against them. Obama, too, wanted to give Morsi latitude.

Meanwhile, Egypt had become a far more dangerous place for Americans. On September 11, 2012, the anniversary of the 9/11 attacks, hundreds of protesters attacked the U.S. embassy in Cairo, scaling its walls, shredding the American flag, and replacing it with the black flag of jihad. They were angry over a film produced by a Coptic Christian in the United States that mocked the Prophet Muhammad. The Islamists, like the secular liberals and the military's supporters, took aim at Patterson. "Say it, don't fear: the ambassador must leave," they chanted.

Under international agreement, host nations are responsible for protecting embassies and other diplomatic facilities. But police stood aside for hours during the attack, and the protest continued. Morsi said nothing to condemn the attack for thirty-six hours. Afterward, Obama called Morsi to complain about police inaction.

Patterson pushed Morsi's team to take steps to strengthen the crumbling economy. She hoped, at the beginning, that the Islamist government might be more open to economic reform than the generals, who controlled a huge slice of the country's business and industry and thus had a stake in the inefficient status quo. She hoped the new government might be willing to end some of the economy's distortions by cutting back on heavy subsidies for gasoline. But Patterson was quickly disappointed. While Morsi began with a cabinet that included skilled technocrats, he shuffled through his ministers, including his economic aides, again and again. He saw economics through the ideological lens of an Islamist. Patterson noticed that one of Morsi's ministers had written a monograph, "Islamic Thought and the Money Supply." "I thought, *Oh, God, that shows you we've got issues here*," she said.

Morsi also had an inflated notion of his own importance. When Patterson met for the first time with Morsi's foreign policy adviser,

Essam el-Haddad, he pressed Patterson to arrange for Morsi to address a joint session of Congress. Such speeches are a rare honor, accorded only the closest American allies. Patterson was taken aback by the request. "I said, that's for Mexico and Canada, and countries like that," Patterson said. "I didn't know quite how to squirm out of it."

Patterson did believe that a Morsi invitation to the White House could help the relationship and pushed repeatedly for a Morsi-Obama meeting. Other officials disagreed, arguing Morsi was not living up to his promises to build an inclusive Egypt and that the sight of an Islamist in the Oval Office would only invite conservative attacks on Obama. But in January 2013 it came to light that Morsi had described Zionists as "bloodsuckers" and urged Egyptians to nurse their children on hatred for Jews and Zionists. Patterson recognized this was a fatal blow to plans for a visit. She "said very quickly, 'We should pull it down, and I'll tell him this is beyond the pale,'" recalled Prem Kumar, the former National Security Council official.

In his second month in office, Morsi struck at the power of the generals. He pushed Tantawi and the defense minister into retirement and nullified the edict the generals had put in place before his election that had stripped him of many of his powers. He installed as defense minister Abdel Fattah el-Sisi, an ambitious fifty-seven-year-old general who had been seen, to that point, as a protégé of Tantawi's. Morsi's move alarmed Washington, as well as the Israelis and Gulf leaders, who feared the general might be a closet Islamist.

Patterson offered a different take on Sisi. She knew the general because he had tried to cultivate her, a sign of his desire to strengthen ties with Washington. He had once seemed a loyal supporter of Mubarak but during the revolution had urged the military to force him out. He had undermined the military's second-in-command, General Sami Anan, by providing Morsi evidence of his corruption. Now he had turned on Tantawi, who had been a father figure to him. Sisi was ambitious and ruthless, Patterson wrote

Washington. "Morsi may have bitten off more than he can chew," she told them.

In November, Egypt exploded in crisis again, over a new sign of Morsi's drift toward authoritarianism. Morsi issued a decree declaring that he was immune from any court ruling until the new constitution was completed. The move seemed a clear sign that Morsi wanted to be dictator, and it surprised even some in the Muslim Brotherhood hierarchy. Protesters flowed into the streets, and gunfire crackled in running battles between the government's supporters and opponents. Muslim Brotherhood offices all over Egypt were attacked and some burned to the ground.

Morsi's move, it turned out, was intended to head off actions he believed his rivals were planning against him. He had become convinced that the Supreme Constitutional Court, Egypt's highest, was going to disband the committee drafting a new constitution and possibly annul Morsi's election. Shocked by the violent reactions to his decree, Morsi tried to calm the public in a televised rally but did little to assuage the anger. Within a month he had done an about-face and rescinded the decree's language about the courts. Even so, Morsi's fumbled edict was a fatal blunder for his presidency, defining him for all time as an autocrat. As denunciations of him intensified, so, too, did criticism of the Obama administration for failing to challenge him. Critics said the administration looked like Morsi's enabler.

But Obama and other top U.S. officials clung to hopes that the two governments could cooperate. Those hopes were strengthened in early November when Morsi collaborated closely with Obama to settle bloody fighting between Israel and the Palestinian Islamist group Hamas in the Gaza Strip and southern Israel. Obama talked to Morsi six times in a handful of days, and afterward aides gushed to the press that Obama hoped he had found a pragmatic new ally in the Middle East. A week after Morsi's decree on the courts, Obama had a cordial Oval Office meeting with Morsi's foreign policy adviser, Essam el-Haddad.

As 2013 began, Morsi took further steps to consolidate his

power, silence critics, and sideline civil society groups. In December, crowds protested Morsi's moves to force through a constitution that put vast powers in the hands of the president and limited rights of expression. He moved to strip private political groups of their funding and to impose one-sided election rules. A deepening economic crisis, coupled with power blackouts and fuel shortages, added to the unrest.

Patterson decided it was time to start publicly distancing herself from Morsi's harsh rule. In a January speech in Alexandria, she went after the government's clumsy economic management. Speaking to a Lions Club gathering, she said the most catastrophic path for a government is to "avoid decisions, to show no leadership, to ignore the economic situation of the country." She criticized the new constitution, written by an Islamist-dominated committee, which restricted dissent and encouraged a backlash against Egypt's newly freed press. Patterson's new public challenge to the regime did not go unnoticed. She had shifted from the "velvet glove to tough love," wrote the National Endowment for Democracy, a private American pro-reform group.

As spring approached, it became clear that Morsi's rule was catalyzing a growing resistance from many sides: from the military, the activists in the streets, the business classes, and the rich Gulf states, who feared that Islamism could spread and threaten their own rule. The military began weighing an overthrow of the government. The United Arab Emirates and Saudi Arabia, which had been sending billions to Egypt to stabilize the economy, began quietly lobbying U.S. officials to support such a military intervention.

In March, Patterson warned Morsi advisers in a meeting at the presidential palace that Mohammed bin Zayed, the de facto leader of the United Arab Emirates, was trying to build support for Morsi's ouster. Patterson played down the risks of military intervention, saying she thought there was little chance any such effort would succeed. At the time U.S. officials didn't understand how many billions the Saudis and Emiratis were spreading around to win support for removal of Morsi. Within a month, however, Patterson began to see that she had underestimated the dangers. On April 24, in a meeting with defense minister Sisi and visiting defense secretary Chuck Hagel, Patterson was startled to see that Sisi was now signaling the military was considering overthrowing Morsi—later if not right away. "It was sort of a gee-whiz moment for me," she said. Patterson cabled Washington that she knew Sisi well enough to understand that he was serious. A military coup, she wrote, would be devastating.

Four days later she went public with her concerns. "Let me be clear: a military intervention is not the answer, as some would claim," she said in a speech.

Patterson decided she needed to try to correct the widespread perception that she and the administration were siding with the Islamists over other groups. In a June 18 speech at the Ibn Kaldun Center for Development Studies, a Cairo think tank, she urged unhappy Egyptians to organize and bring their influence to bear through the ballot box. She intended the remarks to be an endorsement of working through the system. But the locals focused on her call for Egyptians not to turn once again to street protests to overthrow a government. "Some say street action will produce better results than elections," she said. "To be honest, my government and I are deeply skeptical." The speech outraged many Egyptians, who saw it as more proof that she was siding with the government and trying to keep protesters at home.

"Ambassador Patterson is continuing the age-old U.S. practice in Egypt of being the last man standing to support an authoritarian regime," wrote the Egyptian-American activist Dina Guirguis.[7] In Washington, critics, including some former administration officials, said the remarks seemed to tilt toward Morsi and looked like intervention in Egyptian politics at a moment when America should be staying out of it. "I cringed when I heard it," said one former administration official.

A day later, Patterson traveled to a dilapidated office building in Cairo's Nasr City neighborhood to try to sell a compromise to Khairat al-Shater, the Muslim Brotherhood's top political strategist. A bearlike six-foot-four businessman with ten children, Shater had made a fortune selling household appliances to the exploding Egyptian population. He was the driving force behind the Muslim Brotherhood's recent ascent, reorganizing it and arranging its financing.

In a two-hour meeting, Patterson warned Shater that the government would be overthrown unless it took immediate steps to give the opposition a greater voice. She suggested they could overhaul the cabinet, and add some non-Islamists to broaden public support. They could start a process to amend the hard-line constitution with new input from the opposition. With these concessions they could announce plans for Morsi to serve out the next two years, she said. Otherwise "we think you're goners," she said.

Shater wasn't buying. He was preoccupied with worries that the Persian Gulf states, and particularly the Emiratis, were conspiring to overthrow the government. "The Emiratis hate me," he told her. Even so, he played down the threat of a coup, convinced the Morsi government still had the loyalty of a majority of Egyptians and could turn out its army of supporters into the streets. He didn't realize that the military, the intelligence agencies, and their foreign allies were already ahead of the government in preparing to mobilize their side.

"We think we can tough it out," Shater said.

"I hope you're right," Patterson replied.

Patterson had gotten nowhere. But when the opposition learned of the meeting, they smelled conspiracy. "History will remember that days before June 30, the world's superpower spent three hours in MB leader Kheirat Shater's office," a secular activist who identified himself as Big Pharaoh wrote on Twitter.

As the month went on, all the warning lights blinked red. On June 23, Sisi made his plans explicit, warning in a speech that the military might be forced to intervene. Still, Morsi continued making clumsy moves that further weakened his position. He appointed as the governor of Luxor, a top tourist destination, an Islamist with ties to a militant group that in 1997 had attacked the Deir el-Bahri archaeological site and killed sixty-two tourists. The appointment sparked public protests, and the official soon resigned.

The opposition had been publicizing its plans to hold a demonstration June 30, the one-year anniversary of Morsi's rule. The protests turned out to be a massive show of force: millions crowded into the streets in Cairo for a gathering that outstripped even the protests before Mubarak's fall. The demonstrators came armed with wooden clubs and metal pipes, prepared for the battles with Morsi supporters they believed were now inevitable. After dark they attacked the Muslim Brotherhood's Cairo headquarters with Molotov cocktails and were met with blasts of birdshot.[8] The following day Sisi gave Morsi an ultimatum: he needed to accept the demonstrators' demands within two days.

Morsi and his team again bumbled in interpreting the meaning of the demonstrations. By their count, there had still been more demonstrators in pro-Morsi protests. Morsi made a televised appeal at midnight, rejecting Sisi's ultimatum and warning that his supporters would react violently if the military tried to mount a coup. "If the price of protecting legitimacy is my blood, I'm willing to pay it!" he declared. He raged on for two and a half hours, denouncing his opponents, judges, and the media. The address, and another one a few days later, "were two of the most terrible, incoherent speeches I've ever heard," Patterson said. "I sat there and thought, *This guy just doesn't get it.*"

On the streets, signs of an impending coup began to appear. Army tanks and riot police appeared around key intersections in Cairo, surrounding government buildings and state media. On television, clock faces ticked down the minutes until Sisi's deadline. Morsi and top aides retreated from their offices in the presidential palace to the protection of a complex of buildings used by the presidential guards.

On the day before Sisi's deadline, Obama called Morsi from Tanzania, urging him to try to find a compromise by including opposition figures in his government. Morsi needed to make "bold gestures," Obama counseled.

In the last hours before the deadline, Patterson and other U.S. officials began frantic attempts to head off the ouster. After Obama's call, Patterson met with the Morsi aides who were huddled in the palace guard complex. What did Obama mean by "bold gestures"? they asked. If Morsi wanted to avoid arrest, Patterson told them, he might now need to resign. She enlisted the Qatari foreign minister to call Morsi with a proposal that he seek to placate Sisi by accepting a new prime minister, cabinet, and provincial governors. Essam Haddad, Morsi's foreign policy adviser, soon called Patterson to let her know Morsi had rejected the proposal. He would sooner let them slit his throat, he told aides, than give in. In a final bid, Patterson called Sisi and asked him to delay seizing power for two days in hopes that a compromise could be found.

Sisi insisted to Patterson that he would prefer not to intervene. And she believed him. It would be easier for him to remain the power behind the throne, with control over much of the nation's economy. But she saw that pressures on him were building. Lower-ranking military officers thought the government was challenging the military's leading role in the country and were demanding action. The crowds on the street were appealing to Sisi to save the country. "Come on, Sisi, make a decision," some chanted. "I thought, '*Oh, God, he's going to have to respond,*'" Patterson said. "You don't just question the manhood of an Arab military leader."

Late on the night of July 3, the military moved. They took Morsi into custody and spirited him to a secret location while also arresting top aides and dozens of other senior Muslim Brotherhood officials. Tens of thousands of supporters in Tahrir Square were jubilant as the military installed an interim government. But only blocks away, at other huge demonstrations, supporters of the Muslim Brotherhood were in tears and threatening violent retaliation. At least seven died and three hundred were injured in the first night as protests spread.

Over the next weeks the Islamists retreated to encampments in Cairo's streets, demanding a return of their power. Then the military, despite pleas from Patterson and a full cast of U.S. officials, moved against them. On August 14 the military killed an estimated 1,000 Muslim Brotherhood supporters in an attack on Rabaa al-Adawiya and Nahda Squares in Cairo. It was the worst political bloodletting in Egypt's modern history.

The Obama administration had failed to foresee the scale of the killings, convinced that the military would be restrained by the Islamists' popular support. In the days after the slaughter, U.S. officials entreated Sisi to release Morsi and to begin shaping a civilian government that included Islamists. Patterson believed there was little chance the generals would take those steps, and urged Washington to focus instead on dealing with Sisi and the new team.

The aftermath of the coup left U.S.-Egyptian relations at their lowest point since the 1970s and subjected the administration to scalding criticism at home. "Critics have howled at the administration's handling of Egypt from all directions," Derek Chollet, an Obama defense official, wrote in a memoir.[9]

Some critics complained the administration had been paying little attention to the crisis. Secretary of State John Kerry was spotted on his yacht off Nantucket the day of the coup and Obama went golfing two days later. Kerry defended himself saying that he had been on the phone with Patterson five times on July 3. The charge of inattention was unjustified. But the limits of American influence were clear.

Bill Burns, the deputy secretary of state, visited Cairo in late July to try to broker a deal that would have brought the release of some Islamists from jail and reduced the threat of the pro-Morsi crowds. The generals heard him out but kept Morsi in jail and continued the crackdown. Some Islamist and reform groups declined to meet with Burns at all. The administration threatened repeatedly to cut off its $1.3 billion in military aid but never did more than delay delivery of some F-16 jet fighters and other arms. As before, they remained convinced they needed to preserve the U.S. security relationship with Egypt in hopes of maintaining leverage over the generals.

The administration faced an embarrassing dilemma on whether

to call Morsi's ouster a coup. Everyone recognized that it was. But under U.S. law, Washington couldn't provide aid to a government once the State Department made a finding that it had come to power in a coup. Patterson was among those who said the administration should avoid the word, arguing it would only further strain relations and limit Obama's choices in dealing with the Egyptians. The administration was mocked for the decision but stuck by it.

The coup brought a new outpouring of criticism of Patterson in Egypt. The state-owned *Al-Ahram* newspaper wrote in a front-page article that Patterson and Shater had struck a secret deal to create a separate country out of Egypt's southern region. Posters in the public squares showed a distorted image of her face with red X's across it and denounced her as a *hayzaboon*, or ogre. "Spinster, Go Home," read a banner. It was no secret that she was married, but that didn't matter.

This time the vilification campaign was led by the United Arab Emirates, which wanted to head off any U.S. attempt to restore Morsi or halt the coming crackdown in the streets on the Muslim Brotherhood. Gulf-based satellite news networks such as Al Arabiya and Sky News Arabia began hammering Patterson as the supposed ringleader of the plot that brought Morsi to power. Emirati leaders were not subtle. Yousef al-Otaiba, the UAE's polished and well-connected ambassador in Washington, sent Obama aide Ben Rhodes a photograph of a poster denouncing Patterson with no explanation attached. It was "one of the most brazen acts I'd experienced in my job," Rhodes wrote in a memoir.[10]

President Obama complained angrily to Mohammed bin Zayed, crown prince of Abu Dhabi, about the attacks on his ambassador. Patterson was grateful Obama had stood up for her but told Prem Kumar, the National Security Council official, that it was unnecessary. "I'm a big girl," she said. "I can deal with it."

In Patterson's two years in Cairo, the embassy there had gone through much of what the embassy in Islamabad had experienced during her earlier posting. The embassy building, occupying a full block, felt increasingly besieged, with new concrete barriers added to the streets around it and security rules tightened and tightened again.

Patterson's Cairo posting had brought her criticism from some human rights advocates, including some officials within the administration, that she should have pressed Morsi's government harder for reform. Some reform activists saw her as a diplomat too comfortable dealing with dictators in back rooms. From the other direction, some conservatives thought she had been too close to the Muslim Brotherhood. Lieutenant General Michael Flynn, then the director of the Defense Intelligence Agency and later President Donald Trump's national security adviser, was among them.

Patterson agreed, in hindsight, that the administration should have pushed Morsi harder at some moments—especially, she believed, in late 2012, when he overreached to consolidate his own power. But from her perspective, many Americans didn't appreciate how little running room the administration had in pressing the Egyptians. American civilian aid to Egypt had dwindled over the years and provided little leverage, she said. The foremost U.S. priority had always been maintaining the security tie to preserve the 1979 peace treaty with Israel, she pointed out. Washington had intermittently pushed for democratic reforms, she noted, "but when push comes to shove, these all took a back seat to maintaining good relations with Israel."

There were limits to the value of trying to make Morsi a more democratic leader, she said, because "the problem with Morsi was not that he was an Islamic extremist, but that he simply didn't know what he was doing."

Patterson concluded Washington needed to rethink the way it funded pro-democracy NGOs because foreigners saw these efforts as American manipulation. "The policy backfired," she said.[11]

Deputy Secretary of State Bill Burns also decided in hindsight that the Obama administration should have made some different tactical choices. Officials should have pushed harder against Morsi's seizure of power in late 2012, he wrote later, and should have labeled the ouster of Morsi a coup, to send a message to the military and gain leverage with other political players. But, like Patterson, he suspected that "American influence was fundamentally incapable of shifting the course of events." Also like Patterson he believed Egypt never really had a democratic government in those two years, but remained under the control of the military throughout.[12]

After the coup, Sisi became president and began what became the most repressive dictatorship in the country's modern history. The Gulf states wrote checks for $20 billion to Egypt within weeks of Morsi's arrest to strengthen Sisi's hold on power.[13] Morsi was jailed for six years, then collapsed and died during a court hearing in June 2019.

When Patterson's Egypt tour ended, the administration nominated her to be assistant secretary for Near Eastern affairs. It was the department's top Mideast job and a post that rarely went to officials without decades of experience in the region. Some Gulf states and the Jordanians lobbied against her, arguing she had been tied too closely to the Muslim Brotherhood, but Obama himself wanted her in the new job. He ran into her at a meeting at a Brookings Institution event in December and told her the administration would push for her. "We'll get you through," he said. The Senate approved her nomination by a vote of 78 to 16. During her Senate confirmation hearing, lawmakers did not even raise the criticism of her time in Egypt.

Patterson was taking over the Middle East portfolio at a moment of rare turmoil, including in Syria, Yemen, Libya, and Egypt. Like her last three postings, the job would be a long, uphill climb. Her new boss, Secretary Kerry, was confident she could do it. On the day of the military coup in Egypt, when she was taking the most heat, he put out a statement defending her. "She does her best work in the most challenging places," Kerry wrote.

# CHAPTER 16

# In Good Conscience

Hundreds of members of the Syrian opposition jammed into the Dusit Thani LakeView hotel in Cairo in July 2012 for a gathering aimed at finally unifying their squabbling organizations. The delegates spent two days together drinking tea, smoking, and arguing over a joint statement their foreign backers hoped would show the world they were capable of governing a new Syria. As the night grew late on the second day, word came that the leaders would soon emerge into the main hallway to make a statement to the news media.

When TV crews flipped on their lights and the doors parted, a crowd spilled forth in a din of shouting. Men pushed and scuffled while, at the center of the scrum, a Kurdish delegate and an Arab traded punches. On the sidelines, a plump woman in a head scarf began weeping. Robert Ford stood at the edge of the crowd clutching a red folder and looking on. "This is not good," he told a colleague. He waded into the group and began trying to peel the combatants apart.

For the past five months Ford had been working from Washington as U.S. envoy to the Syrian opposition and the Obama administration's point man on the expanding civil war. Uniting a fractured opposition was a constant struggle. Coordinating the administration's unsteady approach to the war was no easier.

Ford and his team of about twenty worked from a suite of rooms on the second floor of State Department headquarters. They were in their offices by dawn, using Skype and other channels to gather support for arming the moderate Syrian rebels. "We all need to get in this game," Ford told him. If the Islamists in eastern Syria joined forces with those in western Iraq, "it's going to be terrible," he said.

The following month Ford rode the State Department elevator up to the seventh floor to make the same pitch to Secretary of State Clinton. Ford feared Clinton would not welcome his prodding and "it would be another unhappy, unpleasant meeting." Ford ran through his talking points: Washington needed to provide aid to strengthen the moderates, restrain the growth of the Al Qaeda–linked Nusra Front, and build pressure on Assad to negotiate. To his surprise, Clinton was already on his side. "Absolutely," Clinton told him. She said there was another reason to provide aid: it would also give Washington more leverage over the opposition groups. Clinton had already been thinking about ways the administration could try to steer the upcoming negotiations toward a resolution. Over the coming months Clinton, Petraeus, and Defense Secretary Leon Panetta all argued internally that the administration needed to arm the rebels to pressure Assad to negotiate peace.

In trying to unite the opposition, Ford had to deal with fault lines between religious and secular, Sunni, Christian, and Alawite, Arab and Kurd. The tensions between Arab and Kurd were especially high. The fistfight at the Cairo hotel in July 2012 was over the Kurds' demands to be granted a measure of autonomy in a new Syria, just as Kurds had been given one in postwar Iraq. The Syrian Arabs claimed some of the same territory in northeastern Syria and were in no mood to compromise.

Ford succeeded in breaking up the fight that night in Cairo. Afterward he rounded up Arab and Kurdish delegates in a conference room and haggled until 3:00 a.m. He told them they needed to focus on uniting the group against Assad and shouldn't be sidetracked by other issues. "Don't worry about the status of the Kurds," he said. "You need to worry about how you're going to stop this guy from killing people."

But the Arabs batted down everything the Kurds wanted. They wouldn't accept language acknowledging Kurdish "autonomy"

news of the war from rebel generals, academics, journalis
other contacts inside Syria. By 7:40 a.m. they would present
status report to Beth Jones, the acting assistant secretary i
Middle East. They were also briefing the CIA on internal
opments, because they had the administration's best contac
freshest information.

Even before he returned to Washington from his posti
ambassador in Damascus, Ford had been warning the admir
tion about the troubling drift of the conflict. Ford and his team
the first to warn, by October 2011, that jihadists were swar
into Syria in numbers that could enable them to seize contr
the uprising from the more moderate Syrians who began it. 7
was a flow of Al Qaeda–linked militants from Iraq. Other rec
were entering from Europe and the Middle East across the 7
ish border. With money from rich Saudis, Kuwaitis, and Qat
Islamist groups were taking over pockets of territory in law
eastern Syria.

In cable after cable Ford and his team urged the adminis
tion to step up support for the moderate opposition, including v
arms. Ford's position on the war had shifted. In the first months
urged the opposition to avoid violence. By the fall of 2011 he I
come to the view that the protest movement was now a civil v
and Washington needed to help the moderates.

Officials in Washington were painfully divided on the confli
As killings and refugee flows grew, many wanted more U.S. actic
But President Obama doubted the United States could have mu
influence over the outcome and was intent on winding down Ame
ica's Mideast wars, not joining new ones.

In the summer of 2012, the State Department team had prepare
a classified memo for Washington warning that unless Washingto
helped the moderate opposition in the eastern side of the country
the extremists would take over there. "By 2012, we were in full
scale alarm about it," Ford said.

In April 2012, Ford went to Langley, Virginia, to visit retirec
general David Petraeus, then the CIA director, to try to enlist his

or references to a "decentralization" of government. Ford finally won the two sides' commitment to a joint statement. But its language on the Kurdish issue was weak, providing only that the new government, once installed, would review the structure of governance. "It was incredibly painful," said Ford. "And both sides went away mad."

The meeting was a new blow to the opposition's image. Only three days earlier, world leaders meeting at UN offices in Geneva had signed a communiqué intended to lay the groundwork for negotiations to create a new government in Syria. U.S. officials had hoped that the Cairo conference would show that a unified opposition was ready to create a new country that would share power among all of Syria's diverse groups. Instead the world saw video clips of a fistfight.

Ford traveled an endless circuit of opposition meetings in the Middle East and Europe, some of them nearly as acrimonious as the summit in Cairo. One of the most disappointing was a gathering in Qatar in November 2012.

The opposition organizations were linked by an umbrella group called the Syrian National Council. But as the months passed, it became clear that the group was a fractured and incoherent organization dominated by expatriates who had only weak ties to the armed groups actually battling the government in Syria. The leaders of many of these political groups seemed more interested in raising money from Western governments and securing luxury hotel accommodations abroad than with what was going on in their homeland. "They're just coming from their Swedish spas and have no credibility inside Syria," Beth Jones, the acting assistant secretary, told officials of allied governments.

The American team tried to develop a plan to create a new opposition organization that would give a more prominent role to groups that were actually fighting the war. The British, Germans, and French were open to this idea, as were some Middle Eastern states. Qatar volunteered to host the meeting and, with the Turks, organized it. But what seemed a generous offer turned out to be much less.

When Ford showed up in Doha on November 11, 2012, he was barred from sitting in on the deliberations over the new organization. "They'll come out when they're finished and brief you," a Qatari official told Ford at the door. Ford had given the organizers a list of groups who were now active in the fighting in Syria, urging that they should be invited and given a role in the deliberations. None had been invited.

The Qataris and Turks, fearful that the groups they backed would be marginalized, had outmaneuvered the Americans, arranging the meeting so that the opposition groups who were their strongest allies would retain their central influence. The new group was largely the same as before—old wine in a new bottle. "The Qataris and Turks cooked the whole thing up," Ford said. The French had gone along because Lebanese Christians, influential with Paris, had pressed to keep the old pecking order. The Germans and British, bound to preserve European unity, followed the French lead. The outcome was a troubling sign that Washington, though providing billions in humanitarian aid, had little influence in the diplomacy because of its peripheral role in the fighting.

Meanwhile, President Obama had rejected the proposals from the CIA and State Department to arm the rebels. Through much of 2012, the debate over the aid to the rebels continued through many meetings, with the same arguments and counterarguments repeated over and over.

Ford took part in the so-called deputies meetings—the interagency sessions that included the deputy agency heads—until the end of 2012. One day he stopped getting invited. It seemed the group had heard all they wanted of Ford's arguments for military assistance. Ford raised the issue with Denis McDonough, Obama's chief of staff, and McDonough said he would look into it. But Ford heard no more and was never invited back.

In August 2012, Obama heard a proposal backed by Clinton, Petraeus, and Defense Secretary Leon Panetta for the United States to begin arming vetted opposition fighters. By the following month

Obama had decided against the plan, fearing it could draw Washington into a war without winning it. He approved plans for U.S. agencies to help provide public services in liberated areas of the country, as well as aid, food, blankets, computers, and phones for the rebels. But "all these steps were Band-Aids," Clinton wrote in her memoir.[1] "The battle raged on."

Opposition leaders agreed with her and shared their frustrations with Ford. In November 2012, the reshaped umbrella group chose as its new president Moaz al-Khatib, a popular and respected Syrian imam who was considered a moderate Islamist. Khatib, a former geologist from a prominent family, had been jailed repeatedly by the Assad regime. He wanted to see a multiparty system and an end to sectarianism in the new Syria. He gave an inspiring speech when he was chosen, raising hopes that the opposition finally had the charismatic leader it badly needed.

Khatib clashed almost immediately with Ford. The American diplomat flew to Cairo in February 2013 to warn Khatib that the opposition needed to stop collaborating with the Nusra Front, the Al Qaeda–linked jihadist group that was the most aggressive of the rebel forces. Nusra had been recently added to the U.S. list of foreign terrorist organizations, a step that made it illegal for Americans to have contacts with it. Ford told Khatib that they needed to stay away from Nusra if his group wanted American help.

"You don't know who you're dealing with," Ford told Khatib. "As soon as Assad's gone, they'll kill you next." Khatib was outraged by the American demand, arguing that the opposition needed Nusra's military help, since the Americans and other Western countries were providing so little. Washington was standing by, Khatib raged, while Sunnis were slaughtered. "They're being bombed and killed and you aren't doing anything," he told Ford. Ford reminded him that he had warned from the beginning that U.S. troops would never join the war, as the rebels hoped. He pressed Khatib to finally start preparing for negotiations with Assad over formation of a new government. Khatib said the opposition group had no interest in negotiations and didn't need them, because they would soon win a victory on the battlefield. "We'll be in Damascus the next time we meet," he told Ford.

But the rebel advances soon became retreats. The rebels lost a key battle at the small western city of Qusayr in April when 7,000 troops of the Iranian Revolutionary Guard Corps joined the fight. It was the first time the elite Iranian unit had gotten into the war as combat forces, and a turning point in the military struggle. The same month Khatib quit his job, complaining about Western inaction and his organization's internal squabbles.

Ford was talking to dozens of fighting groups and carrying on similar conversations with each. The first thing they asked for was American protection from Syrian aircraft. They wanted shoulder-fired surface-to-air missiles, like the Stingers that the U.S. had supplied Afghan fighters during their 1980s war with the Soviets. They would also ask Washington to set up a no-fly zone to protect them from Syrian aircraft, or a no-bombing zone. "They tried every different version, angle and possibility of that," said Wa'el Alzayat, a former foreign service officer who was part of Ford's team. The opposition groups were always persistent and always disappointed.

Ford also had a tempestuous relationship with Colonel Abdul Jabbar al-Oqaidi, a ranking officer of the armed rebel group called the Free Syrian Army. Oqaidi, a burly defector from the Syrian army, hung up his brown and green camouflage and wore a suit when he met Ford for the first time in an Istanbul hotel. The conversation turned combative after the first greetings.

Ford, eager to show a U.S. commitment, told Oqaidi that the Americans were giving the rebels thousands of American field rations along with medical supplies.

"I don't want your food," Oqaidi told him in Arabic. "My men can eat the bark off the trees. We want weapons."

"I have strict instructions to tell you the president is not willing to provide weapons," Ford said. "And you should not expect we will ever provide weapons. Why don't you take the food? Then you won't have to eat the bark off trees."

Ford urged Oqaidi to try to build a close relationship with U.S. officials. If officials in Washington knew him and his group better, they might at some point consider providing some arms, he said.

"In my country, a boy meets a girl, they talk, they go out to lunch, go to a movie. And eventually, they might get married," Ford said.

"Mr. Ambassador, in my country you get married before you have lunch or dinner," Oqaidi said.

Ford later described that exchange to White House officials. It didn't get a laugh.

Ford saw Oqaidi again two months later, in an encounter that brought him face-to-face with the new reality of the war. Ford flew to an airport in southern Turkey near the Syrian border to watch the unloading of 65,000 U.S. military field rations for Oqaidi's troops. Afterward, Ford and his team decided to cross into Syria and pose for some pictures with Oqaidi to publicize America's support for the rebels.

Ford and his team drove across the Turkish-Syrian border at the Bab al-Salameh crossing point, then walked a kilometer through a no-man's-land to Oqaidi's local base. But their quiet conversation with the commander was disrupted by the arrival of a group of angry fighters from an Islamist militia called Suqour al-Sham, the Hawks of the Levant. The fighters roared in in pickup trucks mounted with machine guns, firing their weapons and angrily denouncing Oqaidi. A fighter from their group had just been killed and they blamed Oqaidi for failing to provide enough ammunition. They hinted that he was selling off the rebels' ammunition supply to enrich himself.

The appearance of the fighters was shocking. They were in their early twenties but had long hair, piercing eyes, and a wild look from years in battle. After two years of killing and fighting to stay alive, they seemed no longer fully human, Wa'el Alzayat thought. "They were so much tougher looking, hardened by the fighting. They had been transformed into something else."

Oqaidi finally calmed the fighters and they left. But the Americans knew the encounter could have ended badly, in a shoot-out that would have drawn attention around the world—and possibly set off a political crisis in Washington. It was only one year since U.S. ambassador to Libya Chris Stevens had been killed in a terror attack in Benghazi, and the GOP-led congressional investigations that followed had made the State Department more anxious than ever to keep diplomats out of danger. Ford and Alzayat hadn't asked clearance to go into Syria. They knew the trip held danger but believed they need to publicize U.S. support for the rebels.

Ford had another unhappy encounter with Oqaidi three months later. Oqaidi's forces had teamed up with Islamist fighters to seize the Menagh Air Base, near Aleppo. Afterward, Oqaidi had posed for triumphant pictures with their captured weapons and the jihadists who had collaborated with them. The Syrian regime and its Russian allies circulated pictures of Oqaidi and the jihadist leader Abu Jandal, along with the earlier photos of Oqaidi with Ford. The Syrians and Russians viewed the pictures as proof the Americans were in bed with terrorists, just as they had been arguing. The pictures were an embarrassment for the Obama administration, which had been trying to convince the American public that it wasn't collaborating with terrorists. It was also a disturbing sign that the extremists were becoming the core of the opposition's military effort.

Ford called Oqaidi to complain about his collaboration with the jihadists. The Syrian blew up at him, much as Khatib had. "God damn you, I've told you we need weapons," Oqaidi exploded. "I've got Assad on my head. If I can't get weapons from you, I'll go somewhere I can get them."

Ford kept arguing, but he had some sympathy for Oqaidi's impossible position. He understood that the opposition was losing thousands of fighters, surrendering ground, and that there was nothing they could do about it. The conversations kept getting harder and harder for him. As Assad and his allies the Iranians and Russians gained strength, the moderates were leaning more and more on the Islamists. Some key U.S. officials resisted giving arms to the moderates out of fear that the opposition could be highjacked by more radical elements. In Ford's view, the lack of U.S. help made the radical takeover a self-fulfilling prophecy.

Another hinge point came in late August 2013 when President Obama backed off his threat to attack Assad with missiles for killing 1,400 civilians in Ghouta with the deadly chemical agent sarin. Obama had declared a year earlier that a chemical strike would be a "red line" that would bring U.S. retaliation. But on August 31, Obama backed away from the strike at the last minute, saying he would need congressional support for such an action. The support never materialized. Instead, Obama reached an agreement with Russia and Syria to remove Syria's stores of chemical weapons. The administration hailed the deal as a better outcome than a one-off missile attack. But as the years passed, the regime's chemical attacks resumed, confirming fears that Assad never intended to surrender all of his chemical stocks. In 2018 a UN-convened investigative commission found there had been thirty-four confirmed chemical attacks in the past five years.[2]

Obama's reversal convinced Ford he was making no headway and needed to find another job. Frederic C. Hof, another administration adviser on Syria, had quit in frustration in September 2012. Ford's arguments were going nowhere. He had been urging an expansion of the covert program of training rebels in Jordan and southern Turkey, but U.S. agencies had been training so few that they had no practical effect.

Obama's decision not to strike had further strained Ford's relations with his Syria contacts. "They're deeply disappointed that we chose not to use military force," Ford testified to the Senate Foreign Relations Committee. "I have just heard anguish from people I have talked to over there."

While Ford was pressing behind the scenes for stronger action, in public he was the face of the administration's Syria policy, and was getting bashed for it. At meetings of the Senate Foreign Relations Committee, Ford was a piñata.

Senator John McCain had been cordial to Ford in the past. He was one of the senators who had put a hold on Ford's 2011 nomination to be ambassador to Syria. But McCain had privately assured Ford the dispute was about the wisdom of sending a U.S. ambassador to repressive Syria, not about him personally. He had told Clinton that she should make Ford ambassador to Iraq, not Syria. But McCain's attitude about Ford had changed as his frustrations over the Syrian war boiled over. McCain was taking out his frustrations on Ford.

In April 2013 McCain asked Ford why the administration wouldn't agree to set up a no-fly zone in Syria, when the four-star officers in charge of NATO and the U.S. regional command in the Middle East all said it could be done. Ford demurred, saying his training had been in economics and he didn't have the military background to challenge those military leaders' judgment.

McCain blew up. "You were the ambassador there," McCain told him. "If anybody is supposed to know what is going on in Syria, it is you. For you to answer me that you are an economist . . . Maybe you are suited for a job as an economist over at the State Department, not as a lead on Syria."

In October, Senator Bob Corker, the Tennessee Republican who was the committee chairman, assailed Ford because the administration was still providing nothing more lethal than delivery trucks and had succeeded in training only a handful of rebel fighters. "I cannot imagine that you can sit here with a straight face and feel good about what we have done," Corker said. "I could not be more embarrassed by the way our country has let people, civilians, down on the ground the way we have." Ford sat there knowing, of course, that he shared many of their views and had been arguing for them in private. But he could say nothing.

After the October hearing, Ford decided he'd had enough. He had continued to serve in Iraq through five postings, despite his misgivings about the invasion, because he felt he was contributing. Now he sensed he was making no headway and found it agonizing to hear the complaints of the Syrians and watch the war's destruction at close range. He put in for a transfer to another job, intending to leave the Foreign Service soon. When Bill Burns, the deputy secretary of state, heard that Ford had applied for a transfer, he canceled it and persuaded Ford to stay for another six months. "We can't replace you," Burns told him.

John Kerry, who'd become secretary of state in Obama's second term, had proposed to make Ford the new ambassador to Egypt. The post was traditionally the most coveted ambassadorship for Arabists, and Ford was eager to take it. But when the idea was broached to the military government that had taken power in a coup in July 2103, they rejected it out of hand. They had watched Ford challenge Assad in Damascus and saw him as the kind of ambassador who would side with dissenters, perhaps including Islamists, and cause trouble for them. The State Department offered another ambassadorship in another country. But it was damp, peaceful, and far from the Middle East.

"That is not you," said his wife, Alison. "Wouldn't you rather move to Vermont?"

"Vermont sounds a lot better," he agreed.

Ford thanked Kerry for the offer but joked that it was simply too far from his world. "I've never been east of Dubai," he said.

Ford had one final Syria assignment—a tough one. The United Nations was bringing together the parties in the Syrian war in Geneva in January 2014 in hopes they could begin negotiating, for the first time, the formation of a new government. The U.N. had announced the meeting, with support from Russia, the Assad regime, and the United States, in late November 2013. Kerry had assigned Ford to see to it that the opposition groups showed up. They had long resisted such negotiations, as they were reluctant to sit at a table with Syrian officials they considered mass murderers.

"You have a big job in front of you," Mikhail Bogdanov, a Russian deputy foreign minister, told Ford at a meeting in New York. Ford noticed that Bogdanov showed no interest in ensuring that all the parties showed up. He suspected that Moscow would be just as happy if the opposition stayed away, the talks collapsed—and it was all blamed on Washington.

With help from key players and laborious effort, Ford convinced the opposition leaders to show up. The armed groups had been planning to stay away and criticize the other groups for going. But the Turks and the Qataris had leaned heavily on the brigades they supported, threatening to cut off their aid if they didn't show up.

When the Geneva conference entered its second weeklong round, in mid-February, it became clear that negotiations over a new government were going nowhere. It wasn't because of the rebels. They made an unexpected last-minute offer to begin negotiations over the composition of a new Syrian government without requiring as a precondition that Assad step down. That was an important concession: the opposition had previously insisted Assad's departure had to be part of any deal. But the Syrian regime refused to even talk about the proposal. And their patrons the Russians refused to make them, despite their earlier commitments to do so. Wendy Sherman, the undersecretary of state and the ranking U.S. official at the negotiations, ripped into them. "You agreed to this," she told the Russian delegation. "You say you want to deal with us in good faith, then you do this." After watching the Russians frustrate the peace negotiations for three years, Ford found Sherman's performance satisfying. "She was tough," he said. "I loved it."

The talks sputtered to an end on February 15, and the diplomats left town with no plans to restart them. Ford told Kerry, in a final word of advice, that the secretary shouldn't waste time trying to convince the Russians to force the Syrians into negotiations, because Moscow would never do it. Kerry, eager for every challenge and convinced of his powers of persuasion, spent the next three years pressing the Russians on negotiations. He made no headway.

Twelve days after the Geneva talks ended, Ford walked out of the State Department for the last time, carrying an assortment of photos, awards, and personal effects. One memento he valued was the American flag Bill Burns, the deputy secretary, gave him at a retirement ceremony. He had been in the Foreign Service twenty-eight years.

After helping guide the country's Syria policy for three years,

Ford wanted to explain himself. As a foreign service officer, if he couldn't defend the policy, "it was time for me to leave," he wrote in a June op-ed column in the *New York Times*. The Geneva talks had collapsed, he wrote, because Assad and his Russian and Iranians allies didn't feel enough pressure to negotiate an end to the war. And the way to build that pressure was for the United States to strengthen the opposition with supplies, salaries, and arms, including surface-to-air missiles to vetted groups. More delay in strengthening the moderate opposition against the regime and the jihadists, he wrote, "simply hastens the day when American forces will have to intervene against Al Qaeda in Syria."[3] Within days of Ford's op-ed, Obama was forced to start sending U.S. troops back to the region, first to Iraq and then to Syria, to help halt the expansion of the new jihadist threat, the Islamic State.

Ford's exit and op-ed brought little visible reaction from the administration, in part because his views were widely shared among insiders. "Everybody knew that was the feeling of almost the entire administration, except the president," said Beth Jones, who was the senior State Department official for the Middle East until December 2013. Deputy Secretary of State Bill Burns, who retired from the State Department later in 2014, ended up with a view on Syria that was not far from Ford's. The administration would have improved its chances for a successful outcome by pressing for more limited, gradual reforms and taking earlier, stronger action to strengthen moderate rebels, he concluded. "It is hard not to see Syria's agony as an American policy failure," he wrote in his memoir.[4]

Some in Washington seemed pleased to read Ford's exit lines. Senator McCain tweeted that Ford's op-ed was "devastating." But Ford wasn't interested in patching up relations with his former tormenters in the Senate. When McCain invited him over for a goodbye meeting, Ford declined.

CHAPTER 17

# Cool Heads in Hot Spots

Robert Ford was riding uptown on a clattering New York subway train in late September 2015, when his cell phone rang. "This is the White House," a voice said. "The president would like you to come for lunch Friday." Ford was not sure he had heard that right over the din of the rush-hour Lexington Avenue line. "The president is inviting me to lunch?" he shouted into the phone. The weary commuters around him fell silent and stared.

Ford had been out of the Foreign Service for almost two years. He had quit his final post, as envoy to Syria, over his unhappiness with the administration's policy. Barack Obama was the last person he was expecting to hear from. But when he got off at Eighty-Sixth Street and called back to make sure this was no hoax, he was assured it wasn't. He showed up at the wrought-iron gate of the White House three days later. Standing in front of him in line was his former boss, Ryan Crocker.

The president wanted to have lunch alone with the two top Mideast hands at a dire moment in the Syrian civil war. Only days before, the Russians had officially entered the war on the Syrian government's side, a development that undermined peace talks and ultimately swung the war in the Syrian regime's favor. At the same time the Pentagon had closed down its $500 million effort to train Syrian rebels, a major piece of its participation in the conflict, acknowledging it had prepared only a handful of fighters. "Robert and I realized, *Wow, it's come to a point where the president is going to be asking some serious questions*," Crocker said.

During lunch in a small room off the Oval Office, Obama probed their thoughts on the civil war and the intertwined struggle against the Islamic State militant group in eastern Syria and Iraq. Crocker and Ford urged a limited increase in U.S. military involvement in hopes of forcing the Syrians and their allies, the Iranians and Russians, to finally negotiate seriously on peace. Without a show of U.S. determination, they told him, the three countries were likely to continue to escalate their fight with the rebels, further reducing the chance of a settlement. Crocker, a former ambassador to Syria, argued that the Pentagon could ground pro-government warplanes with a no-fly zone, and said there were ways to set it up to limit risk to U.S. troops. Obama was skeptical, arguing that U.S. escalation would only provoke the Russians to step up their campaign. He doubted, too, that there would be public support for direct military involvement. But Crocker and Ford tried to make the case that only through the combination of force and diplomacy could Washington end the most devastating war of the new century. Obama listened, asked questions, and took notes. A president's time is Washington's most precious commodity. Obama spent ninety minutes with them.

Later that day Crocker and Ford went out for a beer. It felt good to have a chance to air their thoughts on a situation that had been haunting them. They felt they had made a good case. "We congratulated ourselves on how brilliant we had been," said Crocker. The glow faded as weeks passed. "The president did not do a single thing we put on the table," Crocker said.[1] For foreign service veterans, the feeling was familiar. The top officials valued your advice and sought it out. They might follow it and they might not. That's how it worked.

After her return from Egypt, Anne Patterson stayed in the State Department for three years as assistant secretary for Near Eastern affairs, the top Middle East job. The bureau was traumatized from a dozen years of turmoil in the region. The upheavals meant that embassies were periodically forced to evacuate family members and so-called nonessential staff, increasing the burden on those who remained. In the past year the bureau had been under intense scrutiny from higher-ups and Congress following the terror attack that killed Ambassador Chris Stevens in Benghazi, Libya. All of it made it far harder to recruit staff for the posts in the conflict zones. Lawmakers and other diplomats were surprised but impressed that she would take the job. "I don't know anyone who would have wanted that job," said one diplomat. "But she doesn't shrink from the hard stuff."

Her team's top priority was the war in Syria, where casualties continued to rise and an exodus of refugees was destabilizing the country's neighbors and Europe. Secretary of State John Kerry had Patterson and the Mideast experts up until late at night trying to devise new strategies to get Assad's government to the negotiating table. The secretary of state wanted the White House to build military pressure on Assad to negotiate a peace, and urged more covert aid to the rebels and, at some points, strikes on the Syrian military. But Obama didn't want the U.S. drawn into another war, leaving Kerry with a weak diplomatic hand. He tried to persuade the Russians to pressure their Syrian allies to negotiate. But the Kremlin would not be moved. In September 2015, when the Russians began direct military involvement with air attacks on rebels, "that was the beginning of the end," Patterson said. They bombed not only the rebel encampments but hospitals, water plants, and sewage facilities, making civilians' lives ever more miserable. "We were simply overwhelmed by Syria. No one knew what to do. It kept getting worse and worse and worse."

The State Department team offered a series of initiatives to try to get negotiations going, but they varied little from one to the next. As the years passed, pressure only grew. Behind closed doors, Kerry encouraged a candid back-and-forth with his Mideast staff, and he got it. He sometimes yelled at the staff over their work. And they sometimes pushed back, telling him his approach was based on a flawed understanding and would accomplish nothing. Kerry kept trying, but when Obama's presidency ended, the war ground on, and so did criticism of the administration for failing to stop it.

Patterson left the job and ended her forty-three-year foreign service career in December 2016, a month before the end of the Obama administration. But some of her former colleagues still wanted her help. In February 2017 the Trump administration's new defense secretary, retired Marine General James Mattis, asked Patterson to serve as his number three, the undersecretary of defense for policy. Some former colleagues told Patterson she ought to stay away from a new administration that seemed intent on upending foreign policy tradition and sidelining diplomats. But Patterson had had a good relationship with Mattis when he was U.S. military commander for the Middle East, and she hoped the new team might be able to make progress after the retrenchment of the Obama years. "I just didn't feel I could say no to Mattis," she said. "I thought we had a chance to redeem some of the mistakes, particularly on Syria," she said. Obama's moves to limit U.S. involvement in Syria and elsewhere in the Middle East "were, in retrospect, very damaging," she said.

Patterson's nomination seemed to have the support of a majority in the Senate, including Senator John McCain, who was chairman of the Senate Armed Services Committee. But opposition grew in some conservative circles. Patterson, in their view, had been too close in her Egypt posting to the Muslim Brotherhood, which conservatives wanted Trump to designate an outlawed terrorist group. Supporters pointed out that Patterson had, of course, been following the administration's policy in dealing with a democratically elected government. But Mira Ricardel, an adviser on Pentagon staffing who had long had friction with Mattis, tried to stop the appointment. When senators Ted Cruz (R-Tex.) and Tom Cotton (R-Ark.) said they would block the confirmation, the White House decided it didn't want the fight. Mattis was forced to drop the nomination.

But Patterson, like Ryan Crocker, Robert Ford, and Chris Stevens, had already made a mark. They had gone to the hardest places, as their superiors had asked, and done the hardest things. In a time of confounding challenges, they were sent repeatedly on the toughest assignments because they could improvise policy, manage teams of thousands, and sometimes, in a crisis, help run their host governments as well.

These diplomats followed in a long tradition of Western envoys sent past the horizon to deal with states in turmoil. Among their predecessors were famous names: T. E. Lawrence, the British officer who led an Arab insurgency in World War I; Gertrude Bell, the colonial envoy who shaped modern Iraq in the 1920s; and Edward Lansdale, the American adviser who sought political solutions to insurgencies in the Philippines and Vietnam in the middle of the twentieth century. Like those emissaries, these ambassadors sometimes relied on military force and great-power pressure. But their main tools were persuasion and an understanding of local ways. When Washington lost all patience with the leaders of Iraq, Pakistan, and Afghanistan, the ambassadors kept knocking on their doors and found a way to do business with them day after day.

Crocker began building a relationship with Hamid Karzai in 2002, when the Afghan was a former schoolteacher who had become the accidental leader of a state that existed only on letterhead. While Crocker was ambassador to neighboring Pakistan between 2004 and 2007, he visited Afghanistan regularly to tend the relationship. And in 2011, when Karzai was barely speaking to U.S. officials in Kabul, Crocker could step in as ambassador and conduct business.

Foreign leaders who complained about American meddling sometimes asked U.S. diplomats to resolve their crises. In 2009, when a confrontation between Pakistan's two most powerful politicians had brought the country close to a coup, the army chief, civilian officials, and even Islamist leaders turned to Anne Patterson to find a way to end the dispute.

These ambassadors reminded Washington of the hard realities. In late 2008, when President Bush wanted a deal with the Iraqi government that would set no departure date for U.S. troops, Crocker explained to him that that was out of reach. Average Iraqis had lost patience with the five-year-old occupation.

They told officials in Washington, always under domestic

pressure to end overseas missions, of the importance of patiently following through on the grand plans they had put in motion. Ryan Crocker, as head of the governance team in chaotic post-invasion Baghdad, told his bosses they would need to "hunker down and prepare for a long stay." Anne Patterson, asked by the Obama White House in 2009 how to end the Afghan war, counseled that it would require years of laborious effort to stabilize the country and extend Pakistan's control over the wild tribal areas where militants took refuge. The ambassadors knew the German sociologist Max Weber's observation that conducting foreign policy is like slowly boring a hole through hard wood.

The ambassadors sometimes offered good counsel to contacts outside government, too. Robert Ford, seasoned by years in Iraq, urged Syrian dissidents in the first days of their uprising to try to negotiate limited reforms with the Assad government rather than opening an all-out conflict they had little chance of winning. He told opposition leaders in mid-2011 that the Obama administration would never send U.S. troops to fight beside them, as the rebels firmly believed they would. He was right.

Some of their best advice was ignored. Crocker began 2002 cautioning Washington that leaving too few troops in Afghanistan could allow the insurgency to take root and organize a comeback. By the summer he warned that invading Iraq could be disastrous. The Bush administration didn't heed his advice on either occasion. Over time, most in Washington came to the view that they should have.

These ambassadors built a new model for relations between diplomats and generals on the battlefront. In the first years after 9/11, the generals and ambassadors often worked around or against each other. Crocker and commanders like Generals David Petraeus and John Allen mapped strategy at morning meetings, then spoke as one. Their roles were hybrid: the generals had a hand in local politics and the diplomats sometimes played war planners. Patterson built a network of U.S. military and intelligence officials who all supported each other as they moved from job to job in the national security world as the wars continued.

Most Americans at home had little idea what these ambassadors were doing in their remote postings. But the public would get a peek as of November 2010, when the Wikileaks anti-secrecy group released 251,000 classified U.S. diplomatic cables. The papers revealed what top diplomats, including Crocker, Patterson, Stevens, and Ford, had been saying about foreign governments and leaders. The disclosures were an earthquake that strained American ties to other governments for years. But they had the unexpected effect of raising the public's appreciation of the diplomatic corps. "My personal opinion of the State Department has gone up several notches," wrote the British historian and journalist Timothy Garton Ash. Beneath their "dandruffy" exteriors, he concluded, the ambassadors were sharper than they looked.[2] Patterson was praised as a truth teller for her assessment of war in Pakistan and Afghanistan. Her candor was "heroic," wrote Simon Jenkins, a British author and columnist. "Patterson's cables are like missives from the Titanic as it already heads for the bottom."[3]

After they left the Foreign Service, Crocker, Ford, and Patterson took posts at universities and think tanks and spoke to groups interested in foreign policy. Crocker and Ford testified to congressional committees. They had all invested blood and sweat, and sometimes, in public appearances, a deep disappointment spilled out about U.S. efforts in the Middle East. Crocker could be caustic about what he saw as the administrations' folly. He criticized the drone strategy he had helped supervise in Pakistan. He had come to the view that it was a stopgap substitute for a real counterinsurgency strategy and that U.S. officials, despite their claims, never knew how many civilians they were killing.[4] In early 2019, Crocker became one of the most outspoken critics of the Afghan peace negotiations that his former partner, Zalmay Khalilzad, was carrying on with the Taliban. He contended that the Trump administration's search for a quick deal to withdraw U.S. troops would mean the abandonment of the country, much like the Nixon administration's Paris peace talks to end the Vietnam War. But both Crocker and Ford supported the Trump administration's plan to withdraw the U.S. troops fighting the Islamic State militants in Syria.

Crocker made progress in dealing with his movement disorder. He found a physician in Houston who could treat his symptoms, allowing him to resume his beloved jogging routine.

Their predictions for the region were not optimistic. In their view the Middle East, which had seemed on the threshold of a bright new era in 2011, was doomed to disorder for years to come. The period revealed that weakness in these states was not just in newer and fragile civilian institutions but in pillars of the old order, like the militaries, which Washington had assumed to be strong. "I don't think we knew how bad they were—how rotten in the core," said Patterson. The Egyptian military, despite $45 billion in U.S. aid since 1978, had become a hollow force that was unable to defeat 1,000 insurgents in the Sinai Peninsula without Israeli help, she said.[5]

The Mideast's crises were fundamentally about failures of governance, the diplomats believed. Since Britain and France carved up national boundaries during World War I, the region had tried Arab nationalism, socialism, communism, simple authoritarianism, and political Islamism, Crocker told students at Georgia State University. "There's nothing out there I can see that's going to reverse this 100-year-old tide and produce good governance," he said.[6]

The years since 9/11 pointed to the limits of U.S. influence and how hard it was to engineer a quick transition to democracy and rebuild an economy from ruins. Many of the foreign service hands Robert Ford knew in Iraq had as their personal goal to restore just enough order that the United States could scale back its presence and get young American soldiers out of danger. Their perspective, he said, was "This is just way too complex and we don't want to be in the middle of it." His years in the region convinced him that the United States should set its sights on more limited goals: supporting moderate elements in their struggle against extremists, mediating political crises, helping lay the foundations for better government institutions and economies. The multibillion-dollar rebuilding programs of the period fell short, he said, but U.S. agencies could help with more limited projects and trade agreements. "It's a question of gradual steps," Ford said.

Yet though they saw the limits of U.S. influence, these diplomats, like most foreign service officers, believed the country should take a leading role in the world. "We have to be out there," said Anne Patterson. "Otherwise, somebody else will be: Russia, China, ISIS." And many other countries, for all their complaints about domineering Americans, preferred having the United States trying to lead a world order than the others that might seek the role, she said. Patterson admired Obama but thought his moves to reduce U.S. involvement overseas were "in retrospect, very damaging."

In Crocker's view, many of the country's foreign policy blunders were due to its fitful approach. Americans are confident they can solve complex international challenges and charge in. Soon the public and its leaders grow frustrated by casualties and costs and want to go home. "Americans want to identify a problem, fix it and move on," he said. "Sometimes this works, often it does not. What's needed in dealing with this world is a combination of understanding, persistence, and strategic patience to a degree that Americans, traditionally, have found difficult to muster."[7]

Over the course of his career, Crocker saw the same pattern repeatedly in American military interventions in the Middle East and South Asia. In Lebanon, Iraq, Afghanistan, and Pakistan, American adversaries know that their forces can't stand up to the American military. "But they also know that soon enough, American leaders will lose patience and leave," he observed. "They know they can wait us out."[8] Crocker said his thirty-eight-year career could be boiled down to two lessons: Be careful what you get into, and how you get out.

In truth, many career diplomats were privately uncomfortable with the White House approach for much of the period since the 9/11 attacks. They thought President Bush's first term was too interventionist and that Obama's second term, in its retrenchment, represented a retreat from the traditional American leadership role. They were charter members of the Washington foreign policy establishment, which Obama disparaged as an insular elite too worried about preserving U.S. "credibility" and too inclined to use force. They believed in America championing a liberal world order and trying to preserve global security using alliances and, if required, military interventions. They thought each president had veered from the template of the previous seventy years. "The Foreign Service believes deeply in the traditional game plan," said James F. Jeffrey, a foreign service veteran and former ambassador to Iraq and Turkey, in a 2016 interview.[9] "Bush's first term and Obama's second were abominations for them."

They also found troubling the Trump administration's downgrading of the Foreign Service and the president's declarations that the country needed to scale back military involvement, foreign aid, and other efforts to help foreign countries. But they did not fail to notice that even the Trump administration soon found it needed the talents of experienced Mideast hands.

When he took office, Trump and his inner circle barred top jobs to "Never Trumpers," former officials who opposed Trump's candidacy, and other former officials of the Bush and Obama administrations. But when Trump's second secretary of state, Mike Pompeo, began his tenure in April 2018, he sought guidance in a round of consultations with former top diplomats, including Crocker.

In August 2018 the administration hired former ambassador Jeffrey, a thirty-five-year foreign service veteran, to be an envoy on issues related to Syria's war. Jeffrey had been a "Never Trumper" in 2016 and was among fifty former officials of Republican administrations who signed a letter saying Trump "lacked the character, values and experience to be president." In January 2019 the administration supplemented Jeffrey's duties with a second post, as U.S. representative to the coalition of countries fighting ISIS. Also, in August 2018, the administration hired for the State Department's number three post David Hale, an Arabic-speaking thirty-four-year foreign service veteran who had been Obama's special envoy on Arab-Israeli peace, and executive assistant to Madeleine Albright, secretary of state under President Bill Clinton. A month later the administration put Zalmay Khalilzad, a former ambassador to Iraq and Afghanistan, and a Bush White House insider, in charge of peace talks with the Taliban.

In Jeffrey's view, administrations eventually come around to relying on experienced foreign service hands because they want results. Americans generally believe the country can achieve diplomatic successes with limited time and effort, Jeffrey said, and presidents often begin their terms relying on political appointees who promise quick solutions. Foreign service veterans tell the White House that overseas projects will take time and great effort. "That makes us unpopular," he said. "But normally in the end presidents follow our lead."[10]

The number of diplomats sent abroad to help in broken countries has been on a downward slope since Obama's second term. But even if Washington avoids new missions on the massive scale of Iraq and Afghanistan, administrations will still need to send diplomats to try to strengthen weak and endangered countries. Some will be sent, again, to deal with insurgent threats. Though Americans are weary of the battle, transnational terrorism is not going away. The yearly count of terror attacks has grown fivefold since 9/11.[11] At the end of 2018, the Trump administration was pursuing joint counterterror programs with eighty countries.[12] Former secretary of state Condoleezza Rice said Washington would continue to need frontline diplomats wherever it was helping partner countries overcome insurgencies. "Unless you can strengthen the governments of your partner, the bad guys are going to be back," she said. "I don't see that, particularly in these hard places, there's going to be another option."[13]

U.S. diplomats will also be sent abroad to try to deal with the root causes of dysfunction, to prevent weak states from collapsing and threatening all around them. The last four administrations all began with vows that they would conduct nation-building only in the United States. It was easy to promise and hard to deliver. Presidents "don't like the term 'nation-building,' but they're sort of condemned to the activity," said former foreign service officer

James F. Dobbins, who, as a U.S. envoy, led postwar rebuilding efforts in Afghanistan and four other countries.

Some foreign service hands will be ready to go. One year after he ended his second tour in Afghanistan, Ryan Crocker confided that even at sixty-four, and with a chronic illness, he would go to Syria to try to work out a peace deal if he were asked. "In a heartbeat," he said.[14] On campuses he urged young people planning foreign service careers to bypass the comfortable posts for the violent and chaotic places where the need is most urgent. "Do you really want to spend your career in Brussels, Paris, or Berlin?" he asked students at Stanford University. "Or do you want to be out where the action is?"[15]

# ACKNOWLEDGMENTS

Soon after I began writing about U.S. foreign policy, I began noticing the special role of a small group of seasoned career ambassadors. When a new crisis erupted in the world's unstable belt, top State Department officials of successive administrations turned again and again to the same circle of proven hands. Facing a breakdown in the U.S. effort in Afghanistan, they brought in a troubleshooter who had led the U.S. mission in Iraq two years earlier, and the American teams in Pakistan, Lebanon, Syria, and Kuwait before that. When revolution staggered Egypt, a crucial ally, Washington sent a career officer who had been managing the embassy in Pakistan and earlier was in charge in turbulent Colombia.

This inner circle must have a lot to say, I thought, both about their postings and, more broadly, about America's trials in the greater Middle East. When I sat down with them, I was not disappointed. Their accounts rank with the best of American diplomatic memoirs. At a time when the Foreign Service has been downsized and marginalized, they attest to its contributions.

Former ambassadors Ryan Crocker, Anne Patterson, Robert Ford, and the family and friends of Christopher Stevens have my gratitude for their patient help over four years. At times, I'm sure, they would have preferred not to have to relive their time in the molten core. I was also helped by dozens of other diplomats, military and intelligence officers, and White House aides. Among them were former senior officials with a special understanding of U.S. policy and the ways of the diplomatic corps. These included former secretary of state Condoleezza Rice, deputy secretary of state William J. Burns, undersecretaries of state Marc Grossman and R. Nicholas Burns, and assistant secretaries Richard A. Boucher,

James F. Dobbins, Jeffrey D. Feltman, and A. Elizabeth Jones. I drew on the insights of many former ambassadors who have been through the crucible, including Patricia A. Butenis, Gene A. Cretz, James B. Cunningham, J. Adam Ereli, Gerald M. Feierstein, Gordon Gray III, James F. Jeffrey, Stuart E. Jones, Thomas C. Krajeski, David Mack, Ronald E. Neumann, Thomas R. Pickering, Laurence E. Pope II, and Charles P. Ries. Among the retired military officers who offered their perspective were Generals John R. Allen and David H. Petraeus, Vice Admiral Michael A. LeFever, Lieutenant Colonel Brian E. Linvill, and Lieutenant Colonel Gregory Arndt. Kevin Hulbert, former CIA station chief in Islamabad, helped, as did other former intelligence officers who did not wish to be identified.

Many others who were part of the overseas missions or knew the principal subjects in other settings made important contributions. Among them were Wa'el N. Alzayat, Jeffrey Beals, Jonah Blank, Sharon E. Burke, Leslie Campbell, Elizabeth L. Dibble, Benjamin Fishman, Patrick A. Garvey, Bubaker Habib, Roya Hakakian, Mounir Ibrahim, Ali Khedery, Prem Kumar, Robert Loftis, Daniel Markey, Stephen McInerney, Eileen O'Connor, Emma Sky, Jordan Stancil, and Austin Tichenor. Others who helped preferred to remain unidentified.

The oral histories of the Association for Diplomatic Studies and Training were invaluable.

I got important advice in shaping the book from former colleagues at the *Los Angeles Times*, David Lauter, James Mann, and Doyle McManus. Doyle suggested over a brainstorming lunch that if I found that any of the diplomats had been involved in action sequences, I should be sure to include them. There were plenty, it turned out.

My editor, Alice Mayhew, believed in the project from the beginning and steered it through shoals and sandbars. We liked the same things about the story and agreed on everything. My agent, Gail Ross, was first to suggest there might be a book in what I had seen in Foggy Bottom and Bab al-Aziziyah. I received advice and encouragement on gray days from my wife, Karen Tumulty, who often sat nearby, under a pile of dog-eared volumes, writing her own book.

# NOTES

## CHAPTER 1: THE BEST PEOPLE FOR THE WORST PLACES

1. Farrow, Ronan, *War on Peace: The End of Diplomacy and the Decline of American Influence* (New York: W. W. Norton & Co., 2018), page xi.
2. Estimated from "Significant Attacks Against U.S. Diplomatic Facilities and Personnel, 2006–2017," Bureau of Diplomatic Security, State Department.
3. Clinton, Hillary Rodham, *Hard Choices* (New York: Simon & Schuster, 2014), page 383.
4. Crocker, Ryan, interview with Erik Spanberg, "Charlotte Talks: Causes and Consequences in the Middle East with ambassador Ryan Crocker," WFAE Radio, Charlotte, N.C., September 5, 2018.
5. Haass, Richard N., "The President's Inbox," Council on Foreign Relations podcast, January 18, 2018.
6. McManus, Doyle, "Almost Half the Top Jobs in Trump's State Department Are Unfilled," *Atlantic*, November 4, 2018.
7. Crocker, Ryan C., and R. Nicholas Burns, "Dismantling the Foreign Service," *New York Times*, November 27, 2017.

## CHAPTER 2: GO FIGURE SOMETHING OUT

1. Krajeski, Thomas, Oral History, Association for Diplomatic Studies and Training, page 358.
2. Coll, Steve, *Directorate S: The C.I.A. and America's Secret Wars in Afghanistan and Pakistan* (New York: Penguin, 2018), page 130.
3. Khalilzad, Zalmay, *The Envoy: From Kabul to the White House, My Journey Through a Turbulent World* (New York: St. Martin's, 2016), page 139.
4. Ibid., page 132.

5. Filkins, Dexter, "The Shadow Commander," *New Yorker*, September 23, 2013.

6. "U.S. Amb. Ryan Crocker on Iraq and Afghanistan," *Newsweek*, September 4, 2009.

7. Filkins, Dexter, "The Shadow Commander."

8. Burns, William J., *The Back Channel: A Memoir of American Diplomacy and the Case for Its Renewal* (New York: Random House, 2019), page 165.

9. Partlow, Joshua, *A Kingdom of Their Own: The Family Karzai and the Afghan Disaster* (New York: Knopf, 2016), page 61.

10. Dobbins, James F., *Foreign Service: Five Decades on the Frontlines of American Diplomacy* (Santa Monica, CA, and Washington, DC: Rand Corp. and Brookings Institution Press, 2017), pages 258, 259.

## CHAPTER 3: THE PERFECT STORM

1. Duelfer, Charles, *Hide and Seek: The Search for Truth in Iraq* (New York: PublicAffairs, 2009), page 197.

2. Burns, William J., *The Back Channel: A Memoir of American Diplomacy and the Case for Its Renewal* (New York: Random House, 2019), page 162.

3. Gray, Gordon, III, Oral History, Association for Diplomatic Studies and Training, page 88.

4. Armitage, Richard, Comments in "Green Zone a New Hot Zone for Iraq Pick," *Morning Edition*, National Public Radio, February 7, 2007.

5. Burns, William J., *The Back Channel*, page 171.

6. U.S. Special Inspector General for Iraq Reconstruction, *Hard Lessons: The Iraq Reconstruction Experience* (Washington, D.C.: U.S. Government Printing Office, 2009), page 15.

7. Crocker, Ryan C., comments at Modern War Institute at West Point, March 26, 2018.

8. Burns, William J., *The Back Channel*, page 169.

9. Woodward, Bob, *Plan of Attack* (New York: Simon & Schuster Paperbacks, 2004), page 284.

10. Rice, Condoleezza, *No Higher Honor: A Memoir of My Years in Washington* (New York: Crown, 2011), page 17.

11. Krajeski, Thomas, Oral History, Association for Diplomatic Studies and Training, 2017, page 176.

12. U.S. Special Inspector General for Iraq Reconstruction, *Hard Lessons*, page 37.

13. Ibid.

14. Ibid., page 45.

15. Ibid., page 53.

16. Krajeski, Thomas, Oral History, page 169.

17. Khalilzad, Zalmay, *The Envoy: From Kabul to the White House, My Journey Through a Turbulent World* (New York: St. Martin's, 2016), page 164.

18. Bremer, J. Paul, III, with Malcolm McConnell, *My Year in Iraq: The Struggle to Build a Future of Hope* (New York: Simon & Schuster, 2006), page 13.

19. Chandrasekeran, Rajiv, comments in "Green Zone a New Hot Zone for Iraq Envoy Pick," *Morning Edition*, National Public Radio, February 7, 2007.

20. Sky, Emma, *The Unraveling: High Hopes and Missed Opportunities in Iraq* (New York: PublicAffairs, 2015), page 103.

21. Dobbins, James, et al., *Occupying Iraq: A History of the Coalition Provisional Authority* (Santa Monica, CA: Rand Corp., 2009), page xxiv.

22. Khalilzad, Zalmay, *The Envoy*, page 173.

23. Dobbins, James, et al., *Occupying Iraq*, page 116.

24. Filkins, Dexter, The Shadow Commander, *New Yorker*, September 23, 2013.

25. Rice, Condoleezza, *No Higher Honor*, page 238.

26. Bremer told Rand Corp. researchers that he tried to convince Crocker to extend his commitment but didn't persuade him. Crocker said Bremer didn't try to change his mind.

## CHAPTER 4: A GOVERNMENT OF ONE

1. Krajeski, Thomas, Oral History, Association for Diplomatic Studies and Training, 2017, page 201.

2. Ford, Robert, email to CPA officials in Baghdad, September 21, 2003: "Subject: Najaf Sitrep." Cited in Dobbins, James, et al., *Occupying Iraq* (Santa Monica, CA: Rand Corp., 2009).

3. Bremer, J. Paul, III, Oral History, Association for Diplomatic Studies and Training, page 224.

## CHAPTER 5: WITH US AND AGAINST US

1. Musharraf, Pervez, *In the Line of Fire: A Memoir* (New York: Simon & Schuster, 2006), page 204.
2. "Drone Strikes: Pakistan," America's Counterterrorism Wars, New America. https://www.newamerica.org/in-depth/americas-counterter rorism-wars/pakistan/
3. Bush, George W., *Decision Points* (New York: Crown, 2010), page 214.
4. Crocker, Ryan C., "U.S. Ambassador Ryan Crocker on Iraq and Afghanistan," *Newsweek*, September 4, 2009.
5. Crocker, Ryan C., State Department cable, "Tribal Areas: Talibanization Threat Persists Despite North Waziristan Jirga Agreement," December 14, 2006, Wikileaks.
6. Crocker, Ryan C., State Department cable, "Political Scenesetter for PM=A/S John Hillen," March 8, 2006, Wikileaks.
7. Crocker, Ryan C., comments at Georgia State University, November 29, 2016.
8. Crocker, Ryan C., State Department cable, "Musharraf on Chief Justice Controversy, FATA, and Jirgas." March 26, 2007, Wikileaks.

## CHAPTER 6: TALENT HUNT

1. Ford, Robert S., State Department cable, "Governor in Trouble-Ridden Anbar Province Held Hostage," August 3, 2004, Wikileaks.
2. Rice, Condoleezza, *No Higher Honor: A Memoir of My Years in Washington* (New York: Crown, 2011), page 320.
3. Gordon, Michael R., and Bernard E. Trainor, *The Endgame: The Inside Story of the Struggle for Iraq, from George W. Bush to Barack Obama* (New York: Pantheon Books, 2012), page 137.
4. Ibid., page 141.
5. Ford, Robert S., State Department cable, "Jaafari's Farewell: Parting is Such Sweet Sorrow," May 11, 2006, Wikileaks.
6. Ford, Robert S., State Department cable, "Baghdad Provincial Governor's Assassination Shakes Capital," January 4, 2005, Wikileaks.

## CHAPTER 7: FROM ENEMIES, FRIEND

1. Hakakian, Roya, "A Friend's Tribute to Ambassador Chris Stevens," *Daily Beast*, September 13, 2012.
2. Stevens, J. Christopher, State Department cable, "Muammar al-Qadhafi Quietly Involved in Process to Write New Constitution," December 5, 2008, Wikileaks.
3. Stevens, J. Christopher, State Department cable, "Libya Seeks to Purchase 130,000 Kalashnikovs for Unknown End Users," August 18, 2008, Wikileaks.
4. Stevens, J. Christopher, State Department cable, "Libya Seeks to Blackmail European Missions for Visa," July 3, 2008, Wikileaks.
5. Stevens, J. Christopher, State Department cable, "A River Runs Through It: A Case Study in Libyan Infrastructure Management," August 8, 2008, Wikileaks.
6. Rice, Condoleezza, *No Higher Honor: A Memoir of My Years in Washington* (New York: Crown, 2011), page 703.
7. Burns, William J., *The Back Channel: A Memoir of American Diplomacy and the Case for Its Renewal* (New York: Random House, 2019), page 314.


## CHAPTER 8: NOT PEACE BUT MORE PEACEFUL

1. Rand Corp., "Ending the U.S. War in Iraq," 2013.
2. Crocker, Ryan C., comments at Modern War Institute at West Point, March 2018.
3. Nessman, Ravi, "Veteran Diplomat to Lead Iran Talks," Associated Press, May 26, 2007.
4. Interview with Ryan Crocker, "Bitter Rivals, Iran and Saudi Arabia," *Frontline*, PBS, 2018.
5. Interview with Ryan Crocker, "Losing Iraq," *Frontline*, PBS, 2014.
6. Petraeus, David, comments at the Modern War Institute at West Point, March, 2018.
7. Gates, Robert M., *Duty: Memoirs of a Secretary at War* (New York: Vintage, 2014), page 60.
8. Kessler, Glenn, "Embassy Staff in Baghdad Inadequate, Rice Is Told," *Washington Post*, June 19, 2007.
9. Holmes, J. Anthony, "Where Are the Civilians?" *Foreign Affairs*, January–February 2009.

10. "Tough Days for the State Department," the Burbank Park Project show, National Public Radio, November 2, 2007.

11. Kessler, Glenn, "Embassy Staff Is Inadequate, Rice Is Told," *Washington Post*, June 19, 2007.

12. Crocker, Ryan C., and David Petraeus, comments at Modern War Institute at West Point, Class of 2006 War Studies Conference, March 26, 2018.

13. Crocker, Ryan C., "A Discussion on Afghanistan with Ambassador Ryan Crocker," Comments at Brookings Institution event, September 18, 2012.

14. Parker, Ned, "Special Report: How Mosul Fell; An Iraqi General Disputes Baghdad's Story," Reuters, October 14, 2014.

15. Crocker, Ryan, State Department cable, "Ambassador, CG Meet with PM Following Samarra Shrine Attack," June 14, 2007, Wikileaks.

16. Gates, Robert M., *Duty: Memoirs of a Secretary at War* (New York: Vintage, 2014), page 74.

17. Council on Foreign Relations, "Haass: Petraeus, Crocker Blunt Congressional Criticism on Iraq," Comments of CFR President Richard N. Haass as interviewed by Bernard Gwertzman, September 11, 2007.

18. Crocker, Ryan C., appearance at Modern War Institute at West Point, March 26, 2018.

19. Gates, Robert M., *Duty*, page 75.

20. Rice, Condoleezza, author interview.

21. Crocker, Ryan C., "Bitter Rivals: Iran and Saudi Arabia," *Frontline*, PBS, February 20, 2018.

22. Rice, Condoleezza, *No Higher Honor: A Memoir of My Years in Washington* (New York: Crown, 2011), page 663.

23. Gordon, Michael R., and Bernard E. Trainor, *The Endgame: The Inside Story of the Struggle for Iraq, from George W. Bush to Barack Obama* (New York: Pantheon, 2012), page 528.

24. Gates, Robert M., *Duty*, page 236.

25. Sky, Emma, *The Unraveling: High Hopes and Missed Opportunities in Iraq* (New York: PublicAffairs, 2015), page 266.

26. Crocker, Ryan C., comments at Brookings Institution, September 18, 2012.

27. Gordon, Michael R., and Bernard E. Trainor, *The Endgame*, page 555.

28. Baker, Peter, *Days of Fire: Bush and Cheney in the White House* (New York: Anchor, 2013), page 620.

29. Crocker, Ryan C., State Department cable, "Strengthening the Center or Emerging Strongman?," February 11, 2009, Wikileaks.

30. Gray, Gordon, Foreign Affairs Oral History Project, Association for Diplomatic Study and Training, February 2016, page 93.

31. Sky, Emma, *The Unraveling*, page 276.

32. Gordon, Michael R., and Bernard E. Trainor, *The Endgame*, page 582.

33. Hill, Christopher, "How the Obama Administration Ignored Iraq," *Politico*, October 2, 2014.

## CHAPTER 9: LOST IN TRANSLATION

1. Constable, Pamela, *Playing with Fire: Pakistan at War with Itself* (New York: Random House, 2011), page 162.

2. Patterson, Anne W., State Department cable, "Focusing the U.S.-Pakistan Strategic Dialogue," February 21, 2009, Wikileaks.

3. Patterson, Anne W., State Department cable, "Ambassador Discusses Elections with Fazl-ur-Rehman," November 27, 2007, Wikileaks.

4. Patterson, Anne W., State Department cable, "The Best Thing That Could Happen in Pakistan," February 1, 2008, Wikileaks.

5. Shifter, Michael, "Plan Colombia: A Retrospective," *Americas Quarterly* (Summer 2012).

6. Rice, Condoleezza, *No Higher Honor: A Memoir of My Years in Washington* (New York: Crown, 2011), page 316.

7. Schweich, Thomas, "Is Afghanistan a Narco-State?," *New York Times Magazine*, July 27, 2008.

8. Ibid.

9. Rice, Condoleezza, *No Higher Honor*, page 606.

10. Rice, Condoleezza, author interview, September, 2017.

11. Rice, Condoleezza, *No Higher Honor*, page 611.

12. Patterson, Anne W., State Department cable, "Heavy Handed Implementation of Pakistani State of Emergency," November 4, 2007, Wikileaks.

13. Patterson, Anne W., State Department cable, "Bhutto Says She Must Protest State of Emergency," November 8, 2007, Wikileaks.

14. Patterson, Anne W., State Department cable, "Pervez Musharraf Resigns," August 18, 2008, Wikileaks.

15. Patterson, Anne W., State Department cable, "Ambassador's Condolence Call on Asif Zardari," January 28, 2008, Wikileaks.

## CHAPTER 10: THE LID STAYS ON

1. Abedin, Huma, "Notes from Anne," August 14, 2010, Case No. F-2014-20439, Secretary Clinton Emails, State Department Freedom of Information Act archive.

2. Patterson, Anne, State Department cable, "Ambassador's Condolence Call on Asif Zardari," January 28, 2008, Wikileaks.

3. Patterson, Anne W., State Department cable, "Profile: PPP Co-Chair Asif Zardari," March 31, 2008, Wikileaks.

4. Nasr, Vali, *The Dispensable Nation: American Foreign Policy in Retreat* (New York: Doubleday, 2013), page 61.

5. Patterson, Anne W., State Department cable, "Zardari-Nawaz Reconciliation: Pleas for Intervention," March 7, 2009, Wikileaks.

6. Patterson, Anne W., State Department cable, "Zardari's Planned Approach to Holbrooke," February 9, 2009, Wikileaks.

7. Patterson, Anne W., State Department cable, "Little Movement on Reconciliation," March 12, 2009, Wikileaks.

8. Patterson, Anne W., State Department cable, "The Fat Lady Rarely Sings in Pakistan," March 21, 2009, Wikileaks.

9. Coll, Steve, *Directorate S: The C.I.A. and America's Secret Wars in Afghanistan and Pakistan* (New York: Penguin, 2018), page 310.

10. "Drone Strikes: Pakistan," America's Counter-Terrorism Wars, New America, https://www.newamerica.org/in-depth/americas -counterterrorism-wars/pakistan/.

11. Patterson, Anne W., State Department cable, "US Media Leaks Have Pakistani Military 'Reviewing Contingencies,'" Wikileaks.

12. Patterson, Anne W., State Department cable, "Taskings for IDP, Refugee Information," October 6, 2008, Wikileaks.

13. Patterson, Anne W., State Department cable, "U.S. Direct Assistance to on-Ground Pakistani Military Forces," October 9, 2009, Wikileaks.

14. Patterson, Anne W., State Department cable, "Pakistan: Fixing Coalition Support Funds," December 14, 2007, Wikileaks.

15. "Drone Strikes: Pakistan," America's Counter Terrorism Wars, New America, https://www.newamerica.org/in-depth/americas -counterterrorism-wars/pakistan/.

16. Patterson, Anne W., State Department cable, "Reviewing Our Afghanistan-Pakistan Strategy," September 23, 2009.

17. "Obama's War," interview with Anne Patterson, *Frontline*, PBS, August 2009.

18. Patterson, Anne W., State Department cable, "Reviewing Our Afghanistan-Pakistan Strategy," September 23, 2009.

19. Dobbins, James, *Foreign Service: Five Decades on the Frontlines of American Diplomacy* (Washington, DC: Brookings Institution, 2017), page 271.

20. Patterson, Anne W., State Department cable, "Scenesetter for CJCS Admiral Mullen," February 5, 2008, Wikileaks.

21. Patterson, Anne W., State Department cable, "Scenesetter for National Security Adviser Jones," June 20, 2009, Wikileaks.

22. Patterson, Anne W., State Department cable, "U.S. Removal of Pakistani Research Reactor Fuel on Hold," May 27, 2009, Wikileaks.

23. Rice, Condoleezza, *No Higher Honor: A Memoir of My Years in Washington* (New York: Crown, 2011), page 719.

24. Coll, Steve, *Directorate S: The C.I.A. and America's Secret Wars in Afghanistan and Pakistan* (New York: Penguin, 2018), page 347.

25. Ibid., page 721.

26. Feierstein, Gerald M., State Department cable, "Scenesetter for FBI Director Mueller's February 24 Visit," February 22, 2010, Wikileaks.

27. Constable, Pamela, *Playing with Fire: Pakistan at War with Itself* (New York: Random House, 2011), page 249.

28. Patterson, Anne W., State Department cable, "Scenesetter for FBI Director Mueller's Visit," February 22, 2010, Wikileaks.

## CHAPTER 11: FLOWERS, AND STONES, FOR THE AMBASSADOR

1. Shadid, Anthony, "Envoys Stay in Syrian City Where Protests Continue," *New York Times*, July 8, 2011.

2. Clinton, Hillary Rodham, *Hard Choices* (New York: Simon & Schuster, 2014), page 449.

3. Mills, Cheryl D., State Department email, "Ford (Syria) Confirmed," October 2, 2011, Case No. F-2014-20439, Secretary Clinton emails, State Department.

## CHAPTER 12: ENVOY TO THE REBELS

1. Landler, Mark, *Alter Egos: Hillary Clinton, Barack Obama and the Twilight Struggle over Foreign Policy* (New York: Random House, 2016), page 171.

2. Kennedy, Patrick, State Department email to Jacob J. Sullivan, March 30, 2011, cited in Report of the House Select Committee on Benghazi, page III-20.

3. Clinton, Hillary Rodham, remarks at Chris Stevens's swearing-in ceremony, May 2012.

4. Worth, Robert F., "Can American Diplomacy Ever Come out of Its Bunker?," *New York Times Magazine*, November 14, 2012.

5. Polaschik, Joan A., testimony to House Benghazi committee, August 12, 2015.

6. Wehrey, Frederic, *The Burning Shores: Inside the Battle for the New Libya* (New York: Farrar, Straus & Giroux, 2018), page 117.

7. Stevens, J. Christopher, State Department special press briefing, August 2, 2011.

8. Feltman, Jeffrey, "Jeff Update," email to Secretary of State Clinton, August 21, 2011, Case No. F-2014-20439, Clinton Email Collection, State Department.

9. Sullivan, Jacob J., et al., note to Deputy Secretaries of State William J. Burns and Thomas Nides, September 28, 2011, cited in Report of House Select Committee on Benghazi, page iii–57.

10. Chorin, Ethan, Testimony to House Benghazi Committee, March 11, 2016.

11. Hakakian, Roya, "A Friend's Tribute to Ambassador Chris Stevens," *Daily Beast*, September 13, 2012.

## CHAPTER 13: THE LONG GOODBYE

1. Rice, Condoleezza, *No Higher Honor: A Memoir of My Years in Washington* (New York: Crown, 2011), page 636.

2. Gates, Robert M., *Duty: Memoirs of a Secretary at War* (New York: Vintage Books, 2014), page 359.

3. Norland, Rod, et al. "Gulf Widens Between U.S. and a More Volatile Karzai," *New York Times*, March 17, 2012.

4. Crocker, Ryan C., remarks at U.S. Institute of Peace, November 5, 2014.

5. Crocker, Ryan C., "A Discussion of Afghanistan with Ambassador Crocker," remarks at Brookings Institution, September 18, 2012.

6. Crocker, Ryan C., "Ambassador Ryan Crocker on Afghanistan," comments at Carnegie Endowment for International Peace, September 17, 2012.

7. Partlow, Joshua, "Cat Fight at U.S. Embassy in Kabul," *Washington Post*, August 3, 2011.
8. Gates, Robert M., *Duty*, page 490.
9. Rosenberg, Matthew, "Court Convicts Allied Soldier in Attack on Allies," *New York Times*, July 17, 2012.
10. Whitlock, Craig, "U.S. Troops Tried to Burn 500 Korans in Blunder, Investigative Report Says," *Washington Post*, August 27, 2012.
11. Crocker, Ryan C., "A Discussion of Afghanistan with Ambassador Crocker," comments at Brookings Institution, September 18, 2012.
12. Partlow, Joshua, *A Kingdom of Their Own: The Family Karzai and the Afghan Disaster* (New York: Knopf, 2016), page 350.
13. Crocker, Ryan C., interview on *NewsHour*, PBS, March 16, 2012.
14. Clinton, Hillary Rodham, *Hard Choices* (New York: Simon & Schuster, 2014), page 166.
15. Crocker, Ryan C., "Ambassador Ryan Crocker on Afghanistan," comments at Carnegie Endowment for International Peace, September 17, 2012.

## CHAPTER 14: LIBYA LOSES A FRIEND

1. Hakakian, Roya, "A Friend's Tribute to Chris Stevens," *Daily Beast*, September 13, 2012.
2. Wehrey, Frederic, *The Burning Shores: Inside the Battle for the New Libya* (New York: Farrar, Straus & Giroux, 2018), page 76.
3. "Report of Accountability Review Board on Benghazi," U.S. State Department, December 19, 2012, page 17.
4. Stevens, J. Christopher," State Department cable, September 11, 2012, released by House Oversight Committee.
5. Wehrey, Frederic, *The Burning Shores*, page 119.
6. Burns, William J., *The Back Channel: A Memoir of American Diplomacy and the Case for Its Renewal* (New York: Random House, 2019), page 319.
7. "Review of the Terrorist Attack on the U.S. Facilities at Benghazi," a report of the U.S. Senate Select Committee on Intelligence, January 1, 2014.
8. "Report of Accountability Review Board on Benghazi," U.S. State Department, December 19, 2012, pages 4–7.
9. Wickland, Scott, Testimony in U.S. District Court Trial of Ahmed Abu Khatallah, October 3, 2017.

10. Burns, William J., *The Back Channel*, page 320.
11. Crocker, Ryan C., "Former Diplomat: Doing a Good Job Invites Risk," interview with host Scott Simon, Weekend Edition Saturday, National Public Radio, September 15, 2012.
12. Wright, Robin, "Chris Stevens's Family: Don't Blame Hillary Clinton for Benghazi," *New Yorker*, June 28, 2016.
13. Burns, William J., *The Back Channel*, page 321.
14. Jones, Deborah, "The Benghazi Aftermath," podcast, American Military University, September 10, 2018.
15. Clinton, Hillary R., *Hard Choices* (New York: Simon & Schuster, 2014), pages 369, 411.
16. Norris, John, "How to Balance Security and Openness for America's Diplomats," *Atlantic*, November 4, 2013.
17. Burns, William J., *The Back Channel*, page 322.
18. Wehrey, Frederic, *The Burning Shores*, page 270.

## CHAPTER 15: ARAB SPRING AND FALL

1. Allem, Hannah, "New Ambassador Faces Cooler Relations in Egypt," *Miami Herald*, August 17, 2011.
2. Hosnein, Mohsen, "Ambassador from Hell Who Ignites Tahrir Square," *October*, July 31, 2011.
3. Patterson, Anne W., "The Arab Uprisings Eight Years Later," Comments at Center for American Progress, February 14, 2019.
4. Clinton, Hillary Rodham, *Hard Choices* (New York: Simon & Schuster, 2016), page 346.
5. Sullivan, Jacob J., email to Hillary Clinton, "Egyptian Presidential Election Sitrep," June 17, 2012, Case No. F-2014-20439, Hillary Clinton Email Archive, State Department Freedom of Information Act Archive.
6. Clinton, Hillary R., *Hard Choices*, page 349.
7. Guirguis, Dina, "In Response to U.S Ambassador Anne Patterson," Atlantic Council, June 27, 2013.
8. "Tension Roils Egypt as Protests Grow," *Washington Post*, June 30, 2103.
9. Chollet, Derek, *The Long Game: How Obama Defied Washington and Redefined America's Role in the World* (New York: PublicAffairs, 2018), page 123.

10. Rhodes, Ben, *The World as It Is: A Memoir of the Obama White House* (New York: Random House, 2018), page 204.

11. Patterson, Anne W., "The Arab Uprisings Eight Years Later," comments at Center for American Progress, February 14, 2109.

12. Burns, William J., *The Back Channel: A Memoir of American Diplomacy and the Case for Its Renewal* (New York: Random House, 2019), page 312.

13. Patterson, Anne W., "The Arab Uprisings Eight Years Later," comments at Center for American Progress, February 14, 2019.

## CHAPTER 16: IN GOOD CONSCIENCE

1. Clinton, Hillary R., *Hard Choices* (New York: Simon & Schuster, 2014), page 464.

2. "Most Chemical Attacks in Syria Get Little Attention: Here Are 34 Confirmed Cases," *New York Times*, April 14, 2018.

3. Ford, Robert S., "Arm Syria's Opposition," *New York Times*, June 10, 2014.

4. Burns, William J., *The Back Channel: A Memoir of American Diplomacy and the Case for Its Renewal* (New York: Random House, 2019), page 322.

## CHAPTER 17: COOL HEADS IN HOT SPOTS

1. Crocker, Ryan C., comments to World Affairs Council of Atlanta at Georgia State University, December 2, 2016.

2. Garton Ash, Timothy, "US Embassy Cables: A Banquet of Secrets," *Guardian*, November 28, 2010.

3. Jenkins, Simon, "US Embassy Cables: The Job of the Media Is Not to Protect the Powerful from Embarrassment," *Guardian*, November 28, 2010.

4. Shinkman, Paul, "The Drone Age," *U.S. News*, November 16, 2016.

5. Patterson, Anne W., "The Arab Uprisings Eight Years Later," comments at Center for American Progress, February 14, 2019.

6. Crocker, Ryan C., comments to World Affairs Council of Atlanta at Georgia State University, December 2, 2016.

7. Crocker, Ryan C., "Amb. Ryan Crocker on Iraq and Afghanistan," *Newsweek*, November 4, 2009.

8. Crocker, Ryan C., remarks at Stimson Center, December 6, 2014.

9. Jeffrey, James F., interview with the author, April 4, 2016.

10. Jeffrey, James F., comments on *1A*, National Public Radio, December 4, 2017.

11. "Final Report of the Task Force on Extremism in Fragile States," U.S. Institute of Peace, February 26, 2019.

12. "Costs of War Project," Watson Institute for International and Public Affairs, Brown University, January, 2019.

13. Rice, Condoleezza, author interview, September 2017.

14. Crocker, Ryan C., "Interview with Ryan Crocker: Assad Will Prevail, 'Yard by Bloody Yard," Defense One, August 5, 2013.

15. Crocker, Ryan C., comments to Abassi Program in Islamic Studies, Stanford University, May 2013.

# BIBLIOGRAPHY

Baker, Peter, *Days of Fire: Bush and Cheney in the White House*. New York: Anchor, 2013.

Bremer, J. Paul III, with Malcolm McConnell, *My Year in Iraq: The Struggle to Build a Future of Hope*. New York: Simon & Schuster, 2006.

Briggs, Ellis O., *Proud Servant: The Memoir of a Career Ambassador*. Kent, Ohio: Kent State University Press, 1998.

Burns, William J., *The Back Channel: A Memoir of American Diplomacy and the Case for Its Renewal*. New York: Random House, 2019.

Bush, George W., *Decision Points*. New York: Crown, 2010.

Chandrasekaren, Rajiv, *Imperial Life in the Emerald City: Inside Iraq's Green Zone*. New York: Knopf, 2007.

Chivers, C. J., *The Fighters: Americans in Combat in Afghanistan and Iraq*. New York: Simon & Schuster, 2018.

Chollet, Derek, *The Long Game: How Obama Defied Washington and Redefined America's Role in the World*. New York: PublicAffairs, 2018.

Clinton, Hillary Rodham, *Hard Choices*. New York: Simon & Schuster, 2014.

Coll, Steve, *Directorate S: The C.I.A. and America's Secret Wars in Afghanistan and Pakistan*. New York: Penguin, 2018.

———, *Ghost Wars: The Secret History of the CIA, Afghanistan and Bin Laden, from the Soviet Invasion to September 10, 2001*. New York: Penguin, 2005.

Constable, Pamela, *Playing with Fire: Pakistan At War With Itself*. New York: Random House, 2011.

DeYoung, Karen, *Soldier: The Life of Colin Powell*. New York: Knopf, 2006.

Dobbins, James F., *Foreign Service: Five Decades on the Frontlines of American Diplomacy*. Santa Monica, CA, and Washington, DC: Rand Corp. and Brookings Institution Press, 2017.

———, et al., *Occupying Iraq: A History of the Coalition Provisional Authority*. Santa Monica, CA: Rand Corp., 2009.

Duelfer, Charles, *Hide and Seek: The Search for Truth in Iraq*. New York: PublicAffairs, 2009.

Farrow, Ronan, *War on Peace: The End of Diplomacy and the Decline of American Influence*. New York: Norton, 2018.

Feith, Douglas J., *War and Decision: Inside the Pentagon at the Dawn of the War on Terrorism*. New York: Harper, 2008.

Gates, Robert M., *Duty: Memoirs of a Secretary at War*. New York: Vintage, 2014.

Gordon, Michael R., and Trainor, Bernard E., *The Endgame: The Inside Story of the Struggle for Iraq, from George W. Bush to Barack Obama*. New York: Pantheon Books, 2012.

Gurman, Hannah, *The Dissent Papers: The Voices of Diplomats in the Cold War and Beyond*. New York: Columbia University Press, 2012.

Jones, Seth G., *In the Graveyard of Empires: America's War in Afghanistan*. New York: Norton, 2009.

Kaplan, Robert D., *The Arabists: The Romance of an American Elite*. New York: Free Press, 1993.

Khalilzad, Zalmay, *The Envoy: From Kabul to the White House, My Journey Through a Turbulent World*. New York: St. Martin's, 2016.

Kirkpatrick, David D., *Into the Hands of the Soldiers: Freedom and Chaos in Egypt and the Middle East*. New York: Viking, 2018.

Landler, Mark, *Alter Egos: Hillary Clinton, Barack Obama and the Twilight Struggle over Foreign Policy*. New York: Random House, 2016.

Lawrence, T. E., *Seven Pillars of Wisdom: A Triumph*. New York: Penguin, 1978.

Mazzetti, Mark, *The Way of the Knife: The CIA, A Secret Army and a War at the Ends of the Earth*. New York: Penguin, 2013.

Moskin, J. Robert, *American Statecraft: The Story of the U.S. Foreign Service*. New York: Dunne, 2013.

Musharraf, Pervez, *In the Line of Fire: A Memoir*. New York: Simon & Schuster, 2006.

Nasr, Vali, *The Dispensable Nation: American Foreign Policy in Retreat*. New York: Doubleday, 2013.

Neumann, Ronald E., *The Other War: Winning and Losing in Afghanistan*. Washington, DC: Potomac, 2009.

Packer, George, *The Assassin's Gate: America in Iraq*. New York: Farrar, Straus, and Giroux, 2005.

Panetta, Leon, with Jim Newton, *Worthy Fights*. New York: Penguin, 2014.

Partlow, Joshua, *A Kingdom of Their Own: The Family Karzai and the Afghan Disaster*. New York: Knopf, 2016.

Rhodes, Ben, *The World as It Is: A Memoir of the Obama White House*. New York: Random House, 2018.

Rice, Condoleezza, *No Higher Honor: A Memoir of My Years in Washington*. New York: Crown, 2011.

Robinson, Linda, *Tell Me How This Ends: General David Petraeus and the Search for a Way out of Iraq*. New York: PublicAffairs, 2008.

Rumsfeld, Donald, *Known and Unknown: A Memoir*. New York: Sentinel, 2011.

Shultz, George, *Turmoil and Triumph: My Years as Secretary of State*. New York: Scribner, 1993.

Sky, Emma, *The Unraveling: High Hopes and Missed Opportunities in Iraq*. New York: PublicAffairs, 2015.

U.S. Special Inspector General for Iraq Reconstruction, *Hard Lessons: The Iraq Reconstruction Experience*. Washington, DC: U.S. Government Printing Office, 2009.

Warrick, Joby, *Black Flags: The Rise of ISIS*. New York: Doubleday, 2015.

Wehrey, Frederic, *The Burning Shores: Inside the Battle for the New Libya*. New York: Farrar, Straus, and Giroux, 2018.

Woodward, Bob, *Plan of Attack*. New York: Simon & Schuster, 2004.

# INDEX

An italicized page number refers to a text illustration

# ABOUT THE AUTHOR

Paul Richter has written about foreign policy and national security for the past three decades. As a Washington-based reporter for the *Los Angeles Times*, he traveled to sixty countries and appeared in U.S. and international media. He is principal author of *California and the American Tax Revolt,* University of California Press, 1983. He lives in the Washington, D.C., area.